The
Shadow of Calvary

The
Shadow of Calvary

Gethsemane, The Arrest,
The Trial

HUGH MARTIN

THE BANNER OF TRUTH TRUST

THE BANNER OF TRUTH TRUST
3 Murrayfield Road, Edinburgh, EH12 6EL
PO Box 621, Carlisle, Pennsylvania 17013, USA

★

First published 1875
Reprinted by the Free Presbyterian
Church of Scotland 1954, 1955, 1956
First Banner of Truth edition 1983
ISBN 0 85151 373 5

★

Reproduced, printed and bound in Great Britain by
Hazell Watson & Viney Ltd, Aylesbury, Bucks

PREFACE

An able writer in the "Quarterly Review" (January, 1875), in an article on "Farrar's Life of Christ," shrewdly desiderates an "interpreting idea" of "the last great crisis of the Sacred Life"—a "divine idea," which by its "grandeur," shall "transfigure the Cross and, through it, the whole sphere of moral and religious conflict."

So far as it goes, this is good—eminently good. But it is extremely melancholy to find how completely, in professing to implement his own desideratum, this writer misses the divine idea which effectually transfigures the Cross, removes the scandal, and swallows up the shame in glory. He uses, indeed, the phrase, "atonement for sin," but he renders it significant of nothing more than the "revelation of the Son of God," "consummated in the passion of the Son of Man"; and he asserts that this revelation is the "criterion by which all doctrines, whether of sacrifice, satisfaction, or substitution must ultimately be tested," adding that it is "through participation in this ideal Sonship that obedience unto death has become possible to sinful man."

Had the author of these expressions obtained the slightest glimpse into the Catholic doctrine of "atonement for sin," he would have known that "obedience unto death," in the only sense in which that Scripture phrase is ever used, was never meant to be rendered "possible to sinful man," and that in the nature of things it is impossible to creatures, sinful or holy. "Obedience unto death" was the absolutely unique priestly action of a Divine Person in human nature, competent only to a Divine Person, and morally possible to Him because, in human nature, he was the substitute of sinful men, offering himself a sacrifice to God to satisfy divine justice for their sins. When

this is seen to be the "atonement for sin," the Son of God is
recognised as Redeemer: and when it is accepted in faith,
redemption is accepted—complete redemption as the gift of
God; and men do not profess according to the strange doctrine
of this writer, to be joint redeemers of themselves along with
Christ, "obedient unto death," as He was.

Of course, I can do nothing more, here and now, than simply
state the doctrine which the Catholic Church of Christ has in
all ages held as the "divine idea which transfigures the Cross
and, through it, the whole sphere of moral and religious conflict." The demand for some such "interpreting idea," from
whatsoever quarter it comes, is fitted to awaken esteem: and
the deeper is the grief, inevitable, when we find God's own idea
rejected. Had the following pages been written in controversy,
I might have presented the truth on this point in forms of
expression more exactly shaped to meet the lines of thought
pursued, and the vocabulary of expression adopted, by the more
recent writers. But if there be one predominant thought in the
volume, it is just this, that "the last great crisis of the Sacred
Life" is unintelligible, and (in the scriptural meaning of the
word) invincibly scandalous, except in the light of "the interpreting idea" which the Holy Spirit jealously insists upon,
both at the commencement (Luke xxii. 37) and at the close
(Mark xv. 28) of "the last great crisis of the Sacred Life";
namely, that the Scripture was fulfilled which saith, "And he
was reckoned among the transgressors." In this light,
"sacrifice, satisfaction, substitution," instead of appearing, as
in the hands of the "Quarterly Reviewer," as so many discrete
and separable doctrines, requiring to be tested separately, are
seen blended into one great divine achievement, in what is not
the mere "passion," but the glorious and unapproachable
priestly action of the suffering Messiah, offering himself to God
in the room of sinful men, a sacrifice of sweet-smelling savour,
in expiation of sin, unto the satisfaction of divine justice and the
reconciliation of sinful men to God, the Judge of all, the God

and Father of our Lord Jesus Christ, and of all who believe unto the saving of the soul. If, in examining the history and doctrine of the death of Christ, men will not recognise in his death his own action as a priest, offering himself a substitutionary expiatory sacrifice to God, they will find themselves doomed to slip through their hands perpetually a knotless thread: and the further they carry their inquiries, and the more they attempt to redeem one another's and their own successive failures, they will but exhibit a continually increasing ingenuity to evade a scheme of thought which really can—and alone can —"interpret" and "transfigure" the cross.

I consider that the friends of orthodox evangelism in Scotland owe their generation a very solemn duty in the line of depriving intelligent inquirers of every inducement or temptation to seek any other "interpreting idea" of Christ's sufferings than that which the Westminster and Puritan theology has so clearly affirmed, and so powerfully established and so richly illustrated. A "glib evangelism" will not do for the days on which our lot has fallen. An indolent repetition of old phrases will not do. A more exact and profound study, and a more rich preaching of the priesthood of Christ are indispensable, if the covenant and gospel of God's grace are to abide among us. "Other gospels" are already rife, and in many quarters the covenant of grace seems to be forgotten. But the theology of the Confession of Faith and the pages of Boston and the Erskines are still dear to the Scottish people. And the same truth, sent through the living fire of a spiritual preacher's soul, will force out for itself new and fresh expression, assert itself in ever-varying combinations, and adorn itself in unexpected cross-lights and side-lights, so as to put to shame, even in a literary point of view, the pretentious but feeble literature (in many cases only semi-Christian) which in some quarters is supplanting the solid Scriptural instruction in which our fathers rejoiced.

I am ashamed to say these things, when I think how poor a contribution the following pages are to the discharge of the duty which I counsel. Still I cast them, as my mite, into the treasury. It is as well to state frankly that they are just specimens of the Scottish Lecture—an instrument of instruction which, since the days of Principal Rollock, has been a great favourite with the pious people of Scotland. So far as they deal with "the last great crisis of the Sacred Life"—(and I have entitled the volume "The Shadow of Calvary" because it does not dare to attempt to carry the reader into the thick darkness)—these pages are an attempt to view the history of Christ's sufferings in the light of the doctrine and the fruits thereof. May the Lord graciously give a blessing with what I have thus written! "Gird thy sword upon thy thigh, O most Mighty, with thy glory and thy majesty." "The Lord hath sworn, and will not repent, Thou art a Priest for ever, after the order of Melchizedek."   H. M.

June, 1875.

CONTENTS

CONTENTS

THE SHADOW OF CALVARY.

GETHSEMANE—I.

THE INCIDENTS.

"Then cometh Jesus with them unto a place called Gethsemane, and saith unto the disciples, Sit ye here, while I go and pray yonder. And he took with him Peter and the two sons of Zebedee, and began to be sorrowful and very heavy. Then saith he unto them, My soul is exceeding sorrowful, even unto death: tarry ye here, and watch with me. And he went a little farther, and fell on his face, and prayed, saying, O my Father, if it be possible, let this cup pass from me: nevertheless, not as I will, but as thou wilt. And he cometh unto the disciples, and findeth them asleep, and saith unto Peter, What! could ye not watch with me one hour? Watch and pray, that ye enter not into temptation: the spirit indeed is willing, but the flesh is weak. He went away again the second time, and prayed, saying, O my Father, if this cup may not pass away from me, except I drink it, thy will be done. And he came and found them asleep again: for their eyes were heavy. And he left them, and went away again, and prayed the third time, saying the same words. Then cometh he to his disciples, and saith unto them, Sleep on now, and take your rest: behold, the hour is at hand, and the Son of man is betrayed into the hands of sinners. Rise, let us be going: behold, he is at hand that doth betray me."—Matt. xxvi. 36-46.

BETWEEN the city and the Mount of Olives lay the Valley of Jehosaphat, traversed by the little streamlet, or winter-brook, called the Cedron. Across this brook Jesus and the eleven now wend their way by the light of the moon—for at the Passover the moon was full—to a place called Gethsemane, where was a garden.

The transaction of which this ever-memorable garden now becomes the scene is, with the exception of our Lord's actual crucifixion, perhaps the most awful and solemnizing which even the Scriptures of God contain. How can we approach the consideration of it with sufficient reverence? How can we be deeply enough affected with the insight which it gives us into the sorrow of the blessed Redeemer's soul? Shall we not feel and own our utter helplessness to speak or think of this scene in a manner befitting its amazing and affecting disclosures? The Lord give us the Spirit of grace and supplications, that we may look on him whom we have pierced!

Leaving the nature and causes of Christ's mysterious sorrow, and the nature and meaning of his prayers, to be considered more fully afterwards, and in the meantime speaking of the agony itself only very generally, let us try to place the affecting facts clearly before our minds.

He cometh, then, with the disciples "unto a place called Gethsemane."

The account given by John is more circumstantial, though he passes over the events of which the garden was the scene. He says, "When Jesus had spoken these words, he went forth with his disciples over the brook Cedron, where was a garden, into which he entered and his disciples. And Judas also, which betrayed him, knew the place: for Jesus oft-times resorted thither with his disciples" (John xviii. 1, 2).

From this we learn that the garden of Gethsemane was a well-known retreat of the Redeemer. Though about to be the scene of a conflict unparalleled in his history, it had oft-times been the scene of his prayers —the place of his secret meditations and communings with God. For he was emphatically a man of prayer. It was by prayer that he kept up fellowship with the Father from whom he had come forth, and to whom he was soon to return. It was by prayer that he vanquished all the trials and sorrows and griefs assigned to him in his pilgrimage in the flesh. It was by praying always with all prayer and supplication in the Spirit, that he sustained his faith in the safety of his person and his cause in the love and faithfulness of his Father. It was by prayer that he sued out all the promises made to him in his covenant with the Father; for concerning his own possession of them, as well as his people's, it may be said that, while they are absolutely given, and must inevitably be fulfilled, " yet for all these things will I be enquired of, saith the Lord."   The law of his humiliation and reward is in these words—" *Ask of me,* and I will give thee the heathen for thine inheritance, and the uttermost parts of the earth for thy possession." And in this, as in other respects, his people must be conformed unto him that he may be the first-born among many brethren, he that sanctifieth and they that are sanctified being all of one.

Gethsemane, then, had witnessed Jesus many times in prayer and supplication, though never so emptied (Phil. ii. 7) and abased as now.   This was the crowning act of what had indeed been a long series—what had been a habit.   " Oft-times he resorted hither."

And so Judas knew the place. " And Judas also which betrayed him knew the place " (John xviii. 2).   Hence Jesus was not fleeing from his fate when he betook himself to Gethsemane.   He was voluntarily going forward to meet the sword of which he had spoken that it should smite him.   It was very necessary that his death should be voluntary—that it should be in the spirit of the ancient oracle: " Lo, I come, in the volume of the book it is written of me; I delight to do thy will, O my God " (Ps. lx. 7).   Without this it could not have been acceptable to God, nor valuable as a sacrifice for sin. And it was needful also that his death should be *seen* to be voluntary, that the eleven might not be utterly offended—stumbling to rise again no more—in the conviction that his power was at length exhausted, that against his will he had been arrested or overpowered by a might which he could not set aside.

How numerous were the methods by which Jesus forewarned them that he went forward of his own accord to all his sufferings. " I lay down my life of myself," saith he; " no one taketh it from me; I have power to lay it down, and I have power to take it again " (John x. 15-18). And now when the hour is at hand, he leads the way to no place of concealment to baffle the traitor's design, but to the place which Judas knew, for he ofttimes resorted to it. Every step towards the garden had in it the voice, " Lo, I come! I come, knowing the things which shall befall me here." Yes: Jesus loved the Church, and gave himself for it. He loved me, says Paul, and gave himself for me.

Arrived within the garden, Jesus stations the larger number of his disciples near the entrance, with the injunction, " Sit ye here, while I go and pray yonder." It is the " Captain of Salvation " making disposition of his forces for a battle in which the weapons of warfare should not be carnal, in which he himself should bear all the fire and terror of the conflict, at once the victim and the conqueror, wounded for our transgressions, and ultimately carrying the victory by yielding himself to death. How solemnizing must this have been to the eight disciples to whom he thus assigned their position! They must have felt instinctively, from their Master's words and tones and manner, that he was himself unusually sad and sorrowful. To the other three, indeed, he was to open up more fully the depths of anguish which now began to distract him. But already even his countenance must have borne traces of the coming conflict of his soul: and his words to them must have implied that such was the crisis now at hand, and such their Master's views of it, that immediate prayer alone could enable him to meet and face it. " Sit ye here, while I go and pray yonder." He speaks with authority, assigning them their post of duty. Yet he speaks to them not as servants, but as friends, telling them plainly what their Lord doeth. " I go," says he, " I go to pray yonder." All my hope now lies in prayer. Where then will *your* strength lie? Remember ye the word that I said unto you, " The servant is not greater than his Lord." Praying always with all prayer and supplication.

"And he took with him Peter and the two sons of Zebedee—Peter and James and John—and began to be sorrowful and very heavy."

Leaving the main body of the disciples, Jesus, we see, advances, as if to meet the adversary in company with the three most valiant of his friends. And yet it is not that he calculates on their strength and aid, for he knows how miserably they will fail in the hour of trial: and their failure serves rather to prove that Jesus wrought a work, and bare a shock in this conflict, to which no mortal power or vigour was adequate. For if these three failed to acquit themselves as the sore exigencies of that dread hour demanded, there were none on earth that could stand when they had fallen. They were the strongest of the disciples; the flower and choice of the little flock. They had been more with Jesus than others. They had been admitted with him where others had been excluded; and especially they had been with him in the holy mount, and were eye-witnesses of his majesty, when he received from God the Father honour and glory. They had seen the Saviour transfigured, his face shining as the sun and his garments white as the light. They had heard the voice from the excellent glory, saying, " This is my beloved Son, hear ye him." They had seen their beloved Lord in the utmost glory in which he had ever appeared on earth in the days of his flesh. And now they were to see him lying prostrate on the ground, crushed with sorrow, weeping tears of anguish, shedding the blood of the "agony." Thus high privileges prepare for sore trials; and the abundance of the revelations needs a thorn in the flesh to balance it!

If Peter could have got his own way, he would have been on the transfiguration mountain still, and there never would have been the agony of Gethsemane. He would have made tabernacles and dwelt there enjoying the glory and shrinking from the shame. But then this proposed arrangement of his would have cost the world's salvation; for it was not amidst the glory and the radiance of the holy mount, but amidst the darkness and anguish of the garden and the desertion of the cross, that redemption was achieved and sealed. Thus the foolishness of God is wiser than men.

Yet, surely those that had seen most of the Saviour's majesty and glory, and of Heaven's testimony to his beloved person and his holy mission, were best selected to see most also of his terrible trial. Their faith, cherished by such precious recollections, might have been expected to withstand severer ordeals. They who had almost reigned with him on the mountain, might have watched and suffered better with him in his agony—but no. Yet such as they were, they were his only confidants —his truest bosom friends on earth. And so when he begins to be sorrowful and very heavy—" to be sore amazed and very heavy " (Mark xiv. 33), he opens up his heart to them, and " saith unto them, My soul is exceeding sorrowful, even unto death." Jesus was not wont to tell his grief. He had ever been a man of sorrows and acquainted with grief. But he had been well accustomed to bear his griefs in secret, and seldom sought relief from making others privy to them. *Now* his soul is filled with sorrow to overflowing, and so it bursts forth, and is poured into the bosoms of his friends. He can conceal his anguish no more.

And what, it must be asked, was the cause of the tormenting sorrow and amazement which now so greatly weakened and agitated the Son of God? It is a solemn question, worthy of long and reverent consideration. But doubtless his sorrow arose from the source that his prayer was concerned with—the vivid view and near approach of that cup which the Father was just giving him to drink. That curse of God, from which he came to redeem his elect people—that sword of the Lord's wrath and vengeance which he had just predicted—the penal desertion on the cross—the withdrawal of all comfortable views and influences—and the present consciousness of the anger of God against him as the surety-substitute, a person laden with iniquity—these were the elements mingled in the cup of trembling which was now to be put into his hands: and the prospect caused him deadly sorrow!

And he told the three. For sorrow seeketh sympathy when it will conceal no more; and the man of sorrows was in all things like unto his brethren. The relief which pouring his anguish into their bosom could bring —even this was precious to him in the crisis of his sore affliction!

But it must be poured into his Father's bosom, for nothing short of that could bring him real relief and strength. And so he plants his three dearest followers on their post of observation, and then advances alone to conflict directly with the hour and the power of darkness.

And now, mark by what successive steps, and how thoroughly, Jesus has separated himself to be alone with God. He and the eleven had left the city, with all its life and stir and care, behind them. Here is the first step. Arrived at the entrance of the garden, he leaves there the greater number of his followers, and advances

further with the chosen three. Here is the second step.
But anon, he must leave these also, and go forward alone,
to meet the danger alone, to wrestle and agonize with
God concerning it. But before he leaves the three, he
gives them also an injunction as he had previously given
to the others: "Tarry ye here, and watch with me."
Now this was the injunction which they so blameably
neglected to observe. And the circumstances were such
as—notwithstanding the excuse which the tender Saviour
made for them—rendered them inexcusable in not
observing it. How affecting was it to hear him whom
they loved imploring the little service which this request
implied! That he whom they had learned to regard as
the Son of the living God, whom the winds and the sea
obeyed, and whom they three had seen as if on the margin
of heaven receiving the homage of glorified just men
made perfect; that he should be reduced to such extremity
as to express his desire that they would help him, by
their watching with him in meeting the sore conflict to
which he was now going forward alone; ought to have
touched all the deepest feelings of their nature; and
doubtless it did do so, and perhaps more truly and ten-
derly than we can understand. But if it made this
impression at the time—if this pathetic appeal struck the
chords of sympathy in their hearts—the evil was that they
did not practically follow up such feelings by a careful,
persevering, "watchful and prayerful" sympathy unto
the end.

"And he went a little farther (or, as Luke says, "he
was withdrawn from them about a stone's cast") and fell
on his face, and prayed, saying: O my Father, if it be
possible, let this cup pass from me: nevertheless, not as I
will, but as thou wilt."

No language can describe the impression which a
statement like this ought to make upon us. The person
who is here set before us—the position of prostrate, yea,

all but abject supplication—the cry of anguish wrung out
from him in the prospect of a stroke about to fall upon
him which he trembles lest his weak, frail human nature
should be unable to bear—all these considerations, and
each of them, ought to fill us with the liveliest and most
inexpressible astonishment. It is deeply to be feared that
too many read the verses before us in a state of mind
indefinitely approaching to unconscious yet real infidelity.
Is it possible that there could be such an amount of
insensibility in any mind that steadily contemplated this
scene as an event which really occurred? Could this
transaction be viewed with more indifference than it is
by multitudes, even though it were announced as a mere
fiction? Nay; suppose it were a fiction, it would be a
grander one unspeakably than the imagination of the
thoughts of any man ever devised. Regarded as a mere
idea, though forgotten as a fact, it is still fitted to produce
a most powerful effect, to arrest and compel attention, to
fill the mind with amazement and with awe. But the
startling idea, the awful conception of the living God,
enthroned in the supreme government of a myriad of
worlds, each one of which with its countless multitudes of
living beings hangs upon his nod: of this great, self-
existent, independent Jehovah, with his Godhead dwelling
in the frail garb of human nature, lying prostrate on the
cold ground in the attitude of deepest abasement and most
prostrate prayer; the idea, combined with the assurance
that it is an idea that was actually realised in this garden
of Gethsemane! Oh! it reveals to us the carnality of our
minds when we feel that we can meet a fact like this with
so little of that adoring wonder and love and praise which
reason and conscience tell us it is worthy and fitted to
call forth. Truly no truth is more fully proved by experience and observation than that we need the Spirit to take
of the things of Christ and show them to us—that we
need the Spirit of grace and supplications to be poured

upon us ere we can look on him whom we have pierced and mourn.

But how could Jehovah-Jesus, the Eternal Son of the Highest, be reduced to such straits as these, to be prostrate on the ground, and lift the cry of helplessness so affectingly? The answer is that this is exactly " the mind that was in Christ Jesus, who, being in the form of God, thought it not robbery to be equal with God: but made himself of no reputation, and took upon him the form of a servant, and was made in the likeness of men: and being found in fashion as a man, he humbled himself and became obedient—obedient unto death, even the death of the cross " (Phil. ii. 5-8). But did he not speak as one whose faith was shaken?—as one whose fear was awakened? As one whose fear was awakened; yes. But not as one whose faith was shaken. For in the very agony of his sorrow, when he groaned in spirit, he groaned in the Spirit of the Son, crying, " Abba, Father." " *Father*, if it be possible." But did not this cry imply that he was begun to regret his covenant engagements, and to repine against the sufferings which they entailed? No: for his language is full of perfect and absolute submission. " Father, if it be possible, let this cup pass from me; nevertheless, not my will but thine be done."

But did not this imply at least that in some respect Jesus longed earnestly to escape from his sufferings? It did indeed. It implied that, save for his Father's will, appointing them and appointing his people's salvation by means of them, save for *this,* it was most desirable that he should have no such sufferings to undergo. Could they have been real; could they have been anything else than imaginary and feigned; had not this been the Saviour's feeling concerning them? Could he have had a true body and a reasonable soul, and not sensitively shrunk from undergoing " the terrors of the Lord "? Could his soul have been holy, could he have truly feared

God, and not trembled in sorrow and in anguish in the prospect of his anger, or the presence of his wrath? And how could he have "learned obedience by the things which he suffered" save by subduing his natural and sinless repugnance to endure them, and thus denying and sacrificing himself?

But still, was it not something like a weakness and imperfection on the part of Jesus that he should speak as if he thought it possible that this cup should pass from him? "Father, if it be possible, let this cup pass from me." And truly it is not to be denied that here we have Jesus revealed to us in weakness, even as the Holy Ghost testifies that he was "crucified through weakness" (II Cor. xiii. 4). Yet let us mark of what nature this imperfection was. It consisted in nothing more than the powerful predominance—or, we may perhaps say, the sole presence—in his mind, for a moment, of the one thought of the desirableness of being exempted from the abyss of misery which yawned before him in his Father's curse. That his holy human nature, considering the matter solely in itself, could not but desire to be exempt from such woe, we have already seen. Considered simply in itself, to desire exemption from the wrath of God was the dictate of his holy human nature, considered as at once sensitive and reasonable and holy. Not to have felt this desire, instead of being holiness unto the Lord, would have argued —what we tremble even to think of while we know it could not be—daring contempt of the divine anger and will! Nay: to have such impressive views as Jesus now had of his Father's wrath, and not be filled with an earnest longing to escape from it (considering the matter simply by itself) would have argued that he did not possess a true human nature with all the sinless sensibilities which are of the essence of humanity. And if Jesus did for a moment consider the matter simply by itself; if he looked to the intense desirableness of this cup passing from him, without for the moment taking the matter in connection with past appointments or future consequences; if there was a moment during which the one only object which stood straight before his mind's eye and filled all his vision, was the terror of the vengeance of the Omnipotent; did this indicate any imperfection but what was absolutely sinless and holy? His true human soul, not infinite (which is a character only of his Godhead) but finite, without which it had not been true, could not possibly behold all elements of truth in one act of con- templation. In unutterable sorrow and sore amazement, the object of dread for an instant engrossed the whole reflective faculty; and in that moment the desire, not unwarrantable but holy, which was suitable to that one instant of his sore experience, in the view of that one object which for the instant exclusively was in view—the desire, which, limiting his emotions to the single object now awakening them, it would have been unnatural, unreasonable, unholy, not to have felt—was emitted as the true and genuine and not undutiful desire of the moment—" Father, if it be possible, let this cup pass from me "—while, immediately admitting other thoughts; looking back on Eternal Counsels and irrefragable Scrip- tures and promises inviolable; the Saviour's soul, admitting these other thoughts, and with them the feelings suitable to *them* also, qualifies his desire with the expression of entire submission—" Nevertheless, not as I will, but as thou wilt." Yea, and the inconceivable intensity with which, without any disparagement of his love to his Father or his love to his Church, he exclaimed—" Father, if it be possible, let this cup pass from me " is just an index by which to mark the truth, or a line by which to fathom the depths, of that love to both, under the force of which he added: " Nevertheless, not my will but thine be done." For is it not unutterably desirable to flee from the wrath to come, whether, O sinner, it be in thine own case, or in

Christ's? And if he fled not, it was not because he was
insensible to the terrors of his Father's wrath, as sinners
are who do not flee; but he fled not, that sinners might
have a hope set before them to flee to; he fled not because
he was not an hireling, but the good Shepherd that giveth
his life for the sheep.

It is here, doubtless, that we should introduce into the
narrative the glorious statement, which is made only by
the evangelist Luke: " And there appeared an angel unto
him from heaven strengthening him " (Luke xxii. 43).

Are they not all ministering spirits sent forth to minister
unto them that shall be heirs of salvation? What
wonder, then, if we find them ministering unto him who
is the elder brother, whom God hath appointed heir of
all things? We know how they announced and celebrated
his advent as the babe of Bethlehem; how they waited on
him as the tempted One in the wilderness; how they
ministered amidst the transactions of the resurrection
morning, rolling away the stone, and guarding the place
where the body of Jesus lay. All these and suchlike acts
of service to the Mediator's person, into whose redemption
work they desire to look, were so many and very obvious
instances of the fulfilment of the Father's glorious oracle
concerning him, as it is written, " When he bringeth in
the first-begotten into the world, he saith, Let all the
angels of God worship him " (Heb. i. 6).

We are not told *how* the angel on this occasion
strengthened the agonising Redeemer. Yet if he came
that he might visibly fulfil the terms of the oracle and
" worship " him, we may see how suitable and seasonable
such a ministration must have been, and how strengthening! For it was not with Jesus at this moment as in the
times when his mighty and miraculous powers went forth;
when the energies of his Godhead were in operation to
attest his Messiahship, or bless and relieve his followers.
The attributes of his divine nature were at this moment

held in abeyance. They slumbered, or retired, to admit
of that humiliation which, had all their glories pressed
forward into view or into action, would have been impossible. And while the Godhead in the second person was
indissolubly and eternally united with humanity in one
person in the man Christ, the sufferings of " the man "
reached their crisis and their complication—just as the
positive action of his Godhead's powers and attributes
was more and more withdrawn and resigned. This was
the precise nature of his abasement, that though it was
no robbery for him to be equal with God, he yet laid
aside the reputation though never the reality thereof; and,
remaining still, as he must ever remain, the same God
unchangeable, he yet appeared in the form of a servant,
not drawing on his divine might and energies, but denying
himself their exercise and forth-putting—concealing,
retiring out of view, withdrawing from the field of action,
those prerogatives and powers of Deity, which in the
twinkling of an eye might have scattered ten thousand
worlds and hells of enemies. He withdrew them all from
action that he might taste the weakness of created nature.
And in thus denying himself the consolation and energy
and support which the action of his divine upon his human
nature, had he chosen, would have furnished to him
boundlessly, in *this* consisted the test and the trial of his
submission to the Father's yoke, in the body which he
had prepared him. To draw unduly on the resources of
his Godhead, and in a manner inconsistent with his relation and his duty towards the Father, as the Mediator
between God and man in the days of his flesh, was
precisely that act to which the devil in vain sought to
tempt him when he said, " If thou be the Son of God,
command these stones that they be made bread."   For
Jesus to have done so would have been to " make himself
of " *some* " reputation."   It would have been to resile

from the form and the duty of a servant. It would have been to abandon his position as one made under the law.

But pre-eminently in the closing scenes of his obedience and sufferings were all manifestation and action and supporting influence of his divine nature withdrawn, as if all divine glories and perfections enfolded and inwrapt themselves into mysterious concealment within. So that the divine suppliant, though he was indeed divine, lay prostrate with his face upon the ground in all the weakness that could overtake a mere—*mere* man.

How unspeakably seasonable and consoling, that at such a crisis, by the adoring worship of an angel, the glory of his own Divine Person should be presented to the view of his created mind, to countervail in some measure the anguish and the shame to which in his human nature he was at this moment reduced! True, the very nature of the case forbade that the arm of his omnipotence should spring forth and bear his enweakened body up against the infirmity and trembling which astonishment and sorrow had evoked; or that the light of his omniscience should gush in upon his human soul, as in God's full flood, and reveal to it the glories and the joys which his sufferings should achieve. Not thus in the hour of his anguish and prostration could his eternal power and Godhead come into action to relieve and comfort him. But if, while all his divine prerogatives were retired, withheld and resigned from his own enjoyment of them, in order that in creature weakness he might expiate the sins of his elect—what if from heaven there come forth one of those ministers of God that do his pleasure, and literally fulfil the commandment of the Father, " Let the angels of God worship him!" To be made the object of divine worship and adoration: to be with profoundest love and reverence reminded, that, though reproached of men and despised of the people; though weakened and abased in body and in soul to the utmost extreme of anguish and of woe; though avenged upon by God as the surety of countless sinners, bearing their responsibilities and visited with all their curse; though reduced in his created nature to all the extremity of helplessness and anguish of which it was susceptible, that still he was the adorable and true God, the living God and an everlasting king: to be worshipped still, while himself a prostrate agonising worshipper: still to be himself worshipped and adored by the messenger from heaven with all the adoration that messenger had been rendering even at the Father's throne. Oh! this was precisely the ministration of strength to his fainting soul which the crisis of his anguish required. This was unto him as the foretaste of his coming glory, when angels and principalities and powers should be subjected to him, and at the name of Jesus every knee should bow. This worshipping angel was unto him as his Father's messenger, meeting him in the moment of profound abasement to tell him of the exaltation that should follow. This answer to his prayer was like the voice of God saying unto the enfeebled man of Gethsemane: "Thy throne, O God, is for ever and ever."

The two great themes which engrossed the whole testimony of the Spirit of Christ as he spoke by all the holy prophets were " the sufferings of Christ and the glory that should follow." The time had been when that glory, as by anticipation, appeared in blessed foretaste to be realised, and the same three witnesses beheld it. While the " glory " seemed thus revealed, the " sufferings " were the theme presented to the Saviour's mind, and heavenly messengers descended on the holy mount and talked with him of " the decease which he should accomplish at Jerusalem." And now, when the " sufferings " begin to be realised, and are already endured even unto the anguish of death, " the glory that shall follow " is the theme suggested to the mind of Jesus; and an angel comes to strengthen and refresh his drooping spirit with the seasonable and assured conviction that he shall yet be glorified with the glory which he had with the Father before the world was.

Alas! that within a stone-cast of the place, in the immediate view of the very scene, where there seemed to meet in one all the intense variety of the unseen world, ranging in its compass from the cords of death and the pains of hell, to the worship and the glories of the heaven of heavens—even in immediate view of such things as these, wherein the powers of the world to come had their action so infinitely momentous, so infinitely important even to themselves, the disciples should have so fallen from sympathy with Jesus as to fall asleep!

" And he cometh unto the disciples and findeth them asleep, and saith unto Peter, What! could you not watch with me one hour?"

Ah! but let us beware lest any of us be chargeable with guilt of a similar or even deeper dye. There is such a thing as having the sufferings and anguish of Christ brought under our view, and seeing Christ set forth in ordinances manifestly prostrated, yea " manifestly crucified," for sin, and yet remaining asleep in sin, yea dead in trespasses and in sins: without fleeing from the hateful evil which entailed upon the Saviour all his anguish, and without, therefore, fleeing from the wrath which Jesus dreaded, yet in love to sinners bore. Oh! awake, thou that sleepest, and arise from the dead. Expose not yourself to such anguish and woe as filled even the soul of the Divine Redeemer with amazement and exceeding sorrow even unto death. You cannot but know, under a preached gospel, that either there must be some distinct and personal transaction, wherein, with hearts alive to the terrible importance of the case, you choose this once wearied, afflicted, abased Redeemer as your own, that in those agonies which he suffered and in that death which he ultimately died, divine justice may accept what is due on your part to the law of your God which you have broken; or else, that same justice of God must find the satisfaction of a broken law in your own eternal endurance of the second death, which is the wages of sin. O careless transgressor! asleep in a world on which the Son of God travailed in spirit, and died a ransom for sin; asleep, it may be, nearer to the unseen world than the three slumbering disciples now were to Jesus, for there may be but a step between you and death. Awake and flee in repentance and in faith to the hope which that suffering Saviour sets before you. Delay no more, lest the sword should find you out of Christ, and slay you with the second death!

But may not even believers be asleep? They were *disciples* whom Jesus found asleep when he returned from his agonising sufferings and prayers. And may not disciples still too often find that an unseemly slumber is upon their souls? Who among us feels that he is awake and alive, as he ought to be, to the powerful lessons which a scene like that of Gethsemane is fitted to teach us? Rather, who does not feel, in review of such a subject as this, that the sufferings of the Saviour's soul, and the unparalleled love which led him to endure them —the " love so amazing, so divine "—deserves not only a larger extent but even another kind of requital than any we have ever rendered? What earnest Christian can fail to be ashamed of the weakness and changeableness of the love which is all that Jesus has ever received at his hands—of the unheartiness and infrequency of the services he has rendered in his kingdom; of the slow and inconstant steps with which he has followed his example, and the much want of faith and fervency wherein he has failed to cultivate as he ought a holy and joyful fellow-ship with him in all his ordinances? Were Christians more with Jesus in the garden of Gethsemane—more studious to enter into the mind and love of a suffering Saviour—more given to cultivate the " fellowship of his sufferings," and to realise the deep glories of their own redemption as upspringing endlessly from the unfathomable abysses of the anguish of the Son of God, and boundless and secure to them only because his anguish was so great and all-sufficient—they would be far more awake to the things that are unseen and eternal, and live both more holy and more blessed under the powers of the world to come. Awake, then, ye children of God, to a livelier faith and a more penitent and grateful love to him who died for you and who rose again. It is high time to awake out of sleep, for now is your salvation nearer than when ye believed. He who lay prostrate on the ground in Gethsemane will soon come to sit upon his great white throne. Awake, and serve him in faith and love. Serve him, and fight for him, under the banner of his own most free and forgiving and sanctifying love—the love that braved Gethsemane and the cross for you. And ever tasting that the Lord is gracious, serve him with godly fear, remembering that the Lord our God is holy. So shall you not be ashamed before him at his coming.

II.

GETHSEMANE—II.

The Agony of Sorrow.

"My soul is exceeding sorrowful, even unto death"
(Matt. xxvi. 38).

THAT the sorrow of Christ in Gethsemane was of a very intense and terrible description, we have many infallible proofs. The Scriptures testify, recording indeed his own testimony, that he "began to be very heavy," to be "sorrowful," to be "sore amazed," and "sorrowful even unto death." And these expressions are far from conveying the great force and emphasis of the original.

The terms in which Jesus himself poured his griefs into the ears of his disciples, combined with the simple fact that he felt induced and constrained to speak of them at all, afford very affecting evidence that they were of a nature and degree which only the overhanging shadow of death with all its woe could have caused to fall upon him. The aid and concert of that vigilance which he implored, as if their sympathy in his sore affliction would afford some comfort and alleviation; the fact that he instantly betook himself to prayer, that mightiest of all instruments which created natures can wield; the paroxysm of earnestness and energy with which he prayed; the frequency with which he recurred to agonising prayer as his only resource; his reiterated but unsuccessful appeals and visits to his disciples; and the bloody sweat which his intense wrestlings in prayer produced, even in that cold night (for it was that same night in which the soldiers " made a fire for it was cold ")—all these are proofs that the anguish of the Saviour's soul in Gethsemane was unparalleled by anything that even he, the man of sorrows, had yet encountered or endured.

In confining our attention at present to the consideration of the sorrow of the Lord, to discover what from the Scriptures may be learned of its nature and causes, we ought to feel that we specially require the Spirit of the Lord to rest upon us, the Spirit of knowledge and of the fear of the Lord, that we may not irreverently intrude where angels might tremble to advance, or gaze with presumptuous eye where angels might veil their faces with their wings. Deep grief, among mere men, is for the most part, generously accounted a sacred thing. Here we have the grief of him who is the ever-blessed God; the sorrow and weakness and fear and trembling of him who is the Lord God Omnipotent; the tears and prostrate agonies and cries of one who is now seated on the right hand of the majesty in the heavens, angels and principalities and powers being made subject to him!

Perhaps the most impressive proof that can be given of the inconceivable terrors of Christ's sufferings considered as a whole, and as constituting the one undivided ransom for sin, results from the fact that the darkness of Gethsemane must be regarded as but the shadow of Calvary, this remark, at the same time, opening to us the nature and sources of what Christ endured when he said, " My soul is exceeding sorrowful, even unto death." The sorrows of the garden arose from the prospect and foresight of the sorrows of the cross.

That this was the case is obvious from the tenor of the Saviour's prayers, for surely the one must throw light upon the other. Without doubt it was the source of his sorrow which formed the subject of his supplication. Now we learn, from the reiterated prayers which this sorrow called forth, that Jesus was not at this time directly drinking the cup of his Father's wrath. *That* he did upon the cross when, there in his own body, on the tree, he bare our sins and was made a curse for us, and suffered once for sins, the just for the unjust. But now, in Gethsemane, the agony or wrestling of prayer which arose from the agony and anguish of grief, concerned not the immediate but the ultimate drinking of that cup—not the immediate drinking of it, but only the immediate and final allocating of it to him as a cup which he should in due time drink, and which it was his now simply to accept and acknowledge as his portion. It is impossible to read the narrative carefully with a view to this question without observing that the Saviour agonises in his deadly sorrow and his oft-repeated wrestlings, not from anguish caused by drinking of this cup, but simply by the prospect of having yet to drink of it, by the foresight of the dreadful and inconceivable travail of his soul which drinking it would cause, insomuch that, were it possible, nothing could be so unspeakably desirable as that this cup should pass from him, and by the clear view of the absolute necessity of accepting it to which his love to his Father's will and his people's salvation finally and irreversibly committed and engaged him— " Nevertheless, not my will but thine be done." And so, this paroxysm of the Saviour's agony passed away, not with the cup being drained, but simply with the cup being put into his hand by the Father's will on the one side and accepted by Jesus in full submission to the Father's will on the other. And that the cup thus given and received was not at this time drained, but simply received, is intimated by the Saviour himself subsequently when, on his entrance on the final and ultimate sorrows of death, by the arrest which Judas effected with his band of soldiers, Jesus reproved the untimely zeal of Peter, saying, " Put up thy sword into his sheath: the cup that my Father hath given me to drink, shall I not drink it."

His submitting to be thus arrested as a criminal was the commencement of his drinking that cup.

From this we may see that the cup which the Father gave him consisted substantially in the imputation to him of a criminal's guilt, and the assignment to him of a criminal's position and destiny. No sooner is the mysterious transaction of Gethsemane over than the secret and spiritual nature of what was there determined immediately begins to be manifest. From this moment, onward to his resurrection, Jesus is seen among men no more in any other character than that of a criminal. Every step now in his history is that of the history of a criminal. The whole may be summed up briefly thus: He is arrested —libelled—judged—condemned—executed. This whole series of his successive positions and endurances as an offender, a transgressor; so immediately begun, so completely sustained and perfected; was the cup which he finally drained upon the cursed tree. This cup, Peter would have had him to refuse; this position of a transgressor, Peter would have had him to renounce; when he set himself against the first element of it, in his Master's arrest. Jesus refused to resist his seizure, on the ground that this were refusing the cup which the Father had given him to drink. Can there be any difficulty, then, in understanding what that cup was? That whole treatment of his person as the person of a malefactor, of which the arrest in the garden was the first step, constituted the cup concerning which the sorrows and wrestlings of the garden had been conversant.

We know how unrighteously the blessed Jesus was forced by men into those attitudes and destinies of an offender. We know that the arrest was unprovoked: the accusation, false: the trial, a mockery: the evidence, perjury: the sentence, unrighteous and malicious: its execution, murder. Yet still, here were all the circumstances and steps, if not the pomp and dignity, of

judgment upon life and death: and if we look beneath
the surface into what infinite wisdom meant in righteousness to shadow forth by the things which the determinate
counsel and foreknowledge of God determined should
thus be done, we will find that, even as to hear of Christ
drinking the cup of wrath, is but to hear in a figure of
the atoning sufferings of the surety; so to see him
arrested, accused, condemned, and led to the death of a
special malefactor, is in like manner only to see in a
figure, to see as in a mirror, the successive footsteps of
the avenging justice of the highest, as, armed with a valid
commission to arrest, and a terrific scroll and handwriting
of ordinances to accuse, and the warrant of the judge of
all to condemn, and the everlasting sword of heaven's
wrath to avenge—she onwardly and unfalteringly pursues
unto the end the Substitute of the guilty, the Seeker and
the Saviour of the lost. That visible seizure of his person
which the traitor accomplished—that libel, judgment,
sentence, death, which in quick succession followed—in
themselves so unrighteous; what were they in the determinate counsel of God, but the outward and visible sign
of the hidden and spiritual process and prosecution
which the incensed, avenging judge carried on against
the man that was "numbered with transgressors"?
Every position in which he now stands, whether as a
captured criminal in the hands of constituted power, or
accused at the tribunal of authority, or condemned by
the highest voices in the Church and in the State, and led
away bearing the cross, and crucified between two
malefactors, one on either side—every one of these
positions, however unrighteous as assigned to him by
man, is but an index and an emblem of a corresponding
and true and righteous position or relation now assigned
to him, and which he now assumes, towards the Judge of
all the earth. Yea, even the preference of Barabbas, who
was a robber and seditious and a murderer, viewed as

the emblem and seal of Christ's hidden condɩ nnation, is but righteous and necessary. Jesus, as the substitute of sinners, is more heavily laden than he!

We see then the cup which the Saviour drank, the doom which Jesus accepted, namely, a malefactor's position and a malefactor's retribution, *symbolized* with minute, prolonged, sustained accuracy by all that the wicked hearts and voices and hands of men now accomplished in him, but *realized* under and along with, yet far above and beyond these emblems, in the reckoning he now had to meet with God and the wrath of God he now had to bear.

And if such was the cup, what could his receiving or consenting to receive it imply, but his submitting to be made sin for us, submitting to be numbered with transgressors, submitting to have the iniquities of his people laid upon him? This was what Gethsemane beheld transacted between the Father and the Son. Finally and formally the Father proposes to Jesus the assumption of the guilt of his Church unto himself. Finally and formally Jesus accepts and confirms what had been determined mutually in the counsel of peace from everlasting. He agrees, or rather solemnly ratifies all his previous agreements to be responsible in all the responsibilities of his elect people. " Not my will but thine be done." " Thy will be done." The Father lays upon him the iniquities of all whom he hath given to him: imputes to him the guilt of all that shall be redeemed: makes him that knew no sin to be sin for us: numbers him among transgressors, as bearing in his own person the sins of many; and looks upon him as lying under the imputation of all their countless transgressions. It is unto this that Jesus says, " Thy will be done." He assumes, therefore, at his Father's will, the sins which he is to bear in his own body on the tree; and the baptism of blood in his agony which follows is the sign and seal of the covenant, which thus by imputation makes him out to be the chiefest and the most heavy laden of transgressors!

Can there be any difficulty now in understanding generally what the nature and emphasis of his sorrow must have been? Think of Jesus coming into this terrible position towards the Judge of all—towards his Father and his God—towards him whose approbation and pleasure in him were the light and joy of his life unspeakable! Think of him consenting to have all the sins of myriads imputed to him by his Father: to underlie, that is, the imputation, in his Father's judgment, of every kind and degree and amount of moral evil—every species and circumstance and combination of vile iniquity! There is a book of reckoning which eternal justice writes in heaven, wherein is entered every charge to which infinite unsparing rectitude, searching with omniscient glance alike the darkness and the light, sees the sons of men become obnoxious. This terrific scroll, so far as the elect of God are concerned in it, was unrolled before the eye of Jesus in Gethsemane: " the iniquities of us all " which God was now about to lay upon him, were therein disclosed: and you have to think of the sorrow with which he should contemplate his becoming responsible and being held of God to be responsible, for all that that record charged—his being accounted of God, in his own one person, guilty of all that that record bore! It was hereupon that the Christ who, in prophetic Scripture as in the fortieth Psalm, proclaimed himself the Father's willing Covenant Servant—" Lo, I come, in the volume of the book it is written of me; I delight to do thy will, O my God; thy law also is within my heart " (Ps. xl. 6)— exclaims also, as one heavily laden with accumulated sins, and trembling, ashamed, and self-doomed because of them—" Innumerable evils have compassed me about: mine iniquities have taken hold upon me that I am not able to look up; they are more than the hairs of my head, therefore my heart faileth me " (Ps. xl. 17). And by the consenting testimony of historic Scripture, he began to be " sore amazed " and " very heavy," and said unto his disciples: " My soul is exceeding sorrowful, even unto death."

In forming a judgment of the sorrow and anguish which the imputation of sin to the holy Jesus must have caused, there is a vexing fallacy to be guarded against. We are ready to suppose that however hard and terrible to bear must have been the wrath and death which were the wages of the sins for which he suffered, yet the imputation of these sins to him could have, in itself, cost him little anxiety, or caused him little sorrow, in the consciousness that he was not personally guilty of them —the consciousness of his own unsullied holiness.

Now let it be remembered that the imputations which even malicious men chose to make him underlie—the reproaches and revilings under which at man's tribunal he was traduced—did, notwithstanding their very certain falsehood, cause him much anxiety and grief in so much that he exclaims in his Psalm of sorrow: " Reproach hath broken my heart, and I am full of *heaviness* " (Ps. lxix.); that same affection of his weary soul which he now endured in Gethsemane, when he was sore amazed and very *heavy*. And if these reproaches thus affected him, let us note these two points of difference, viz., First, that in the one case, the imputations cast upon him were from man and at man's tribunal. In the other case, God laid upon him the iniquity of us all. God made him to be sin. God imputed to him—the Father whom he infinitely loved —the judge whom he infinitely revered as one who could not do but what is right—reckoned him among transgressors. And, secondly, in the one case, the imputations of men which broke his heart and filled it with heaviness, were repudiated and denied by him in all their extent, and to every effect. In the other, there was an imputation admitted as righteous, the proposal of infinitely righteous love and wisdom—the product and decree of divine Triune counsels from everlasting. If, then, misdeeds imputed by man and in every sense denied, and which indeed had no existence at all, were yet unto the breaking of the heart, what when iniquities are imputed by God and in a true and righteous sense admitted—admitted in a sense and to an effect which entailed immediate and full responsibility, avenging and unmitigated reckoning? True, the sins which were charged upon him were not his own, but they were so laid upon him and so became *his,* that he could not merely endure, but accept as righteous, the penalty which they entailed. He did not merely suffer the death which is the wages of sin: he did voluntarily give himself up to death—accepting it as due to him—acknowledging his holy liability to it—justifying as very righteous the doom which he trembled to anticipate. And if the punishment of these sins was thus not in semblance, but in reality accepted by Jesus as justly visited upon himself, must it not have been because the sins themselves had first been made *his*—verily, really *his*—to every effect save that alone of impairing his unspotted personal holiness and perfection? And if they were *his* to bring him wrath unto the uttermost in their penalty, must they not have been *his* to cause him grief and sorrow inconceivable in their imputation? True, they were not personally his own; and so they were not *his* to bring self-accusation, self-contempt, despondency, remorse, despair. But they were *his* sufficiently to induce upon his holy soul a shame, humiliation, sorrow—yea, sore amazement—as he stood at his Father's tribunal, accountable for more than child of man shall ever account for unto eternity!

Still, confessedly, it is difficult to understand the sorrow and amazement and agony of a holy being in having sin thus by imputation imposed upon him. It is only a legal or judicial arrangement; so we reason. It is but a scheme of mercy to relieve the miserable. Or, be it that it is more; that it is a scheme of justice also to absolve the guilty; why should not the Surety's conscious innocence triumph over the sorrow and the shame of this imputed sin? Why should he quail and tremble, filled with anguish and amazement, not merely by the prospect of the penalty which this imputation will ultimately bring, but in the immediate sense of a shame, and the immediate endurance of a sorrow, which this imputation itself inflicts? What can there be in sin, when not personally his own, that can thus cause him agonise in pain and prayer, and offer up supplications with strong crying and tears?

There is nothing that we know of in all the history of God's moral administration that can aid us by comparison in considering how sin imputed by the Judge of all to a personally holy being, should fill his soul with sorrow. But the illustration, which there exists no *comparison* to furnish, may be derived from a *contrast*. The sorrows of imputed sin may be illustrated, perhaps, by the joys of imputed righteousness. Sin imputed to a holy one must produce effects directly the reverse of righteousness imputed to a sinner. And thus, perhaps, in the justification of the believer and the Church, through the righteousness of Christ, we may learn somewhat of the terrible shame and condemnation of him who became responsible for all their sins.

1. To prepare the way for this reasoning from analogy, and in order to justify us in adopting it, let it be observed, first of all, that the contrast which we wish to examine is very emphatically stated in various Scriptures; the one term being represented as the issue and the fruit resulting and contemplated from the other. " He hath made him to be sin for us who knew no sin, that we

might be made the righteousness of God in him " (II Cor.
v. 21). " Ye know the grace of our Lord Jesus Christ,
that, though he was rich, yet for your sakes he became
poor, that ye through his poverty might be rich " (II Cor.
viii. 9). It is very clearly implied in the latter of these
texts that whatever was contained in the poverty wherewith Christ became poor, the very reverse should accrue
to us in the riches wherewith by his poverty we should
be made rich : if sin and sorrow and shame and death in
the one, righteousness and joy and dignity and life eternal
in the other. And in the former text it is very distinctly
asserted that if God imputed our sins to him who had no
sin of his own, it was in order that to us who have no
righteousness of our own he might impute Christ's
righteousness in turn. To effect this marvellous exchange
is the design contemplated in Christ's union with the
Church in federal unity, in one person mystical. He
assumes her sin to taste its bitterness and bear its curse,
that she may be enriched with his righteousness, to taste
its joys, and be endowed with its heavenly rewards. This
contrast, therefore, is of express divine constitution—the
one term moreover being the glorious fruit of the other.
Sinners can be counted righteous, because the Holy One
was reckoned a sinner.

2. Notice, then, secondly, that he that believeth on
Jesus, though ungodly, and who is thereby accounted
righteous, only for the righteousness of Christ imputed to
him, is not the less entitled to rejoice in that righteousness,
even while it is true that it is not his own; yea, while it is
true that he has none of his own; yea, while it is true that
he has nothing but sin of his own. He is entitled to
rejoice, as one clothed in the glorious unsullied robes in
which omniscient holiness can find no spot nor stain.
While in himself, that is, in his flesh, there dwelleth no
good thing, yet in the Lord he hath righteousness, and in
him he may glory and make his joyful triumphant boast.

Even so, Jesus, when he was accounted a transgressor only for the transgressions of his people imputed to him, and received in infinite love to them and submission to his Father, when he said, " Thy will be done," is not the less subjected to inevitable sorrow and shame in that imputed sin, even while it is true that it is not his own; yea, while it is true that he has none of his own; yea, while it is true that he has nothing but glorious and unsullied holiness of his own. He is subjected to sorrow and shame as one clothed in filthy garments in which omniscient holiness—his Father's and his own—alike behold unbounded material for abhorrence. While in himself he is the beloved Son of God—in whom the Father is ever well pleased, yea, delighting in him specially in this very transaction because of his holy acquiescence in this holy liability in the sins of his sinful and unpurged Church, yet identified with his sinful and still unpurged Church in all her unpurged sin, he hath ground only for horror and humiliation. The believers own unworthiness ought not to avail to impair his joy, because a true righteousness is imputed to him, and he hath the blessedness of him to whom the Lord imputeth not his sin. The Surety's own unspotted holiness cannot avail to prevent his sorrow, because sin is imputed to him and he hath voluntarily therefore assumed what misery must belong to him to whom the Lord imputeth—not his holiness—to whom the Lord imputeth nothing but sin.

3. The fact that the righteousness which the believer rejoices in is not his own, not only does not diminish his joy, but on the contrary adds to it an element of wonder, a thrill of unexpected and surprising delight. To be exalted from a relation fraught with guilt and wrath and fear and death, and to be brought at once, on the ground of another's merit, into one of favour and peace and blessedness and eternal life—to have the angry frown of an incensed avenging judge turned away, and

all replaced by the sweet smiles of a Father's love—this, the fruit of the imputation of another's righteousness, hiding all my sin, quenching all my fear, wondrously reversing all my fate, this is not only joyful but surprising —wonderful, the doing of the Lord and marvellous in our eyes!

And so, for Jesus to be accounted a sinner by imputation must have added a pang of amazement to the sorrow and humiliation which ensued. In point of fact, this very element in his sorrow is pointed out. He began to be "*sore amazed.*" Not but that he fully expected it. Yet when it came, the change was in its nature "amazing." To pass from a state of unimpeached integrity to one in which he was chargeable with all grievous sins—from a state in which his conscious and unsullied love and practice of all things that are pure and lovely and of good report caused him to obtain the announcements to his Father's complacency and love—("I do always those things that please him")—to a state in which that love and practice still unimpaired, he nevertheless justified his Father's justice in frowning on him in displeasure by the very horror and the struggle in which he would, but for his Father's will, have refused to be plunged: this must have struck into the very heart of all his sorrow an element of amazement amounting to absolute agony and horror. If an ecstacy of wonder thrills through the believer's joy in the Lord his righteousness, there must have been a deeply contrasted paralysing amazement when the Holy One of God realised himself as worthy, in the sins of others, of condemnation at his Father's tribunal.

4. The justified believer finds his joy in the righteousness of Christ augmented to the highest exaltation by the fact that this righteousness is not only not his own, but is the righteousness of one so beloved, so closely related to him as his living head, his elder brother—" my

Lord, and my God." Had it been the righteousness of
one standing in no endearing relation to him (were this
conceivable) one who in future should be nothing more
to him than any other, or one never more to be heard of,
or at least never to be enjoyed in the embrace of friendship and the offices of love: the believer's joy in such a
righteousness imputed to him would have been unspeakably less. The exulting delight, unspeakable and full of
glory, which the believer cherishes in clasping to his heart
that righteousness of Jesus which is all his boast before
God and angels, and which evermore is as a cordial to
his fainting heart, the ever-reviving fountain to him of
life from the dead, the secret and inexpressible exultation
of his joy in this righteousness of Jesus just springs from
the remembrance that it is the righteousness of one whom
his soul loveth; of one who is all his salvation and all
his desire; of one with whom he shall dwell for evermore
—and thus better to him far than had it been his own.
Imputation, therefore, it is evident, can carry with it a
fervour and intensity of joy to which actual and personal
possession can never reach.

And ah! why may not this principle operate when
imputation infers sorrow, being the imputation of sin? If
Jesus had been *forced* to assume the place and responsibilities of the guilty (were that conceivable) the case in
this respect would have been very different from what it
was. It must not be forgotten that it was love that
induced him to accept the imputation of iniquity—to bear
away, as the Lamb of God, the sin of the world. Had
it been the imputation of the sins of those whom he did
not love (were that conceivable) his resulting sorrow
would have been unutterably less; and there might have
been some scope or place for the idea that the sin being
merely imputed, and not at all his own, he could afford
to let it lie lightly upon his soul. But it was the sin of
those whom he was not ashamed to call, and could not

be induced to refrain from calling brethren—the sin of his children; his Church; his dearly beloved; his elect; his bride—"the Lamb's wife." His electing and everlasting love, therefore—free, sovereign, distinguishing, self-consuming—choosing this sinful Church into this intensely and divinely endearing relation, wherein his delights were with her by anticipation ere yet the morning stars sang for joy—bound her iniquity upon him as his own, even as it bound *her* as a seal upon his heart and as a seal upon his arm. Thus came the Holy One of Israel to have sin to reckon for—sin not his own in his own name, yet still his own in *her* name. And so, having guilt, and having conscience, even while he had not a guilty conscience, his soul was "exceedingly sorrowful even unto death." For he realised that he was "made sin"!

Oh, let us not think that, because personally and in himself perfectly holy, Jesus could on that account have experienced little sorrow from being numbered with transgressors.

Not because in himself he is a sinner is the believer excluded from rejoicing in the imputed righteousness of Christ. Justified by faith in another's merit, he may rejoice in the Lord, and glory in the God of his salvation. Yea, the fact that it is another's merit which is the fountain of all his joy and the ground of all his glorying, infuses an element of admiration and astonishment into his glorying and his joy. And that it is the righteousness of his beloved and his friend, gives to his joy the crowning character of inexpressible delight and sweet and most generous exultation. Oh, blessed is the man to whom the Lord imputeth righteousness without works! "I will *greatly* rejoice in the Lord, my soul shall be joyful in my God: for he hath clothed me with the garment of salvation, he hath covered me with the robe of righteousness, as a bridegroom decketh himself with ornaments, and as a bride adorneth herself with her jewels."

And turning now to the mournful side of this contrast —surely it should break our hearts (Zech. xii. 10) to have to do it—turning to the mournful side of this contrast, which in its deep abasing poverty in sorrow has procured for us all this riches in gladness, we may surely understand how in like manner his personal holiness did not exempt him from sorrow when sin was imputed to him; how, rather, his sorrow was mingled with a peculiar terror and amazement, springing from the fact that the sin was the sin of others and not his own; and how that sorrow must have been deep and terrible in proportion as the love which bound these others to him in love even as his own soul, and thus identified them with himself, did thereby bind upon him as his own, in the name of those whom he was infinitely far from repudiating, all the iniquity which his Father's justice charged against them.

It is not indeed the joy which a believer actually experiences as justified in the merit of Emmanuel which can properly be chosen as the counterpart and contrast to the sorrow of Jesus. It is rather the joy, in its purest form and fullest measure, which there is ground for the believer enjoying, that can alone form anything like an accurate, though even then most inadequate, index to the contrasted sorrow of the Substitute and Surety of sinners. But we have seen enough in the analogy between imputed sin and imputed righteousness to show, that as the latter, though imputed and not personal, does yet lay a ground of righteousness and surprising joy, so the former in like manner, though also not personal but merely imputed, does not on that account any less entail amazing sorrow and shame as its result.

Any aid which this analogy may furnish to us in looking into the amount of the Saviour's sorrow is at the best but small, and the abyss of his troubles must ever be unsearchable—a matter of faith rather than of knowledge. But if the analogy is correct, then, to give to our idea such expansion as it is capable of—measuring still the sorrow of the Redeemer by the joy of the redeemed, we may observe:

1. That the more the believer sees of Christ's righteousness, and the more he realises it by faith as his own, the deeper does that joy become which he is warranted to cherish in the Lord his Righteousness. We can conceive his faith, and his believing consciousness, to attain the consummate strength of a divine and infallible assurance. And, further, we may suppose the glorious spiritual insight he may have attained into the moral loveliness and beauty of the righteousness thus imputed to him to be such, that knowing of God that he is of God invested in this matchless robe of salvation, his joy thereupon should rise above all power of sublunary things to shake or overshadow it. This much as to the measure of the purchased joy—joy in imputed merit—and the conditions on which its rise and increase depend.

Similar are the conditions needful to depth of sorrow in imputed sin. First, infallible assurance (not to be called faith in this case, yet supplying its place in the other), infallible assurance that the imputation is effected; and secondly, a profound insight into the hatefulness and moral deformity of the sin that is imputed. To convey these to Jesus was verily the Father's object in dealing with him in the garden. He gave him a view of the cup such as revealed to him the elements with which it was charged; and accurate and terrible therefore as was the view given him of the iniquities thus laid upon him, profound in proportion must have been that sorrow of which he spoke when he said, " My soul is exceeding sorrowful even unto death."

2. But again, secondly, a believer's joy in the righteousness of Christ rises to its fullest ecstacy of

unmingled exultation and unassailable security, only when he actually enters the home of the redeemed and the presence of his Father on high. Then indeed will he glory in the Lord his righteousness, accepted into everlasting life in virtue of the righteousness of his Lord. And why should his joy then be bounded only by his own capacity of joy? For one reason among others, because the undimmed spiritual eye of his own personal and now unsullied holiness, can look with hitherto unknown appreciation and blessedness upon the transcendent moral beauties of the righteousness in which he walks in light. His perfect holiness now crowns his joy in the righteousness of Christ with its final and celestial radiance.

Ah! does not the contrast again hold, very affectingly? Personal holiness and unspotted purity did not diminish the terrible humiliation and anguish Jesus underwent in being clothed with filthy garments, in being made sin, in being laden with iniquity and accounted a transgressor. Ah! no. The stainless personal perfection of Jesus made him inconceivably sensitive to all the degradation which his position at his Father's tribunal as a transgressor implied. The believer, rejoicing in his Saviour's righteousness, must at death be made perfect in holiness and pass into glory before he can comprehend the glorious depths of perfection in that righteousness which his beloved and his friend hath brought in on his behalf. But Jesus, ever absolutely sinless, did, in virtue of that very sinlessness which we would reckon on as if it alleviated his sorrow, penetrate the depths of moral evil in all its compass and deformity and vileness which was now to be laid upon him: and his soul, because it was holy, was so much the more sorely amazed, and very heavy, and exceeding sorrowful even unto death.

3. But the perfection of the contrast lies not between the joys of a single believer and the sorrows of the one

Saviour who died for all. There shall be a people in the realms of day, blood-washed and redeemed and rejoicing, whom no man can number. Who shall measure the sum of the joy wherewith these millions of once apostate but justified transgressors, saved and sanctified for ever, shall joy in the God of their salvation? The voice of that mighty aggregate of joy shall be loud and long—yea, for ever. It shall be as the noise of many waters, ever springing up yet more and more from exhaustless abyssmal depths. It was *that* mighty aggregate of joy to which Jesus gave being by his sorrow. It is with *that* mighty aggregate of joy—ever deepening in the Holy Ghost unto eternity—that the sorrow of Jesus must be contrasted!

Are we not, then, in some measure prepared to rend our hearts and mourn, to bow our heads and worship, while a still small voice is asking: *" Was there ever sorrow like unto my sorrow?"*

III.

GETHSEMANE—III.

The Agony of Prayer.

"And being in an agony he prayed more earnestly; and his sweat was as it were great drops of blood falling down to the ground" (Luke xxii. 44).

Before entering on the consideration of the import of our Lord's prayer in the garden, there are one or two preliminary considerations requiring our attention.

1.   The Scriptures present Jesus to us as a man of prayer.   At an early period of his ministry we read a statement such as this: "And in the morning, rising up a great while before day, he went out and departed to a solitary place, and there prayed" (Mark i. 35).   Again, after having fed the five thousand, Jesus, we are told, "straightway constrained his disciples to get into a ship and to go before him unto the other side, while he sent the multitude away.   And when he had sent the multitude away, he went up into a mountain apart to pray.   And when the evening was come, he was there alone," remaining there until the fourth watch of the night, when he marvellously and miraculously showed himself to the disciples, walking upon the waters and subduing the storm (Matt. xiv. 13).   In like manner, the night preceding the day on which he chose the twelve to be his special disciples and witnesses, was dedicated to prayer: "And it came to pass in those days, that he went out into a mountain to pray, and continued all night in prayer to God.   And when it was day, he called unto him his

disciples, and of them he chose twelve, whom he also named apostles " (Luke vi. 12). These are instances in which Jesus is set before us as pre-eminently a man of prayer.

2. In the second place, this was of necessity involved in the fact of his being made in all things like unto his brethren, sin only excepted. To identify himself with his people in all their responsibilities, and in all their necessities and sinless infirmities, was the Redeemer's purpose in assuming their nature. He would taste, by experience, all that was implied in their position, bearing by imputation all the sin that was involved in it, and entering by personal sympathy into all in it that was not sinful. He inevitably placed himself, therefore, in a position of acknowledged weakness and infirmity—of absolute dependence on God—a dependence to be exercised and expressed in the adorations and supplications of prayer. He was made of a woman, made under the law—under the law of prayer, as of other ordinances and duties—the law by which a man can receive nothing except it be given him from heaven, and except the Lord be inquired of for it (Ez. xxxvi. 37).

3. That Christ should be a man of prayer was required by the terms or conditions of the covenant between himself and the Father. That covenant, which imposed upon him certain obligations, made him the heir also of many promises. Yet the fulfilment of these promises was suspended on the condition that Jesus should solicit them in prayer. Whatsoever was needful for the preservation of his person, or the erection of his kingdom, the Father engaged to bestow, requiring only the Son to ask.

The strength, the grace, the support, the consolation needed by Jesus personally, had all to be sued out in prayer; as also the fruits of his death and the ingathering of his children. In all things by prayer and supplication, with thanksgiving, he had to make his requests known unto God. For such was the law of his office. Such, accordingly, was the decree concerning him, as he himself rehearses it in the second Psalm: " I will declare the decree: Jehovah hath said unto me, Thou art my Son, this day have I begotten thee. *Ask of me,* and I will give thee the heathen for thine inheritance, and the uttermost parts of the earth for thy possession." And the prayers of the Son of God, David's Son and David's Lord, are predicted also, when in the eighty-ninth Psalm Jehovah speaketh in vision to his Holy One, and saith, " He shall cry unto me, My Father, my God, and the Rock of my Salvation."

4. The subjection of Christ's divine person, in his Mediatorial office, to this necessity of prayer, illustrates the true nature of his humiliation. Prayer is a confession of weakness, of insufficiency. But how singular is this in one who is a divine person—the Eternal Son of God! For he who thus prayed was God manifest in the flesh. Surely, therefore, he was God in an estate of humiliation. For observe. From whom did Jesus seek the grace and power whch his frail human nature needed? From what source did he desire and expect to be supplied with grace sufficient for him, with strength made perfect in his weakness? Surely from Godhead—from the infinite resources and all-sufficiency of Godhead in the person of the Father. But, dwelt there not all the fulness of the Godhead in his own person bodily? And if so, why did he not directly, and without supplicating the Father, lay hold at once on all the resources of strength and consolation which his own Godhead, in the unity of his Mediatorial person, could have yielded? Why, if he was, in his own person, true and very God, did he not make way immediately to enrich, from the treasures of his own divine energies, that frail human nature which he had exalted into union with Deity? Surely with such

unimpeded and immediate access to the whole fulness of God, as the man Christ Jesus may be supposed to have possessed, in virtue of the personal indwelling of the Godhead, he might at once have laid his hand on the very gift, or measure of divine grace and strength, which he required, without the circuitous process and the delay, so to speak, of offering up supplications to the Father?

The fact that Jesus did *not* thus spontaneously, and on his own authority, appropriate from his own divine resources and make over to his human nature the upholding energy he so earnestly desired, but humbly and patiently sought and waited for it from his Father, is an illustration of the wonderful statement made by Paul, when speaking of Jesus he says, " Who being in the form of God, thought it not robbery to be equal with God: but made himself of no reputation, and took upon him the form of a servant, and was made in the likeness of men, and being found in fashion as a man, he humbled himself and became obedient unto death, even the death of the cross " (Phil. ii. 6-8). It was the very God that was found in fashion as a man, in the likeness of men, in the form of a servant. At his disposal were all the attributes of which Godhead is possessed—all the strength and graces and gifts which Godhead can bestow. From his own Godhead he, the God-man, could have supplied gloriously to his own human nature, as he supplies to other created natures, all that is required for maintenance and wellbeing. It would not have been " robbery " had he done so. Yet he had emptied himself. His humiliation implied that he should refrain from seeking in this manner to strengthen his humanity. He was to be found simply " in fashion as a man," resigning all claims to wield in his own behalf the powers of that Godhead which he still possessed unimpaired, though concealed. Though he was " in the form of God "—possessing, exhibiting, exercising the prerogatives of

God—he took upon him " the form of a servant," exercising himself unto all the subjection of a servant—the servant's form alone appearing, the form of God retired from view. Hence, while still the true God, *his* were the infirmities and necessities of a man, and his Father's Godhead was his refuge and his strength, his very present help in every time of trouble. Hence Jesus prayed. He required to pray: for in his humiliation, he emptied himself, and it was to his Father he applied, that according to his day his strength might be. His miracles were thus wrought by the Father's power: " My Father doeth the works." And he received that power by prayer. As in the eminent miracle of raising Lazarus we find Jesus " lifting up his eyes and saying, Father, I thank thee that thou hast heard me. And I knew that thou hearest me always; but because of the people which stand by I said it, that they may believe that thou has sent me. And when he had thus spoken he cried with a loud voice, Lazarus, come forth " (John xi. 41-43).

By the Father's power was this stupendous work achieved—and that given in answer to prayer. For in the depths of his soul Jesus had prayed, and received secretly the consciousness of an answer: nor would he have given audible expression to his communion in prayer with the Father save for the people which stood by. But for their sakes he said it, that they might believe that the Father had sent him, that the Father did the works.

Thus the very nature of Christ's humiliation explains the necessity and nature of his subjection to the ordinance of prayer: while it made prayer as truly indispensable to him as to any of his believing people. For in his resignation of all right to wield at pleasure the powers of his own Godhead, he " became poor " as his own poor and needy children, and left for himself only what *they* may ever draw upon—the fulness of the Father's Godhead and his promises. How truly he became in all things like unto his brethren! In his exaltation in our nature he reassumed his Divine rights and glories, reaccepting full access to the spontaneous employment, for the Father's glory and his own, of all that was his as the co-equal Son of God. "Father, glorify thou me with the glory which I had with thee before the world was." And as he humbled himself that he might be made like unto his brethren, so in being exalted in our nature, it is that the brethren may be made like unto him, as he testifies in his intercession for them. "And the glory which thou gavest me I have given them."

Proceed we now to consider the prayer in Gethsemane. And here there are three things calling for attention. *First,* the subject; *second,* the nature; *third,* the success —of this prayer.

1.   The subject or the matter of this prayer. "O my Father, if this cup may not pass from me except I drink it, thy will be done."

Now we are apt to regard this as an expression of resignation and submission, and nothing more, as a mere negative willingness to suffer the will of God. And the expression which Jesus employs often means this merely. Thus the friends of the Apostle Paul, when told by the Prophet Agabus the things that should befall him in Jerusalem, entreated him most vehemently that he would change his purpose, and when Paul would not be persuaded, they ceased, saying, "The will of the Lord be done." In this they merely gave a pious yet bare acquiescence when they found that matters could not be otherwise; and henceforth they were willing, but not at all desirous, that Paul should go up to Jerusalem. But there is much more than this in the prayer of Jesus: "O my Father, thy will be done." As when he commanded his disciples to pray, saying, "Our Father, who art in heaven, thy will be done on earth, even as it is done in heaven"—meaning thereby that we ought to pray to be willing to know, *obey,* and submit to his will in all things as the angels do in heaven—so, in his own person, he exhibits an example of a positive and strong desire that the will of God should be done. He prays desirously that the will of God may positively be done—prays this " more earnestly " than when he went the first time and said, " Father, if it be possible let this cup pass from me "—prays this " with strong crying and tears "—prays this in a vehement agony of wrestling, more vehement than Jacob's when he would not let the angel of the covenant go except he blessed him—prays this in an agony of blood. We do not enter at all into the mind of Christ if we limit his language to a mere expression of his willingness to drink that cup which could not pass from him. We must understand the Saviour as intensely desiring that the will of God should be done.

What was that will of God? Clearly the two sides of the statement are directly contrasted. " O my Father, since this cup may not pass from me, thy will be done." Since it is thy will that it should *not* pass from me, I desire to drink it. I desire to drink this cup, and thereby fulfil thy will—fulfil thy will in all its extent, in measure and in manner to secure thy full approbation, and so as to secure all thy most holy and most gracious eternal purpose.

O my Father *thy will* be done! Sacrifice and offering thou wouldst not, but a body hast thou prepared me: In burnt-offering and sacrifice for sin thou hast had no pleasure. Then said I, Lo I come (in the volume of the book it is written of me)—Lo I come *to do thy will,* O God. By the which *will* those whom thou hast given me shall be sanctified through the offering of my body once for all. For their sakes therefore I sanctify myself—I consecrate myself a sacrifice for sin—that they also may be sanctified, separated from the world, consecrated to thee, holy to the Lord (Heb. x. 5-10, John xvii. 19). The will of the Father evidently was that Jesus should be an offering for sin—the surety in the room of the guilty—that he should be made sin. " Sacrifice and offering thou didst not will, but in the body prepared for me I come to do thy will." And farther, the will of the Father was that hereby the Church should be sanctified or consecrated, or, in short, saved with an eternal salvation and with exceeding joy. " By the which will we are sanctfied." Hence two things are implied in Jesus' prayer:

1. He prays for support and grace sufficient to enable him to fulfil the whole will and appointment of God in his coming death. That death was one in which his covenanted engagement was not merely that he should passively endure what should be laid upon him, but that he should actively and positively and obediently offer himself unto God—and pour out his soul unto death—and make his soul an offering for sin. With this before him, he prays for such measures of divine grace—such supply of the Spirit of God—such communications and degrees of faith and love and zeal—such ardour of love to God and to the Church, as shall sustain him not only in uncomplaining submission, but in fervent and unimpaired obedience unto the end. For so long as in the spirit of active devotion of himself to his sufferings, the spirit of ardent *obedience,* he embraced every pang of sorrow, every infliction which it was his to bear in " dying the just for the unjust," so long would he be a conqueror. In being positively obedient unto death he would be the conqueror of death; and exactly by dying in such a manner he would be saved from death. Hence in alluding to his prayer, Holy Scripture says " that he offered up prayers and supplications with strong crying and tears unto him that was able to save him from death " (Heb. v. 7). This does not mean that Jesus prayed that he might be saved *from* dying, but saved *in*

dying; saved from being swallowed up of death, by being enabled through death to swallow up death in victory. He prayed to him who, by the boundless riches of his sustaining grace, was able to enable him to meet death in the spirit of obedience and of zeal for his Father's commandment, namely, that he should lay down his life for the sheep. He prayed to him who was able to strengthen him unto all endless love, that he might give himself, by positive " obedience unto death," a sacrifice to God, a substitute for sinners. For so long as thus, by holy and obedient resolution, he presented himself unto death, he met and faced down death—never conquered by death so long as his own obedience was sustained. And should that obedience be sustained " unto death," then would he be " saved from death " exactly by dying, and through death he would destroy him that had the power of death.

Accordingly it was renewed communications of strength from God that he prayed for in his weakness. With the burden of his Church's guilt laid upon him, and the avenging penalty due to it about to be exacted from him in the wrath of God poured into his soul—or his own soul, under that wrath, poured out a victim to divine justice, a sacrifice of a sweet smelling savour unto God —he feels that his weak human nature is utterly inadequate of itself to bear this burden, or come forth from beneath this ordeal with his obedience still unviolated. He calls therefore on the Lord. In an agony he wrestles earnestly. He offers up supplication and prayers with strong crying and tears. He is filled with holy fear. " According to thy fear, O God, so is thy wrath " (Ps. xc. 11). According, therefore, to *his* fear, Messiah knoweth the power of the Father's wrath as no other knows it. He trembles, dismayed. He casts himself prostrate on the ground. And as in the fortieth Psalm, which is his prayer in full, he who said, " I come to do thy will," and who, on the imputation to him of his people's sins, exclaimed, " Mine iniquities have taken hold upon me so that I am not able to look up," exclaimed also in contemplating the wrath which this imputation involved: " Be pleased, O Lord, to deliver me: O Lord make haste to help me: I am poor and needy, yet the Lord thinketh upon me, thou art my help and my deliverer, make no tarrying, O my God " (Ps. xl. 13, 17).

With what earnestness and strong crying Jesus lifted up his voice and sought the Father's strength may be learned from those Psalms that are manifestly prophetic of the Messiah, containing indeed the Messiah's prayers. That the twenty-second and sixty-ninth Psalms are such every reader of the Bible knows; and from these, therefore, we bring forward the following supplications as part of those which Jesus offered up: " Save me, O God, for the waters are come in unto my soul. I sink in deep mire where there is no standing: I am come into deep waters where the floods overflow me. I am weary of my crying: my throat is dried: mine eyes fail while I wait for my God. But my prayer is unto thee, O God, in an acceptable time. O God in the multitude of thy mercy, hear me, in the truth of thy salvation. Deliver me out of the mire, and let me not sink; let me be delivered from them that hate me, and out of the deep waters. Let not the water flood overflow me, neither let the deep swallow me up, and let not the pit shut her mouth upon me. Hear me, O Lord, for thy loving-kindness is good; turn unto me according to the multitude of thy tender mercies. And hide not thy face from thy servant; for I am in trouble: hear me speedily. Draw nigh unto my soul and redeem it; deliver me because of mine enemies. But I am poor and sorrowful; let thy salvation, O God, set me up on high " (Ps. lxix.). " Be not far from me; for trouble is near; for there is none to help. For I am poured out like water, and all my bones are out of joint; my heart is like wax; it is melted in the midst of my bowels. My strength is dried up like a potsherd; and my tongue cleaveth to my jaws: and thou hast brought me into the dust of death. Be not thou far from me, O Lord: O my strength, haste thee to help me. Deliver my soul from the sword; my darling from the power of the dog" (Ps. xxii.). "Withhold not thy tender mercies from me, O Lord; let thy loving kindness and thy truth continually preserve me. For innumerable evils have compassed me about" (Ps. xl. 11, 12).

In these supplications the one unvarying object of desire is divine help, preservation, grace that he may victoriously do and suffer the whole *will* of God. His crushing anxiety is that he may not fail nor waver from his obedience till he shall have done all that *will* of God on account of which a body was prepared for him. For the upholding power of his covenant God he prays, that his strength may not give way in bearing the condemnation of the Church and his Father's wrath due to their iniquities. His work is very dear to him, and he agonises in prayer that he may be sustained unto the discharge of all that it involves. That work was assigned him by the Father's will, and with intense desire he cries: " Thy will be done!"

2. But another thing involved in this prayer was a desire for the fruits of his work—the glory of the Father in the salvation of his people. For saith the Scripture, speaking of this will of God, " By the which will we are sanctified through the offering of the body of Christ once for all." Hence the prayer of Jesus implied in it a supplication for his Church that they may be sanctified —that is, separated, consecrated to God, and finally and fully saved. He prayed that he might so execute all that will of God, as that the covenanted result might follow in many sons and daughters being brought to glory. Hence in those Psalms which we have already quoted, in

the midst of the petitions which supplicate grace for Jesus personally under his baptism of suffering and expiation, there occur, not seldom, petitions that refer to his people and their salvation—his anxiety to be preserved from failing in his work being increased by the thought that otherwise all hope of salvation would be cut off from the Church.

Thus, in the sixty-ninth Psalm, when he represents himself as the surety of the guilty, amenable in obligations not his own—for sins which he nevertheless so embraces in the imputation of them to himself and in the penalty due to them as to call them indeed his own, he says: " I restored that which I took not away: O God, thou knowest my foolishness, and my sins are not hid from thee: Let not them that wait on thee, O Lord God of hosts, be ashamed for my sake; let not those that seek thee be confounded for my sake, O God of Israel." Again when anticipating the all-sufficient grace which he implored, and the glorious issue in the full expiation of his people's sins and the full satisfaction of his Father's justice, he says in the same Psalm (verse 32): " The humble shall see this and be glad, and your heart shall live that seek God." It is the same in his prayer in the fortieth Psalm: " Be pleased, O Lord, to deliver me: O Lord, make haste to help me: Let those that seek thee rejoice and be glad in thee; let such as love thy salvation say continually, The Lord be magnified." Let me so be sustained unto all gracious and holy obedience to thy will, that my offering of myself shall be indeed an an acceptable sacrifice to God—a ransom infinitely precious—a ground of salvation and of boundless hope to all that seek Jehovah and his face—a fountain of redeeming grace so wonderful that all who love thy salvation shall shout for joy and magnify the Lord with me for ever.

Such, then, in substance were the two topics of this most marvellous prayer. *First,* the Lord Jesus implores all needful grace in the discharge of his duty of being " obedient unto death "—in his priestly office presenting himself through the Eternal Spirit a sacrifice without spot unto God. *Secondly,* he implores therein the everlasting salvation of his people and the glory of his Father thereby.

That " will of God " was the offering of the body of Christ once for all: to accomplish this he prayed for all needful strength. By that " will of God," also, his people are sanctified and perfected: to obtain this also was the object of his prayer. He had both these things in view when he said, " O my Father, thy will be done."

2. Consider the nature of this prayer. And in one word this was a prayer of importunate faith. It was the prayer of faith and importunity.

(1) It was the prayer of faith.

Jesus, the Eternal Son of God, was a man of faith. By his incarnation he assumed a nature and a position in which nothing but faith could have sustained him. And the very fact that he found it possible and necessary for him to exercise faith, notwithstanding his glorious possession of Godhead dwelling in his person, resulted from that humiliation to which he subjected himself and of which we have already spoken. Though he was in the form of God, he emptied himself, and was found in fashion as a man—in all things like unto his brethren, sin only excepted. Hence the faith of the man Christ Jesus is stated by the writer to the Hebrews as a proof of the full extent to which Jesus, the living head of the Church, hath identified himself with his members: " For both he that sanctifieth and they that are sanctified are all of one: for which cause he is not ashamed to call them brethren, saying, I will declare thy name unto my brethren, in the midst of the Church will I sing praise unto thee: And again; I will put my trust in him " (Heb. ii. 11-13).

So eminent and obvious was the faith which Jesus reposed in God that it was made especial matter of reproach to him. " All they that . see me laugh me to scorn: they shoot out the lip, they shake the head, saying, He trusted on the Lord that he would deliver him; let him deliver him seeing he delighted in him." Such was the prophetic testimony of the Spirit. And it was literally fulfilled; for " the chief priests mocking him, with the scribes and elders said, He trusted in God; let him deliver him now if he will have him " (Ps. xxii. 7; Matt. xxvii. 43). His faith was conspicuous even to his foes.

Now in order to the prayer of faith, there must be both the Word and Spirit of the Lord. It must be prayer in the Spirit, and prayer according to the Word. It must be so with every member of the Church. And Jesus, the Church's head, is under the same law. He also must pray in the Spirit, if he would be heard. He also must have God's words abiding in him, if he would ask what he will and it shall be given to him. But the covenant under which he lives and dies, and rises again, provides for this abundantly. For, thus saith Jehovah to his Christ, thus hath the Lord said to our Lord, " As for me, this is my covenant with them, saith the Lord: My Spirit that is upon thee, and my words that I have put in thy mouth, shall never depart out of thy mouth, nor out of the mouth of thy seed, nor out of the mouth of thy seed's seed, saith the Lord, from henceforth and forever " (Isa. lix. 21).

(1)   Had Jesus the warrant of the Word for his prayer? Was it the promise of Jehovah that he pleaded? Was it as one who could say, " Remember unto thy servant the word on which thou hast caused me to hope "? Most certainly. When seeking the Father's upholding power he had only to make mention of the Father's covenant

promise to him: " Behold my servant whom I uphold,
mine elect in whom my soul delighteth; I have put my
Spirit upon him, he shall bring forth judgment unto the
Gentiles. He shall not fail nor be discouraged till he
have set judgment in the earth, and the isles shall wait
for his law " (Isa. xlii. 1-4). Or again, thus had Jehovah
said in the prophets concerning him " whom man
despiseth," " In an acceptable time have I heard thee,
and in a day of salvation have I helped thee; and I will
preserve thee and give thee for a covenant of the people "
(Isa. xlix. 8). Hence did he say in faith: " The Lord
God will help me; therefore shall I not be confounded;
therefore have I set my face like a flint, for I know that I
shall not be ashamed. He is near that justifieth me: who
will contend with me? Let us stand together. Who is
mine adversary? Let him come near unto me. Behold,
the Lord God will help me: who is he that shall condemn
me?" (Isa. l. 7-9). Yes, Messiah had abundant promises,
exceeding great and precious promises, all Yea and Amen
in himself. And his prayer was simply an inquiring for
the thing which the Lord had spoken.

(2) But was Christ's prayer also in the Spirit as well
as according to the Word? Now we know that the Spirit
of the Lord was given him without measure; and if so,
he must have prayed in the Spirit.   Believers receive
from Christ the promise of the Spirit. According to the
measure of the gift of Christ to each member, the Spirit
comes forth to the Church from her living head to whom
the Spirit was given without measure. And if in the
believer the Holy Ghost is a Spirit of grace and supplications, he must have primarily wrought in this same
character, in all his fulness and in his highest efficacy, in
Jesus.   There is not indeed any express passage in
Scripture in which Jesus is said to have prayed in the
Holy Ghost, yet the inference is valid and unavoidable.
We find it stated by the Apostle that the Spirit helpeth

our infirmities and maketh intercession for us according to the will of God—that he maketh intercession with groanings which cannot be uttered. Bearing this in mind, let us stand for a moment beside Jesus at the grave of Lazarus. We hear him there referring to a prayer which he had presented, and giving thanks that the Father had answered it. " Father, I thank thee that thou hast heard me. And I knew that thou hearest me always." But on referring to the preceding context we find in it no record of any prayer that Jesus had offered up. We find it stated, however, a few verses before, that when Jesus saw Mary weeping and the Jews also weeping which came with her, " he groaned in the Spirit." When we take this in connection with the fact that Jesus afterwards makes mention of a prayer which he had presented, and in connection with the description which Paul gives of the Spirit's work in quickening the children of God in prayer, namely that " he maketh intercession in them with groanings which cannot be uttered," are we not entitled to infer that when Jesus " groaned in the Spirit " he was offering up in the Spirit prayers and supplications, if not with strong crying, at least with tears (for at this time also " Jesus wept ") unto him that was able to hear him, and was heard, even as he immediately rendered thanks and put forth the power of giving life to the dead, even as the Father had given him. And indeed the Spirit of grace and supplications in the Church is just the Spirit of the Son in their hearts crying, Abba, Father, as doubtless that same Spirit it was in whom Jesus cried, " Abba Father, O my Father, thy will be done."

How closely are the brethren conformed to the first-born—he in all things made like unto them—that they might be conformed to the image of the Son! Mark it carefully. He is himself a man of prayer, as they must be. His prayer is the prayer of faith, as their's must be. His prayer of faith is in the power of the Spirit, and on the warrant or promise of the Word; even as they must pray in the Holy Ghost, and with the Lord's words abiding in them.

2. But, secondly, as this was believing prayer, so it was importunate. It was such as would take no denial. It was exceeding earnest: it was with strong and loud cries to God; it was with tears; it was with blood. " His sweat was as it were great drops of blood falling down to the ground."

There was never such prayer offered to God. Jacob's prayer was earnest and persevering, importunate and successful, when he wrestled with the angel of the covenant and would not let him go without the blessing. But when Jesus wrestled, strove, agonised, it was such prayer as heaven and earth had never seen. He was charged with the vindication of his Father's honour—with the maintenance of his Father's law—with the salvation of countless thousands through eternity. He had to discharge himself of all these responsibilities in one only way, by suffering in all the powers and faculties of his created nature, in soul and body, the infliction of those stripes which should satisfy divine justice and be in the scales of equity a righteous equivalent for the second and eternal death of all for whom he gave himself. He had an amazing and appalling view of the justice and terror of such a doom, and his soul became exceeding sorrowful even unto death. No wonder that meeting such a doom with a body such as ours, sensitive in every nerve to every pang of physical endurance—and a soul unutterably more sensitive, in its unspotted purity, to the agony of those spiritual pangs which the frown and displeasure of the Almighty and the All-holy One caused him; he should have laboured in the anguish of his spirit to lay hold, in the prayer of faith, importunate and invincible, on the divine upholding power through which alone he could achieve the eternal wonder of an obedient endurance of the coming Cross. Loving his people also with an everlasting love, and alive to the dreadful doom from which he came to save them; understanding in the depths of his created spirit, as he had never till now understood, the bitter endless woe and shame from which he is about to rescue them; and seeing what that dreadful destiny is which must pass upon them and abide on them for ever, if he cannot obediently, willingly, wholly and successfully endure it all in their stead; with a love towards them rising in its action and intensity the more that he apprehends and appreciates all the endless terror from which it is his office and his work now to save them; and the more he apprehends and appreciates *that,* feeling only all the more unfit for going through with the work assigned him, yet all the more resolved to ransom and redeem his people—no wonder if trembling at the prospect of enduring that wrath of God, and trembling still more at the thought of failing, and so consigning his beloved elect to endure it, he throws himself in agony upon Jehovah as his refuge and his strength—fulfils his Father's prophecy concerning him, " He shall cry unto me, Thou art my Father, my God, and the Rock of my Salvation "—appeals with loud cries to his Father's promise, " My hand shall be established with him, mine arm shall strengthen him; my faithfulness and my mercy shall be with him, and in my name shall his horn be exalted "—and in the depths of holy fear offers up supplications with strong crying and tears unto him that is able to save him from death.

III. What was the success of this prayer? It was an abundant answer. " He was heard in that he feared." He received all needful grace, all sustaining strength, qualifying and enabling him to endure the cross and despise the shame; and gain an eternal title to the joy that was set before him.

Two leading desires were embraced in this prayer. *First,* that he might obtain grace and zeal and love even in such measure as would keep him positively obedient unto death, that hereby he might destroy death and attain the perfection of his own office and power as a Prince of Life. And, *second,* as the sure fruit of this, the seeing of the travail of his soul in the salvation of all whom the Father had given to him. Now these are the very things which Scripture testifies he received in answer to prayer.

1. " He was heard in that he feared, and though he were a Son—the only begotten Son of God—he learned obedience by the things which he suffered." In answer to his prayer to be saved in dying, God taught him—God strengthened him to learn—that obedience unto death, whereby death should be destroyed. The Father bestowed upon him all grace to give himself willingly to death; to obey in positive priestly activity and holy zeal the commandment to lay down his life for the sheep. God taught him the great lesson of destroying death and being saved from death, by not passively suffering death —but by actively and obediently meeting death and offering himself in death a sacrifice to God without spot. God taught this lesson in time of need. God gave this counsel; and his reins instructed him in the night season; so as that being thus obedient unto death, " his soul should not be left in the state of the dead, nor the Holy One suffered to see corruption " (Ps. xvi. 8, 9). And Jesus learned the lesson; learned obedience in the things which he suffered; and in dying obediently he was saved from death, and exclaimed, " It is finished " or " It is perfected." He himself in all his office and work was hereby made perfect (see Heb. v. 7-9).

2. But when Jesus prayed that he might be saved from death, his petition referred not personally to himself alone, but to himself as the head and high priest of the

Church, and therefore to the salvation of all his people. He prayed that he might emerge from the jaws of death, not only safe in himself from all the claims of the king of terrors, but bringing up with him also the eternal salvation of all for whom he died. Hence the Scripture assures us that in this point also he was heard. Not only was he heard on his own behalf, and saved from death, saved from succumbing under the last enemy, Jehovah teaching him the strange lessons of vanquishing death by being obedient unto death. Not only was he heard on this point, and, taught and strengthened for obedience in the things which he suffered, but he received his people's salvation also in and with his own, so that they dying in his death and rising to newness of life in his resurrection, " he became the author of eternal salvation unto all them that obey him " (Heb. v. 9). Hence those Psalms from which we have already quoted, as giving us in full the prayers which Jesus offered up in his sorrow, all point to the salvation of the Church—the promised seed—the prospering pleasure of the Lord—the gathering together of all the elect in Jesus. Thus in the fortieth Psalm— where the answer to the prayer is celebrated in the outset; " I waited patiently—(*he* waited who in the seventh verse says, Lo, I come, in the volume of the book it is written of me)—I waited patiently for the Lord, and he inclined unto me, and heard my cry. He brought me up also out of an horrible pit and out of the miry clay— (the same as in the sixty-ninth Psalm, " I sink in deep mire where there is no standing ")—and he set my feet upon a rock and established my goings: And he hath put a new song into my mouth—(for " he that sanctifieth and they that are sanctified are all of one, for which cause he is not ashamed to call them brethren, saying, In the midst of the Church will I sing praise unto thee ") —he hath put a new song into my mouth, even praise unto our God—*many shall see it and fear, and trust on the Lord.*" Many shall believe to the saving of the soul: many shall put their trust in the perfected author of salvation: many, even the great congregation who shall hear my song! Thus also the sixty-ninth Psalm closes with this joyful answer, " God will save Zion, and will build the cities of Judah. The seed also of his servants shall inherit it, and they that love his name shall dwell therein." And precisely the same in substance is the close of the twenty-second Psalm, " A seed shall serve him; it shall be accounted to the Lord for a generation. He shall come and shall declare his righteousness unto a people that shall be born, that he hath done this "— that " It is finished."

Thus, him the Father heareth alway. " For I know that the Lord saveth his anointed; he will hear him from his holy heaven with the saving strength of his right hand. The king shall joy in thy strength, O Lord; and in thy salvation, how vehemently shall he rejoice! Thou hast given him his heart's desire, and hast not withholden the request of his lips."

Such, then, were the subject, the nature, and the success of our Lord's prayer in the garden.

Deferring the full application, let me close with three words of exhortation.

1. Be ashamed and confounded, ye who pray not for your own salvation! Shall the king of righteousness and peace, the Son of God, thus wrestle in supplication, with cries and tears and agony and blood, for the salvation of sinners, while you yourselves will not wrestle for that salvation which his prayers and his blood have purchased? Will you despise and neglect so great salvation, on which the Lord of glory set such a value that to gain it for such as you, he was content to be prostrate in anguish and extremity and blood in that garden—and terror unutterable and amazement seized him at the bare thought of not succeeding in securing what you despise?

If you live in such prayerlessness, how inevitable and
righteous will be the everlasting loss of your soul!

2. Be encouraged, ye that are seeking salvation, to
come for it most confidently to Jesus. What he agonized
and prayed with tears and blood to procure, he will now
most joyfully and readily communicate. Only be thou
alone with Christ, as he calls thee to himself: and as
assuredly as he was himself heard and " became the
author of eternal salvation," he will hear you and receive
you, and redeem you from all your destructions, and you
shall henceforth obey and love him. Well will you
understand the meaning of the cry: " Saw ye him whom
my soul loveth?"

3. Let believers offer up supplications and prayers, in
the strength of those of Christ. Enter by faith into the
rich inheritance of the prayers of your living Head, and
into all the riches of their answers. Be ye in prayer
beside the Saviour, mingling your strong crying and
tears with his; yea, with what is now his glorious intercession; and when Jehovah looks on his anointed, he will
lift on you the light of his countenance and fulfil all
your petitions.

IV.

GETHSEMANE—IV.

Failing Fellow-Watchers.

"What! could ye not watch with me one hour?" (Matt. xxvi. 40).

If we turn now to consider the aspect in which the disciples present themselves in this crisis, the first thought that strikes us is the perfect contrast between their infirmity and failure on the one hand, and the faithfulness and victory of their Lord on the other. It would seem as if the three chiefest of the apostles had been selected on this occasion expressly in order to prove how inadequate for such an hour—" the hour and the power of darkness "—was the utmost human strength. Jesus was engaged in a work in which none could aid him. The three most eminent believers then on earth, far from being able to take part with him in his sore travail in redeeming his brethren, failed even in the commanded vigilance that was necessary if they were even to be mere spectators of the scene. "When he cometh unto the disciples, he findeth them sleeping."

Now we may consider—the Sin; the Rebuke; the Exhortation; the Apology, or rather the Explanation; the Relapses, and the Issue.

1. In the first place, then, we are to consider their sin. While their Lord, their Friend, their Saviour was wrestling in an agony of sorrow and of prayer, they slumbered and slept. "When he cometh to the disciples, he findeth them sleeping." But in this as in most similar

cases, the chief matter of interest and especially, of general practical application, lies, not singly in the sin itself, but very much in the circumstances by which it was committed, and the aggravations by which it was characterised. It is when we take these into account that we really understand the case; particularly when, as in this instance, the guilt arises solely from the circumstances in which the deed is done. Their sleep was sinful, not in itself, but from the circumstances in which it occurred. And these were such as to render it grievously offensive to their Lord, and deeply humiliating to themselves. For instance, in the first place :—

1. It was a direct breach of their Lord's injunction. For Jesus had said unto them, " My soul is exceeding sorrowful even unto death. Tarry ye here, and watch with me." Even without this special requirement, the whole position of affairs, and the ordinary principles of Christian prudence, not to say personal friendship and love to Jesus, ought to have been sufficient to commend to them unceasing vigilance as very specially the duty belonging to the hour that was passing over them. And so with every Christian and in all circumstances: his position and his principles alone—his position in the midst of an alluring world, of spiritual wickedness, and of the rulers of the darkness of the world; and his principles as one separated from the world and consecrated to God—these alone ought to be sufficient to keep him on his watch against temptation. But if, besides proving unfaithful to these, he be found breaking through express precepts of the Lord—not alive to the danger of his position, nor answering to the promptings of his principles; and even over and above that, deaf to special injunctions of the Lord, then surely he hath the greater sin—as these disciples had.

2. Their sin was committed after very special warnings. " All ye shall be offended because of me this

night." There is evil at the door. There is danger approaching. And the time is *this night.* Ye shall be offended this very night. If ye ever watched before—or ever mean henceforth to watch; if vigilance ever had, or shall have, any place with you at all, let it be " this night " —when your greatest crisis comes. Your chiefest hour of peril passes over you. For it will be Satan's opportunity, and your necessity. The prince of this world cometh. It is the hour and the power of darkness. Satan hath desired to have you, that he may sift you as wheat.

Now after such solemn and reiterated fore-warnings, was not their offence deeply aggravated? Alas! this is not an uncommon aggravation of the sins of believers. May not your sin in this respect have been like theirs? It may have been after warnings from the discipline of God's providence, from the chastisements by which he condemned, and tried to break you from, that sin before. It may have been after warnings given you by experience of the danger of trusting to your own resolution, or leaning to your own understanding. It may have been after very special warnings, seasonably and suitably administered in the preaching of the word; warnings borne home on your heart by the strong action of the good Spirit of God, seeking to conduct you to the land of uprightness; and, possibly, after dreadful warnings of the ruinous and fatal lengths to which others have gone by entering on the temptation against which you have not watched. And if these things be so, surely it is high time to awake out of sleep.

3. Their sin was aggravated by this sore consideration, that it was the refusal of a personal favour to their Lord. There were many grounds on which Jesus could have put the duty he enjoined. His own authority as their Lord and Master was enough. Their own danger, which he had clearly explained, should have been sufficient. But giving them credit for true love to his person, he

chose rather to request their wakeful vigilance as a
personal favour to himself. He opened up to them his
own rent and wounded heart. He showed before them
his trouble. And he implored them, as they loved him,
to watch with him in such an hour—the hour of the
travail of his soul. Oh! who shall tell all the depth and
tenderness of that personal and pathetic appeal which he
made to them? "My soul is exceeding sorrowful, even
unto death. Tarry ye here and watch with me." Surely,
by putting the duty upon a ground like this, Jesus con-
sulted best for the likelihood of its being discharged, and
addressed himself to the strongest motives that could have
engaged them to discharge it. Every one who is alive
to the claims of sacred friendship is aware that the recom-
mendation of a beloved friend is far more likely to be
observed, when he chooses to bind it up with the truth
and evidence of our personal attachment to himself, than
when he puts it merely on the ground of our own interest,
or, if he be a superior, on the ground of his official
authority over us. And when Jesus thus asked their
watchfulness as a personal favour, as a tribute of their
love which he would be gratified to receive, we feel as if
we might almost do well to be indignant at the men who
failed to gratify him.

But let us consider ourselves. Has Jesus never asked
any personal favour at our hands? And if so, have we
never failed as they did? Is it the eleven alone, or is it
these three highly-favoured ones among them only, that
have had it in their power to add this aggravation to
their sin? Was such a possibility limited to the few who
companied with Jesus in the days of his flesh? On the
contrary, Jesus places all our sanctification on the same
footing on which he placed this request to the apostles.
Over and above the unchangeable authority of God, and
the ever-binding obligation of his law as a perfect and
inviolable rule of our obedience; not to speak of the pro-

motion of our own comfort and true moral dignity, or of
the reward which is found in keeping those commandments which are not grievous; over and above all
responsibilities and motives which arise from our relation
to God—the Father, Son and Holy Spirit—and from
unchangeable principles alike of law and gospel; Jesus
has condescended to pour a peculiar tenderness and life
and strength and unflagging freshness and welcome over
all the obligations of his people, by putting their whole
obedience on the footing of a grand series of personal
favours to himself. It is this that wakens up the finest
feelings of the truly Christian or regenerated heart. It is
this, as one element, which differences infinitely the
generous and evangelical obedience of those that are
freely forgiven, from the selfish self-righteous efforts of
those that know not the gospel. It is this, as one element
and ornament of gospel holiness, that makes the king's
daughter all glorious within; that justifies as very holy a
free justification; and almost sanctifies twice the sanctification of the children of God.

They are enlisted and engaged by the gospel to render
many a personal favour to their Lord; to gratify the Son
of God, their beloved and their friend; to promote his
highest satisfaction; to cause him to see of the travail of
his soul; to have a share in causing the pleasure of the
Lord to prosper in his hand. For what else does Jesus
mean, or on what other footing but this does he place
our obedience, when he says, " If ye love me keep my
commandments "? And what else did Paul mean but
this—this, in all its sweetest and most engaging power
—when he said, " The love of Christ constraineth us to
live not unto ourselves, but unto him that died for us and
that rose again "?

But if these things be so, how aggravated are the sins
of believers, implying, as they must thus imply, a rejection

of the Lord's tenderest appeal, a refusal to do the
Saviour a pleasure!

4. The sin of the disciples was aggravated by this
consideration that Jesus had reposed great confidence in
them. He had selected them from a whole nation to be
his especial followers and companions. He had admitted
them to a sacred familiarity and intimacy which has
almost made them the objects of a holy envy—if the
expression might be used—in all ages since. He had, in
his late discourse with them, at the paschal table, poured
out his heart to them in strains of divine truth and tenderness and love, which have been the ever-fresh study and
astonishment of spiritual minds, in proportion to their
light and holiness and love, ever since they were put on
record. He had brought forward these three highly-
favoured men nearer to the marvellous scene of his agony
than any others, and made them spectators of what he
would have shrunk from the rude, unfeeling world
beholding. And it was very far from being the first
time that these selected three had been allowed to see
and hear things from which all others were excluded.
Surely they had been very generously, very confidingly
dealt with. Surely it touched their honour very closely
that they should not fail in such an hour as this. And if
they did, do we not feel that their offence was aggravated
by the weighty trust and tender confidence which they
belied?

For it is a principle which operates well and powerfully on natures in which generous emotion has any place.
To repose large confidence in such a case, is to create
or call forth the honour which receives and guards and
justifies it. Among the higher order of minds, and often
in the humblest ranks, it may be seen to bind the servant
to his master by one of the strongest ties, and to give a
moral dignity to the relation—He hath counted me
honourable, and I will prove that he was not mistaken.

How beautiful it is to find every fine feeling of our nature seized upon and sanctified and impressed into action by the gospel! That glorious gospel of the grace of God finds the sinner not trustworthy at all towards God—an apostate, an enemy, a traitor: and it slays his enmity; reverses his apostasy; sweeps away all his treachery and guile; transforms him into a trusty and a loyal child of honour; simply by at once reposing in him the highest confidence. It finds him bankrupt—dishonourably so, destitute, his character broken, his credit gone. And it gives him a character by giving him some of the jewels of the crown royal of heaven to keep. It gives him freely, in his unworthiness and untrustworthiness, a plenary forgiveness of all his sins, and a rich reconciliation to his offended Father in heaven; and hopes that he will not abuse a mercy so large and liberal. It gives him free access to the great covenant treasure chest of the unsearchable riches of Christ; and hopes that he will never spend them on his lusts, or sin that grace may abound. It gives him great consolation and good hope through grace, reversing all his destiny and his inheritance; and making him a free son of God without money and without price, it hopes that he will walk worthy of the high vocation wherewith he is called. It gives him a clean heart and a right spirit, and the indwelling of the Spirit of our God, and hopes that when entrusted therewith he will keep that good thing which is committed to him through the Holy Ghost that dwelleth in him. It deals bountifully with him, and trusts that he will live and keep God's law. It places in his hands the honour of his God, necessarily committed in his own character as a professed child of God, bearing the heavenly Father's image; and hopes that he will give no occasion to the adversary to blaspheme, but rather cause men to glorify God on his behalf and to take knowledge of him that he has been with Jesus. In fine, it gives him Christ, to be his for ever, to dwell in his heart by faith, the fountain and the pledge of all—and then leaves it to himself to cry out, "What shall I render to the Lord for all his benefits towards me?"

But if, by negligence and wilfulness, he belie a confidence so generous, how aggravated and heinous must be the believer's iniquity—even as was that of these disciples in Gethsemane!

5. We must remark yet another aggravation of their sin. They failed to discharge a duty for which they had both an example and an encouragement, in the work in which Jesus himself was engaged. Had he retired into the garden for repose; courting the relief of sleep from the fatigues and anxieties of the day, and the still more dread prospects of the morrow; leaving them, the while, to act as sentinels to guard his privacy, or forewarn him of the enemy's approach—even in such a case, with all the duty of unslumbering wakefulness devolved on themselves alone, while their master sought repose; they ought to have been animated by such a holy jealousy to guard their post of honour as would diligently have warded off, or at least eagerly and early descried all signs of danger, and challenged all comers with the challenge of the Bride in the Song, "I charge you, O ye daughters of Jerusalem, that ye stir not up nor awake my beloved till he please."

But the case was very different. Their commanded wakefulness was not designed to minister to his ease or protect his comfort. It was only to second, very faintly, the intense action of his own infinitely trying duty. He left them, himself to pray: "Tarry ye here, while I go and pray yonder." And they had to lay aside every weight and their heaviness, and the sin that did beset them, literally looking unto Jesus. For he was immediately within their view. He was under their very eye, himself watching unto prayer—very eminently "praying with all prayer and supplication in the Spirit, and watching thereunto with all perseverance and supplication for all saints." Ah! he assigned them no work which he shunned himself. And still he assigns his people no difficulty, no duty, unknown or foreign to his own experience. This very duty of watching and praying that ye enter not into temptation, when enjoined by Jesus, ought surely to be felt as coming with all the gracefulness and all the enforcement which example may carry, over and above what may be derived from authority. He was himself intensely wakeful and prayerful. He had an agony of wakefulness and prayer. The disciples ought to have seen this; ought to have kept their eye upon it. They ought to have stimulated themselves, quickened themselves, shaken off the bands of their neck and the spell of slumber, by the sight—the thought—that he was himself assailed as they were; that he too, like them, yea infinitely more, was the mark of Satan's fiery darts; that the skirts only of the cloud of battle troubled *them,* while its central terrors were wrestling with him, who in watchfulness and agony of prayer was wrestling with the very power of darkness. And still the same is true of every tried believer. He ought to watch and pray as at the gate of Gethsemane; as in the view of Jesus' wrestlings; in the remembrance of Jesus' temptations. Is it not to this very end that such frequent assertion is made to the effect that he himself hath suffered being tempted—to assure us also that he is thus able to succour them that are tempted? Is it not to make us watch and pray, as in the very wake of our Lord's own vigilance and prayer, that we are assured we have not an high priest who cannot be touched with the feeling of our infirmities, but was in all points tempted like as we are, yet without sin? Ought it not to have inspired the disciples with unquenchable persistency in watching unto prayer, that they saw the Captain of Salvation precisely so engaged himself

with the powers of evil? Was it not enough to nerve
them with endless resistance—that they could not possibly
fall or fail while they might thus participate in the success
which the Lord's own watchfulness and prayer were
achieving? So that to fall from his example and fellowship was to fail of his triumph, and to refuse the
dominion over evil which Jesus was procuring for them!
For when he called them to " watch with him "—to watch
simultaneously with him, after the example and in the
concert of his own watchfulness and prayer—did not
Jesus imply that they should in that case conquer in and
with his own conquest? And still, when with this model
before them—a model that is strangely fraught, as no
other is, not merely with the elements of an example, but
with the power of a triumph and the pledge of a deliverance—when with this model before them, believers shun
the contest or slumber in it, surely, like the disciples, they
have the greater sin!

Yes, this sin was exceeding sinful. They slumbered
while their Lord was in his sorrow; they did so in breach
of his express injunction; in defiance of special warning;
unto the refusal of a personal favour solicited by their
Lord; unto the belying of great confidence reposed in
them; and in violation of their Lord's own example as it
transpired before them.

No wonder, then, that this exposed them to the rebuke
which might well carry some indignation it it—

II. " What! could ye not watch with me one hour?"
" And he cometh unto the disciples, and findeth them
asleep, and saith unto Peter: What! could ye not watch
with me one hour?"

We mark, at once, the just severity with which this
rebuke, addressed to all, was specially pointed to Peter.
What! Thou that didst so lately speak so resolutely:
" Though all men shall be offended because of thee, yet
will not I be offended "—" Though I should die with

thee, yet will I not deny thee." Is your valour, and is
your love, come to this so soon? "He saith unto Peter,
Simon, sleepest *thou?* couldst not *thou* watch one hour?"
(Mark xiv. 37). Alas! on whom then can I rely?

But while rightfully pointed especially to Peter, the
rebuke was addressed to all; for what Peter had said, the
same "likewise also said all the disciples." Nor were
there any among them whose consciences could refuse it
as a merited and seasonable reproof—a word profitable
for reproof, for correction, for instruction in righteousness that they might be led the better to furnish themselves for good works.

Mark the varied emphasis of this rebuke, applicable in
almost all its force to slumbering believers in any
circumstances.

1. "What! could not *ye* watch with me one hour?"
Could not *ye* watch with me? ye who have sojourned with
me, and suffered with me, and been interested deeply in
me; and are interested, more than ye know, in my
sorrows and my trials, and my successful endurance of
them—my contests and temptations and my triumphant
victory over them. *Ye* who have cast in your lot with
me; who have forsaken all and followed me; who have
perilled all your hope and all your happiness in me. Oh!
who could be expected to watch with me, if it be not such
as you?

And still all these elements of emphasis may be found
in the Saviour's rebuke to every negligent or backsliding
believer. Cannot *ye* watch with me, who have been
taught to know me; to believe in me; to love me, to cast
in all your lot with me; to count me all your salvation
and all your desire? Be it so that the unawakened world
sees little in temptation to break their slumber or arouse
them to prayer: could not *ye,* who have been differently
dealt with, and have otherwise learnt Christ; could not *ye*
watch unto prayer? Ye who have been admitted to my

fellowship, entrusted with my honour, partakers of my love, aspirants to my Father's kingdom on high—could not *ye* watch with me, that ye enter not into temptation?

2. "What! could ye not watch *with me* one hour?" When it is to be "with me"?—in my company; not alone; not in your own cause or battle; not in your own skill nor your own strength; but in every sense "with me." When your watching is to be an act—a trying act it may be, but still an act—of fellowship with me? When it is required in order that you may in *all* things be conformed to me; that you may not lose the blessing of conformity, the bond and benefit of fellowship "with me?" In such circumstances "could ye not watch?" I send you on no warfare at your own charges. I send you indeed on no warfare of your own. I shall myself be your leader, your prototype, your forerunner in the battle—the wakeful prayerful battle—of temptation; in all your afflictions myself afflicted; in all points tempted like as you are; suffering in being tempted. And when you watch "with me," you shall triumph if I triumph: if you suffer with me, you shall also reign. Yes, this is the singular secret of the Christian's success in all things: he is in all things "with Christ." He links on, by faith, his very temptations with those of Christ, and finds therefore all the victory of Christ his own. He watches with Christ; and then in his blindness Christ is eyes to him in the wilderness. He prays with Christ; and Christ is intercessor and merit for him in his unworthiness. The watchings and the prayers of Christ in the days of his flesh are not only his example but his inheritance; and he has more than the disciples could have then asked or thought—he has on his side the vigilance of Israel's shepherd, now watching in the power of an endless life; he has the intercession of one who has laid aside his tears and agonies, and bespeaks his people's welfare in glorious and august state at the right hand of

the majesty in the heavens. So that, ever as the believer is true to his position as one in communion with Christ, he may be tempted with Christ nevertheless he shall triumph, yet not he but Christ that dwelleth in him, and the life of trial that he lives in the flesh shall be a life of triumph by the faith of the Son of God, who was tried and triumphed for him. If I am called to no temptation but after this rule, well may wonder and indignation be expressed if I resile and refuse. What! can you not watch, when you are called to keep watch *with me?*

3. And, "Could ye not watch with me *one hour?*" Is your vigilance already overpowered; your resistance already gone? I gave you to wit that the night would be eventful; that this whole night would call for special anxious wakefulness; that ere its watches were all transpired—by daybreak or at cock-crowing—all might not be among you as it ought to be! But, "Simon, couldst not thou watch *one hour?*" I marvel that ye are so soon removed from me! Where is the constancy you spake of? For I bear you record that, if it had been possible, you would have plucked out your own eyes and have given them to me. "Who hath bewitched you, that ye should not obey the truth, before whose eyes Jesus Christ hath been evidently set forth "tempted, watching unto prayer in an agony? Ah! is not this rebuke often needed? Could you not watch with Christ *one hour?* Your heart warmed with some strong and tender feeling of the love of Christ; coming to him at his gospel call and finding peace and joy in believing; pouring out your heart before him in the first prayer of guileless sonship, so very different from all that went before in the spirit of bondage; you gave yourself to Jesus as one whose decision was for ever irrevocable, and you vowed that though all men should forsake him and his cause, yet would not you—as for you and your house you would serve the Lord. You did this as honestly, as sincerely, as ever the eleven bound

themselves to Jesus; with as little reservation as they, on this eventful night, when acting, at least for the time, as Israelites indeed in whom was no guile, they avowed their resolution that they would not be offended in their Lord. But too soon, like them, you felt the action on your whole nature of an evil power which, in the hour of warm-hearted, generous fealty to Jesus, you had forgot to calculate upon: and erewhile the withering spell of worldly influence, and close-cleaving infirmity, managed by the subtlety of him that beguiled Eve, brought you down from the lofty elevation of your holy purpose; weakened you out of the energy with which you started on the Christian race and by which for a little " you did run well "—a slumber, the same in its nature, though in degree never again so complete, as that from which the grace of God had awakened you, overtook you once more; till roused by the sting of conscience, or the stroke of Providence, or the word of Scripture—any or all of these together—you heard, by means of them, Christ's painful but righteous reprimand: " What! could you not watch with me *one hour?*" Are ye so soon removed?

Was it not well that he came to you at all, in however great severity he spoke? Better far that Jesus should come and find you sleeping, than that he should leave you sleeping and cast you off. Is it not good, if he comes to thee, believer, in this word of reproof and warning now, if such be now thy state of backsliding; especially when he comes to renew his exhortation, and give you as it were, in his grace, a fresh lease of your opportunity to vindicate your integrity, to renew the love and faithfulness of your youth?

For it is thus that he mingles his painful reproof with profitable instruction in righteousness; enjoining once more the duty that had been forgotten: " Watch and pray that ye enter not into temptation."

III. We have said this is the same duty enjoined anew. For, combining the informations given by all the Evangelists, we find from Matthew and Mark that before leaving them at all, ere yet he entered the garden, Jesus enjoined on them the necessity of vigilance: " Tarry ye here, and watch with me "; while we learn from Luke that at the same time he enjoined the necessity of prayer: " He came out, and went, as he was wont, to the Mount of Olives, and his disciples also followed him. And when he was at the place, he said unto them, Pray that ye enter not into temptation " (Luke xxii. 39, 40). So that Jesus had really nothing new to say to them—no fresh or additional advice to give them, but the same which they had heard from the beginning.

And there is a lesson in this. For in the decay or slumber of your Christian life, it is not something new that is to revive you; not some novel doctrine; not some unheard of, or lately discovered, Christian exhortation; not some singular and striking advice, prescribing some royal road different from that in which the usual footsteps of the flock are marked, not prescribing even any means or method of revival hitherto unknown to yourself. No: there is a great snare hid under any such expectation as that. You are to stand in the beaten path, and inquire for the good old ways you trod before, if you would find reinvigorating grace and rest unto your soul.

It is to be desired, indeed, that this old commandment to inquire for the good old way may come as a new commandment to you now. It is to be hoped that by a fresh baptism of the Spirit, and fresh humiliation and sense of danger, and quickened spiritual perception on your part, it may have almost the aspect, in its anew discovered suitableness, and in its striking seasonableness of an absolutely new commandment. But it is the same commandment that ye have heard from the beginning of your Christian life: " Watch and pray that ye enter not into temptation." Yet it need not seem to you an old commandment: or if old, yet it should be welcome as an old and faithful friend. For realise only, in the light of your experience, and especially of the sins and failings that have made it needful that Jesus should come and re-issue to you this injunction—realise your weak and defenceless state, and with this the multitude and power and assailing force of those that are enemies to your soul —and realise your own fearful want of wisdom of experience in spiritual warfare—which is almost the only thing which your incipient experience has taught you: think of the subtlety and wiles of the devil, and of the manifold conjunctures in which you are found of him at great disadvantage, as when weak and weary in body, and faint in mind, even though pursuing: think how the enemy can turn all such disadvantage to account; and realise especially the terrible and fatal issue, if you cannot conquer, in so much that if this battle be finally lost, *you* are lost: and does it not come upon you with the joy of a great and a fresh discovery that the old injunction is still as suitable as ever; that while ever, it may be, surrounded by temptation and assailed, you have ever the liberty—I shall not say the duty—but the privilege, the liberty, the warrant, the high right, to watch and pray that you may not enter into temptation at all; and the high assurance that as the prayer of vigilance and faith moves for your protection the infinite wisdom and love and power and faithfulness of God, this old, this new commandment, be it only observed and obeyed, will, even in the midst of innumerable and more than visible dangers, gird your soul with the glad assurance of a present safety, and the unmisgiving hope of a final triumph?

"Watch ye, therefore, and pray that ye enter not into temptation." For what Jesus said to them, he says to all: Watch and pray. Watch: be vigilant. Be thou a faithful sentinel on thy post of duty—thy post of honour. Let the eye of faith and spiritual wisdom be wide open on your position; and you shall see much that the world can never see, much that it concerns you very greatly that you yourself should see. And first of all—duty peculiar to sentinels and soldiers in the warfare of faith —watch and know thyself. Keep thy heart with all diligence and vigilance, for out of it are the issues of life. Arrest its traitorous lusts and besetting sins: condemn and crucify them. If they will not die at once, as they seldom will, watch them all the more; double the guard upon them, and put them under the surveillance of conscience in its highest force and honour. And while thus, on thy faithfulness and honour towards God, they are crucified and watched, and their dominion prevented, let not their presence prevail to cast thee out of communion with the Holy One, but rather let the peace of God garrison thy heart and let it rule there, to the which also thou art called.

Watch the dangers of your special callings—your companionships—your particular connections with the world—your objects of personal attachment.

Watch very specially the sources and causes of past unfaithfulness and failure. Watch the enemy's approaches —his methods of trying you. He goeth about like a roaring lion. He changes himself into an angel of light. Watch, that you be not ignorant of his devices.

Watch your graces—what state they are in, what strength they are in, what danger they are in. Watch especially your repentance and your faith. Oh! keep them for ever fresh. See if the vine flourish, or if the little foxes spoil the tender grapes. Watch what the Lord hath given you—the gracious and contrite heart, the meek and quiet spirit, which are of great price. Watch the treasure of your renewed heart, that you may be ever able to bring forth good things therefrom. Keep

that good thing which is committed to you, through the
Holy Ghost that dwelleth in you. Be not deceived into
any slumbering, at any time, for Satan by subtlety may
beguile you. Be thou ever aware of the disposition of
the enemies' powers. Set thee with the prophet on thy
watch. Yea, watch thou with Christ on thy tower.
Watch with him. Abide thou in Christ, and watch with
him.

Pray also: yea, with all prayer and supplication,
watching thereunto with all perseverance. Pray that of
God's grace you may be preserved from being tempted
or supported and delivered when you are tempted. He
can, if he please, prevent you, not only from entering into
temptation, from falling into its snare and seducement,
but even from being assailed by temptation at all. And,
doubtless, often in answer to the appeal of conscious
weakness and holy fear, the Lord dispenses with the discipline of temptations, with which, but for such frame of
humble holy depreciation, it might have been indispensable to try his people and to prove them. Pray, therefore,
in subjection to the wisdom and the will of your Father,
that he would prevent temptations from framing and
forming themselves against you. But in any issue, pray
that they may not form themselves against you and
prosper. Pray that he would let you know when temptation is at hand; that he would always forewarn you of
every special danger. Pray that he would make you not
unwise in these things, but understanding the wiles of
the devil and the will of the Lord. Pray that he would
make you strong in himself and in the glory of his power.
Pray for armour, and put it on. Put ye on the whole
armour of God, praying always in the Spirit. Pray,
above all—if you would not enter into temptation—in the
name of him who was in all points tempted like as you
are, yet without sin: and let the remembrance of the
temptations of the Lord feed your faith with nourishment

of new life and hope, in the assurance that he is able and willing to succour them that are tempted.

Thus, " Watch and pray," doing both. Yea more; not only combining, but blending them.

Pray to be enabled to watch. Watch that you may know what to pray for. Pray for the grace of vigilance. Watch for materials of prayer. Watch that you may know temptation by its mere presence : and pray to be preserved from knowing it in its successful power. Pray that your eyes may be purged from dimness, and anointed with eye-salve, so that you may see afar off, and may discern good and evil. And then watch with keen and piercing eye, that you may see the answers to prayer. Watch the efficacy of prayer. Pray for success in watching. Watch, if you would be on the alert to pray. Pray that you may be kept alert upon your watch tower. The enemy is subtle : you must watch his movements. You yourself are weak : you must pray for strength. If you could keep yourself, it might be sufficient to watch, but as God only can keep you, you must join prayer with watchfulness. If God would keep you any otherwise than by strengthening and guiding you to keep yourself, it might be sufficient to pray; but as it is, you must combine watchfulness with prayer—watching for your salvation with fear and trembling, the Lord working in you and enabling you to watch of his good pleasure. Thus he persuaded both to " watch and pray that you enter not into temptation."

Such is the blessed exhortation which Jesus graciously gives, even when he comes to reprove and rebuke his disciples.

IV. Jesus added, in his tenderness, a gracious apology or explanation. For as a father, even when he punisheth, pitieth his children, and maketh all due allowances for true heartedness and love, even so the Lord pitieth them that fear him. Jesus admitted their integrity, while he

indicated and condemned their infirmity.   " The spirit
indeed is willing but the flesh is weak."   " Ye are willing
according to the spirit, but weak as regards the flesh."
" The flesh lusteth against the spirit, and the spirit
against the flesh, and ye cannot do the things that ye
would."

Now this agrees with the testimony of Luke, who
assures us that they were sleeping *for sorrow*.   " And
when he rose up from prayer, and was come unto his
disciples, he found them sleeping for sorrow " (Luke xxii.
45). They were not heartlessly indifferent to their Lord's
sorrows. They sympathised in them all, as their own.
They, too, were exceeding sorrowful. But as fools watch
not the dangers of buoyant prosperity, they foolishly
watched not the dangers of depressing grief : and their
very sorrow, in its heaviness, put them off their guard and
sank them in untimely slumber. Alas! for the wiles of
the devil, wherein, alike from our levity and our heaviness
of heart, he can find occasion for his malice.

Yet when Satan sifts the faithful, no grain of wheat
shall be treated as chaff. The grace which really lives in
the heart renewed, even though for the time it may be
overpowered—the eyes of the Lord are upon it continually. Jesus saw their sorrow; and he interpreted it as
proof that the spirit was willing, even though the
infirmity of their flesh prevailed.

That they were indeed spiritual men, true believers and
faithful brethren, Jesus took for granted both in rebuking
and exhorting them, and he framed his rebuke and
exhortation accordingly. But for this—but for the spirit
being willing—he would have expressed neither wonder
nor indignation at their want of vigilance. The very point
of the reproof—" What! could ye not watch with me one
hour "—lay in the fact that he was addressing spiritual
and " willing " men (Ps. cx. 3)—men renewed in their
wills or in the spirit of their minds. Such a reproof would

have been out of place to a worldly or unrenewed heart. And the exhortation, as well as the reproof, proceeds upon the same consideration. It is not at all suitable, and is not addressed in the first instance, to the unconverted. To you, Christ's first address is not, " Watch and pray that ye enter not into temptation." Ye have never been out of temptation nor out of sin. Ye are in the flesh and dead in sin. His first searching question and rebuke to you is, What! why will ye die? And his first exhortations are like these: Flee from the wrath to come! Come out from among them and be ye separate, and touch not the unclean thing. Awake thou that sleepest, and arise from the dead. Repent and believe the gospel. There can be no watchfulness in the spiritually blind—no prayer against temptation in the spiritual dead.

But if ye be willing according to the spirit but weak according to the flesh, then this exhortation is exactly to the point. For it is possible that it can be obeyed, only because " the spirit is willing "; it is necessary to be observed because " the flesh is weak."

Mark, then, to whom this exhortation is given and con- sider whether it be an admonition to which you can immediately and at once address yourself. Amidst the weakness of the flesh, is the spirit really willing? Is the prevailing bent of your most cherished desires towards universal holiness unto the Lord? Consider and know. See what is really your true and inner man. See what is the real hidden man of the heart, whether it be the old man uncrucified or the new man in God's own image longing after that image of God in its full perfection. See whether in your failures you seek to draw with pleasure, or with sorrow, on this very verdict of Jesus: " The spirit is willing but the flesh is weak." And when you do apply this relief or mitigation, is it to deepen or is it to dispense with repentance? And when you sorrow over your failures, your inconsistencies of Christian character and walk, is it with regret and remorse merely for having failed of what conscience said was duty? Or is it with the special grief for having failed and been thwarted in what your heart tells you—and what God who is greater than your heart knoweth—was not only your duty, but your generous and upright and still unshaken desire? This last will be true when the spirit is willing.

V. Finally: Be warned by the fate of the eleven. They relapsed again, and yet again; and they lost this battle utterly. Jesus had at last to give up exhorting them, and hand them over to be taught by stern and sore experience. " Sleep on now, and take your rest: behold, the hour is at hand, and the Son of Man is betrayed into the hands of sinners. Rise, let us be going; behold, he is at hand that doth betray me. And while he yet spake, lo! Judas, one of the twelve, came, and a multitude with swords and staves." And Jesus, who had watched and prayed, met them with dignity and peace and unshaken constancy. The eleven had lost the opportunity of so arming themselves.

Ah! how was Peter hereby prepared for his greater fall —the others for forsaking Jesus and fleeing—all of them for being guilty of sin and laden with sorrow, till they should be forgiven and restored by a risen Redeemer! Who can trace how very different their conduct and their comfort might have been, during that terrific time, had they watched and prayed like Jesus, and as Jesus had enjoined? They escaped with their faith indeed still in life: for the watching and the prayer of him with whom they would not watch, had been for them even more than for himself. They escaped, yet so as by fire. Even so may you reach heaven at last, if indeed you are Christ's. For if ye are Christ's, the Spirit of Christ dwelleth in you. Otherwise ye could be none of his. And if the Spirit of him that raised up Christ from the dead dwell in you, you are renewed in the spirit of your minds, and the spirit is willing though the flesh is weak, and the Lord will not break his covenant with you. Every true believer, whatsoever may befall him by the way, shall at last appear before God in Zion, and dwell where neither sorrow nor sighing nor sifting can come any more—where the inhabitants shall not say, I am sick, for those that dwell there are forgiven their iniquities, and God shall wipe away all tears from their eyes. But even though the spirit may be willing, yet if you fail to watch and pray against the weakness of the flesh, and so fall into temptation and a snare, you *may* reach heaven in the end, but it may be by a path in which no joy of the Lord shall be your strength until the end come—a path in which you may be left to pierce yourself through with many sorrows, and in which God may mingle for you many a cup of bitterness and trembling—" the wormwood and the gall!"

Watch ye, therefore, and pray that ye enter not into temptation.

V.

GETHSEMANE—V.

Gethsemane a Prayer-Chamber for Disciples.

"Jesus ofttimes resorted thither with his disciples"
(John xviii. 2).

Would it not be well if disciples ofttimes resorted thither
with Jesus? Is there not, indeed, a sense in which
Gethsemane ought to be regarded as the very *oratoire* of
the Church, the closet, spiritually, where we may, with
many precious aids to faith, pray to our Father who seeth
in secret and rewardeth openly, as we shall see he
rewarded the Man of Sorrows?

It has been often said—and well said—that a sinner
should not only come to the cross, but dwell there; that
the believer should abide at Calvary. Inspired warrant
for the saying is found in Paul's experience: "I am
crucified with Christ; nevertheless I live; yet not I, but
Christ liveth in me; and the life that I live in the flesh, I
live by the faith of the Son of God, who loved me and
gave himself for me" (Gal. ii. 20). I am spiritually
identified with Christ in his cross. I am united to Christ
the crucified one. I am always offered up unto God, in
and with him who offered himself in death a sacrifice of a
sweet-smelling savour unto God. "Nevertheless," it is as
a living sacrifice that I am offered up; for he with whom
I am crucified was crucified for me; and even in dying
he was the Living One: therefore I live also; yet not I,
but Christ liveth in me. Therefore I live at the cross,

because I live by the cross.   My home, my fortress, my
high tower and dwelling-place is Calvary.

On the same principles and warrants of faith may not
the believer say, My soul's secret prayer chamber shall
be Gethsemane?

Great shall be his reward.   For there are three things
he will find Gethsemane can furnish him with in prayer:
in the *first* place, a blessed and perfect warrant; in the
second place, a precise and comprehensive subject; and,
in the *third* place, an honourable and a blessed fellowship.

Let these be your inducements to make Gethsemane the
scene of your own believing prayers.   Come ye hither, to
this garden of the Lord, to be the Lord's remembrancers
and give him no rest till he arise and have mercy upon
you and on Zion his holy habitation.   Come ye hither, and
ye shall find a high warrant and assurance of success;
the true topic and full compass of your petitions; and
companionship in prayer that will make you least alone
when alone with Jesus as in Gethsemane.

I.   In the first place, then, by praying as in Gethsemane
you have the blessed advantage of knowing your right or
liberty of praying—your warrant or assurance of being
heard.   For it is in reality here, in Gethsemane, that there
resounds that glorious oracle: " Behold, now is the
accepted time; behold, now is the day of salvation."

See on what foundation the truth of that blessed saying
rests and where it was at first proclaimed.   We must by
no means separate this most precious announcement from
the reason which the Lord himself assigns for issuing it,
nor forget the place from which at first it issued.   Now,
in point of fact, it rests upon the prayers of Jesus and
the answers which were vouchsafed to him.   The time
was when Jesus had to cry for acceptance and salvation
—when he had to watch for the acceptable time and
improve the day of salvation.   " Salvation " was the
burden of what he sought from God in agony with strong

crying and with tears; he cried "unto him that was able
to *save* him from death." And "acceptance" is the
grand leading element in salvation; acceptance as righteous in God's sight; hence Jesus says, in expressing his
faith and prospects, "He is near that justifieth me."
These, then, were what he needed in the days of his flesh:
justification or acceptance as God's righteous servant—
deliverance or salvation from the dominion of death. And
he found them both. He was delivered from death by
obediently dying, vanquishing death by his own
"*obedience* unto death," and thus his "soul was not left
in the state of the dead, nor did he, the Holy One, see
corruption." And he was accepted or justified also—
"justified in the Spirit"—through his willing endurance
of condemnation in the room and stead of his guilty but
beloved people. Of this salvation from death by dying,
and of this acceptance or justification by his willingness
to be condemned, the Prophet Isaiah testifies, or, rather,
by the Spirit of inspiration, Jehovah, the Father, testifies,
in converse with Jehovah, the Son, the covenant-head and
surety. For thus saith "Jehovah, the Redeemer of Israel,
and his Holy One," "to him whom man despiseth"—to
him who was despised and rejected of men: "In an
acceptable time have I heard thee, and in a day of salvation have I helped thee: and I will preserve thee, and
give thee for a covenant of the people, to establish the
earth and to cause to inherit the desolate heritages; that
thou mayest say to the prisoners, Go forth; and to them
that sit in darkness, Show yourselves" (Isa. xlix. 7-9).
Thou shalt be made perfect and become the author of
eternal salvation; thou shalt acquire the right and power
of translating sinners out of darkness, and redeeming
slaves from their bondage; thou shalt have the prevailing
sovereign right of combined authority and grace to say to
the prisoners, Go forth, and to them that sit in darkness,
Show yourselves; on condition that thou criest unto me

for thine own acceptance in an acceptable time. Offering up " supplications to him that is able to save " thee in a " day of salvation," thou shalt be heard and helped— helped from the sanctuary and strengthened out of Zion —saved in that thou hast feared. Yea, " behold the Lord God will help thee; who is he that shall condemn thee?" " Thou art my servant in whom I will be glorified." " Thou art my beloved Son in whom I am well pleased." " In an acceptable time have I heard thee, and in a day of salvation have I helped thee." Such is the covenant promise to the Son.

Surely this promise received a very signal fulfilment in Gethsemane, when there appeared unto him from heaven an angel strengthening him. And his Father strengthened him inwardly with strength in his soul, and filled him with all grace and love and patience, and calm courage and resolve to endure the cross despising the shame. Never more than in Gethsemane did Jesus find his prayer to be unto the Lord " in an acceptable time and in the truth of his salvation " (Ps. lxix. 13).

And now having obtained an acceptable time and a day of salvation to himself, does he keep these great blessings to himself; or does he freely lay them open to participa- tion on the part of all who will count them blessings indeed, all who will consent to accept them at his hands? There is indeed to sinners now a day of salvation, an acceptable time—a time of seeking while the Lord may be found, a time of calling on him while he is near. But what is this accepted time, this day of salvation? What is it but the participation, the prolongation of Christ's own accepted time? It is into *it* that we are called to enter, with all the high warrant and assurance of accept- ance and salvation which *his* acceptable time and his day of salvation afford.

It is thus that the Apostle Paul, according to the wisdom given to him, finds all our warrant for acceptable prayer springing out of the accepted and answered prayers of Jesus himself. Quoting from Isaiah, in his second epistle to Corinth (vi. 2), he rehearses the words of Jehovah the Father to Jehovah Jesus promising to hear and answer and help him, and grounds upon them the glorious assurance, without which we can neither believe nor hope nor pray, " We beseech you that ye receive not the grace of God in vain; for he saith "—he saith to Jesus—" I have heard *thee* in a time accepted, and in the day of salvation have I succoured thee: behold," then, O Corinthians, " now is the accepted time; behold, now is the day of salvation." Yes, it is because Jesus was heard in a time accepted that *you* can now pray with the hope of acceptance: it is because he was heard in that he feared when he prayed to him that was able to save him from death that you have now a day of salvation. Now indeed does the blessed Saviour—the suppliant of Gethsemane, heard and answered—now does he draw near to the slaves of darkness and of sin, to bring them forth to the light and salvation of his own kingdom. Now does he truly say to the prisoner, " Go forth," and to thee, O soul, still in darkness, he saith, " Show thyself." And why shouldst thou refuse, when he comes to share with thee his own " accepted time," to make thee a partaker of his own " day of salvation "—to give as sure salvation to thy person, and as sure acceptance to thy prayer, as he himself found for his own person and his own prayers in Gethsemane, when the Father heard him out of Zion, and saved him from falling under the dominion of death?

In Gethsemane, then, you have your high warrant for prayer. In Gethsemane you find the acceptable time—the day of salvation; true and sure and infallible as the salvation which the person of Jesus found—the acceptance which the prayer of Jesus met with. In Gethsemane you seek the Lord in a time when he may be found, you call upon him in a place where he is very near.

And here let me speak to the prayerless and procrastinating. Knowing the terrors of Gethsemane, we would desire to persuade you to seek the Lord while he may be found, to call upon him while he is near. For, oh! be persuaded that if Gethsemane warrants the prayer of faith and assures its answer, it warrants also the justice and assures the certainty of terrible damnation to those who do not pray. That sufferer and suppliant who wrestles there in such anguish and amazement and heaviness and sorrow inexpressible and unparalleled, is bearing nothing more than what he is bearing away from them that believe, but which will abide for ever upon them that believe not. Such as it was to him who stood in the room of the guilty, such will it be without abatement to the guilty who through love of sin and of the world and in unbelief continue to stand in their own name before the Holy One of Israel, having no lot nor part in the Saviour's salvation, but despising the acceptable time which Jesus found for himself and would willingly share with you. Was *his* soul "exceeding sorrowful" under the imputation of the sins of sinners? And what shall *your* sorrow be if ye awake into eternity with your sins still on your own head—on your own head for ever? Would it be fair or righteous that, with others' sins lying to his charge, *his* soul should be very heavy, crushed within him, pressed down to death with sorrow and *your* sorrow should be less? Nay; "their sorrows shall be multiplied" that live and die impenitent and out of Christ. Was he amazed, "sore amazed"? Sinners that meet their own reckoning, unrelieved and unforgiven through that reckoning which justice had with Jesus in Gethsemane, shall be filled, in their horror and damnation, with terrible amazement. Why should *he* be, and not *you* —you who defy God in your deadly unconcern and reject and despise his Son by your careless and prayerless unbelief? " The sinners in Zion are afraid; fearfulness

hath surprised the hypocrites; who among us shall dwell
with the devouring fire?   Who among us shall dwell with
everlasting burnings "?

Ah! if with the holy and spiritual and far-sighted soul
of Jesus, imputation of sin when it came near upon him,
took even *him* by surprise; filled him with sore amazement,
assumed an aspect of horror which, when at a distance,
though he had all along expected its advent and laid his
account in holy intelligence with being made a curse, he
could not have expected to be so crushing, so full of the
wine of astonishment, and thus in trembling and in tears
and in blood, the Lord God Omnipotent in the likeness of
sinful flesh threw himself upon the cold ground and
moaned in the anguish of his spirit and his sweat was as
it were great drops of blood: what horrible surprise and
amazement and blank terror for ever shall seize on you, O
prayerless soul, when, awakened from your carnal sleep,
arrested by the ministers of divine vengeance, and flung
out, a cast-away, on the dread plains of eternity, you find
that the accepted time is past, the day of salvation that
Gethsemane secured gone, and nothing yours from Gethsemane at all, except the sorrow and the amazement and
the agony, remediless and merciless for ever!   Choose
ye this day which ye will accept: the agony of prayer in
a time of acceptance, the agonising to enter in at the
strait gate in a day of salvation, and glory for ever beyond
—or the agony of sorrow, with nothing but a fearful
looking for of vengeance and fiery indignation.   Choose,
do I say?   O how little room for choice!   Accept at once
and improve the time of acceptance.   Be saved now in
the day of salvation.   Let your prayer be offered now in
the acceptable time, in the multitude of the Lord's mercy
and the truth of his salvation.   Bless God that prayerlessness and procrastination have not already sealed your
doom.   Draw near to Gethsemane to pray, tremblingly
grateful that it gives you liberty and warrant to pray in

the full assurance of faith and of acceptance, and henceforth be followers of them who through faith and patience are now inheriting the promises.

And ye, to whom the high duty and privilege of prayer is not unknown, ye who are the Lord's remembrancers—rest your warrant, your assurance on the answered prayers of Jesus, and ye too shall receive an answer. The battle of believing prayer is won. It was won in Gethsemane. Ye are but following up the victory. Come ye, therefore, to Gethsemane and offer here your supplications. Here was your Lord himself accepted—here was he heard and helped and saved from death; and here, therefore, the living oracle resounds to you: "Behold, now is the accepted time; behold, now is the day of salvation."

II. But, in the second place, you will find also in Gethsemane the true topic and the full compass of all acceptable supplications. Here you will find a distinct and all-embracing subject of prayer. For, as the sum and substance of all that you ask of God, you simply adopt the prayer of Gethsemane, "O my Father, thy will be done."

Now, this does not mean simply that in every prayer of yours you are to seek a spirit of submission to the Father's will and acquiescence therein. That is indeed conveyed under this lesson as part of the truth involved. And it lies in the very essence of prayer that we should seek, and indeed desire, nothing but what is agreeable to the will of God. So very elementary and obvious is this that, to see its truth, we have only to contemplate the proposal of asking something in opposition to the divine will, to feel the recoil which the mind instantly makes from the idea as the worst form of deliberate impiety. Assuredly it is the dictate both of reason and of Scripture that only when "we ask anything according to his will can we have the confidence that he heareth us" (I John v. 14). And this lesson Gethsemane very solemnly con-

firms and enforces. " Father, if it be possible, let this
cup pass from me; nevertheless, not my will but thine be
done. O my Father, since this cup may not pass from
me, thy will be done."

Thus far we are supplied in Gethsemane with a rule
of prayer—a general principle or maxim applicable to
prayer at all times, whatsoever may be the subject of the
petitions, namely, that we must ask what things are
agreeable to the will of God.

But we mean something more than this when we say
that Gethsemane furnishes, briefly yet comprehensively,
the very subject, the topic, the matter of prayer. Come
ye here and learn of Jesus what to pray for. Come ye
here and enter into the mind and spirit of Jesus in reference to that same will of God which he prays may now
be done. And how well may you accept the invitation,
and what a price to get spiritual riches does such an
invitation put into your hand! This will of God is the
same which Jesus came from heaven to do, and not his
own. " Lo, I come; in the volume of the book it is
written of me; I delight to do thy will, O my God." Come
then and lay hold on that same will of God and see how
thou art enriched with all spiritual blessings in heavenly
places in Christ Jesus.

(1)   For, first of all, the immediate blessing which you
receive by doing so is that you are separated at once unto
the Lord. You come out and are separate, and the Lord
is a Father unto you, and ye are his sons and his
daughters. His will separates you in destiny from the
world far as the east is distant from the west, and
separates your guiltiness and sin equally far away from
you. For do we not read concerning this will which Jesus
came to do: " O my Father thy will be done " (Matt. xxvi.
42); " Lo, I come to do thy will, O God " (Heb. x. 9); do
we not read, " By the which will we are sanctified through
the offering of the body of Christ once for all " (Heb. x.

10)? We are sanctified, that is, set apart to God, separated to him as his peculiar possession, consecrated by the blood of Jesus, redeemed to the Lord, not our own but bought with a price. Taking hold, then, on this will of God, you find it separates you from the world; it withdraws and translates you out of darkness into God's marvellous light and into the kingdom of the Son of his love; having in it a resistless efficacy to claim and take and keep you as the Lord's peculiar inheritance. For by this will of God ye are sanctified through the offering of the body of Christ once for all.

How blessed, then, to come into Gethsemane and there to deal in prayer and supplication with that same will of God with which Jesus was so sorrowfully yet so faithfully concerned. You come to give yourself unto the Lord, to surrender your soul and body and love and service to the God of salvation. You do so in Gethsemane. You do so with express reference, in the prayer of faith, to that will of God which Jesus came to do, and for the doing of which a body was prepared him. You learn the topic of your prayer in this garden of the Lord's agony. You lay hold on the will of God and surrender yourself to him. Be assured it is a time of acceptance. Your surrender is accepted in deed and in truth. The Lord cannot reject what is his own; and by this will of God you are sanctified, separated to him as his own, whom he cannot disallow. For the Lord knoweth them that are his.

Is this comfort too high for you? Is it, as it were, meat too strong for thee, O meek and contrite soul, who art in thine own estimation no better than a babe in Christ—glad couldst thou but realise that even that blessed state and character are thine? Still we say to you, come here into Gethsemane and learn from Jesus to pray concerning this same will of God with which all his prayer is conversant.

(2) For, in the second place, you know, do you not, that " all whom the Father giveth to him shall come to him, and him that cometh he will in no wise cast out" (John vi. 37). Ah, this blessed twofold truth! this assurance, so glorious and consoling to Jesus, that " all whom the Father hath given him shall come to him "; and this other assurance, so gracious and consoling to you, that " him that cometh he will in no wise cast out "; they both alike rest upon this same will of God, and by it Jesus will ever vindicate and verify them.

For we often lose the full strength of the sayings of Christ, by detaching them from the connection in which they originally appear. No doubt, we often so detach and isolate them in order that we may hide them in our heart, and perhaps few of the blessed Saviour's ever memorable announcements have been more frequently or more deeply graven on the fleshly tables than that ever precious word which liveth and abideth for ever, to shut out all our dark misgivings and obviate all our guilty and (but for Jesus) well grounded fears, and silence all our doubts and unbelieving objections—the ever gracious word of the Lord—" Him that cometh I will in no wise cast out." Doubtless, also, though it stood alone and by itself, this word of Christ were very precious, and exceedingly abundantly sufficient as a warrant to bring near to him the guiltiest of the children of men, however great and numerous their provocations and their backslidings, however debasing and vile their sin. Still it is best to note the full strength which this word of the Lord derives from other truths which he allies and binds up with it; and to see the foundation or the ground on which Jesus sets forth his warrant to proclaim it as a truth. " All whom the Father giveth me shall come to me, and him that cometh I will in no wise cast out." Why are these things so? Why should it be so certain that all whom the Father hath given to Jesus shall come to him, and why so equally sure that him that cometh, whosoever he may be, or what-soever he may have been or done, shall in no wise be cast out? Does Jesus assign any reason for these things, any evidence that they are true and sure? He does. They are both true and sure, " for," saith he, " I came down from heaven not to do mine own will, but the will of him that sent me." Thus Jesus at once binds in the truth of this two-fold assurance with that will of God which he came to do. Every elect soul shall come and every soul that cometh shall be welcome, *" for* I came down from heaven to do the Father's will; for, lo, I come, to do thy will, O God." But how should this will of God, which Jesus came to do, secure on the one hand the coming of those whom the Father hath given him and secure on the other hand the gracious reception or acceptance of him, whoso-ever he may be, that cometh? Very clearly and very surely because these are the things which that will of God contemplates and provides for and guarantees. For there is a two-fold assurance—the first bearing more upon the secret things of God and relating to his people's election; the second, more upon the things that are revealed, that pertain to his people's calling, and both are founded on that will of God. The first declares that all that are given him shall come to him, for Jesus in this respect came to do the Father's will, and " this is the Father's will that hath sent me, that of all whom he hath given me I should lose nothing but should raise it up at the last day " (verse 39). The second declares that who-soever cometh I will in no wise cast out. *For* I came down from heaven to do the will of him that sent me: and, on this point, " This is the will of him that sent me, that everyone that seeth the Son, and believeth on him, should have everlasting life, and I will raise him up at the last day " (verse 40).

When, therefore, in Gethsemane the Lord said, " O my Father, since this cup may not pass from me, thy will be

done; O my Father, thy will be done "; that will of thine
be done which I came down from heaven to do—for
which thou didst prepare for me a body that I might do
it; the subject of his prayer embraced the coming to him
of all whom the Father gave him, and a blessed and
assured welcome to every one whosoever he may be that
cometh.

Again, then, we say, Come ye to Gethsemane and take
hold on this prayer of Jesus. Learn from him the subject
of your supplication. Take hold with him upon the will
of God, which he came from heaven to do; especially on
that which is revealed in all its fulness, even that every
one that seeth the Son and believeth on him shall have
everlasting life, and Jesus shall raise him up at the last
day; that him that cometh he will in no wise cast out; for
that is the will of God with which Gethsemane's prayer
is so solemnly concerned. Come ye to him in this garden
where the will of his Father is so dear to him and costs
him so much in his agony. And if that very will of his
Father be to the effect that you, coming, shall in no wise
be cast out, Oh! with what readiness, with what joy,
with what full assurance of faith may you come! Oh! let
us draw near with a true heart and in the full assurance
of faith. Yes, and thus having made our calling, let us
make also our election sure, persuaded that it was not
only of the Father's will that on coming to Jesus we have
been welcome, but that it was of the Father's will that we
have come, being indeed of the number whom the Father
hath given to the Son; and so we have not chosen him,
but he hath chosen us, when in the volume of the book
it was written of Jesus, and all his members also were
written (Ps. xl. 7; cxxxix. 16). Here, then, again is the
will of God, the same by which we are sanctified or
separated to him, by the offering of the body of Christ
once for all.

(3) And now, thirdly, being thus in no wise cast out, but rather sanctified and consecrated by this will of God, on which you lay hold in the prayer of faith in Gethsemane, remember now that " this is the will of God, even your sanctification," your sanctification not merely in the sense of your separation to the Lord, but of being *holy* to him now that you are separated. " Be ye perfect and complete in all the will of God "; and be so just by realising that you are separated unto him and have all that freedom from evil, and that access by faith unto all grace, which such separation requires. By that will of God ye are sanctified through the offering of the body of Christ once for all (Heb. x. 10). And by that one offering also Jesus hath for ever perfected them that are sanctified (Heb. x. 14). He hath given you a perfect acceptance, and a perfect adoption. Made perfect himself through the instrumentality of his own prayers and their answer (Heb. v. 9), he hath perfected also those whom he hath consecrated to his God, whom he hath washed from their sins in his own blood and made them kings and priests unto his Father. He presents you to God justified in his sight—justified perfectly, with no taint whatever, and no stain of condemnation on you any more. He presents you to God adopted into the household of faith—adopted perfectly, with no trace of slavery or strangeness or foreign origin at all—no more strangers and foreigners, but fellow citizens with the saints and of the household of God, to go no more out for ever, but to be followers of God as dear children. Oh! what remains, then, but that having acceptance most free and perfect; adoption, also, gratuitous and complete and sure; you should now be perfect and complete also in doing the will of God— walking before him and being perfect? Justified in the righteousness of Jesus, that pure and spotless robe, and the King's eye resting on you with approbation, will you not keep your honour bright and your garments unspotted

from the world? Enrolled for ever among the free born sons of God, will you not go and work to-day in his vineyard, and occupy until he come, your eye beaming keen with love and looking for the glory to be revealed? And praying ever in Gethsemane, in the full compass of Christ's own prayer concerning the Father's will, will you not remember, among other elements of that will, and as indeed crowning the others with the beauties of holiness— that " this is the will of God, even your sanctification "?

Thus praying always with all prayer and supplication in Gethsemane you shall neither want a high warrant and assurance of success, nor a rich, full theme for your petitions.

But there is a third advantage to be found from praying as in Gethsemane.

III. You shall have company most honourable and blessed. Here you will have Jesus for your companion. Here you will have communion or fellowship or partnership in prayer with him. For as on Calvary you have fellowship with him in his sufferings, being crucified with Christ; and as in Golgotha you have fellowship with him in his grave, being buried with him by baptism unto death; and as in his resurrection you have fellowship with him, knowing him in the power thereof and raised up with him unto newness of life; even so, come, and by the same faith have fellowship with him in Gethsemane in prayer. Come here to pray. Resort thither often to pray, as he did. And realise that you do not enter on this high privilege of prayer, which still is a very arduous duty, alone. You have company here, company the highest and the best. Of the people there is One with you, one chosen out of the people, one like unto the Son of Man, your leader and commander, your forerunner in all things, your pattern, your more than pattern, your Prince in prayer. You do not come to ground unoccupied, to ground where you shall stand—or kneel—alone. You do

not betake yourself to prayer in your own name at all or
with your own voice alone, as if you could pray with a
prevailing voice. No. But you draw near to Jesus. You
pray side by side with him. You fall into the fellowship
and concert of his very prayer. By faith you adjoin and
identify your prayer with his. " I beseech you that ye all
speak the same thing" *with him,* " being perfectly joined
with him in one mind, and in one Spirit "—the Spirit of
the Son in you crying, Abba Father!

Ah! your closet, where your Father in heaven seeth in
secret, is no dull, blank, dreary place of enforced resort,
if it thus becomes to you, by faith, as it were the garden
of Olives, where Jesus prayed. There you find the
fellowship of Jesus in his prayer, in his wrestling love to
that will of God. It is to you a place of true and deep
communion. You watch there and pray with Jesus!

True it is that Jesus is not now literally in Gethsemane.
He is in the Most Holy Place not made with hands. But
you do not come to Gethsemane as if Jesus had never
been there. No, it is very much changed to you because
Jesus has been there before you. All is bright to you
and safe because Jesus was there. For wheresoever he
hath been as the forerunner, he hath left some radiance
of heaven and some sweet smelling myrrh behind him.
The grave itself is irradiated to the eye of faith, and its
corruption and offensiveness suppressed in the estimation
of faith because Jesus himself has been there. Come, see
the place where the Lord lay. He is not here, he is risen
as he said. There is no terror here. There is a glory
here that annihilates the shame. There is no dominion
of death here; no destroying sway. For you know that
your Redeemer has been here; and that he was dead and
is alive again, and behold he liveth for evermore. You
know that your Redeemer liveth, and that he shall stand
at the latter day upon the earth; and though after your
skin worms destroy this body, yet in your flesh shall you

see God. O death! where is thy sting? O grave! where is thy victory? There is no divination at all against Israel, and specially no victory and dominion over Israel in the grave, for Jesus has been there. Come, see the place where the Lord lay!

Come, in like manner, to Gethsemane. Come, see the place where the Lord prayed! Here he prayed with supplications and strong crying and tears, wrestling even unto blood. True, he is not here. He is ascended as he said. And his prayers now are glorified, even as his person is. But still, even as the grave is sweetened with the fragrant savour of his burial, and the believer's body there shall rest, still united to Christ, till the resurrection, so now when you enter Gethsemane, is it not fragrant with the savour and the success of him whose strong crying and tears Gethsemane witnessed; and may you not here continue instant in prayer, united to and in communion with him, and having fellowship in the prayer of him who was here as your forerunner? For in leading you forth as his own sheep, he ever goeth before you. In Gethsemane he goeth before you in prayer: he seeks to associate you there in prayer with himself, that so your failure or success may all rest on his responsibility.

Wilt thou not, O my soul, agree with the suppliant sufferer, thy Saviour, in this most blessed proposal to watch and pray with him? Oh! why shouldest thou refuse? For how great shall be thy gain! Thy prayer now placed on the same footing with his; resting on the same promise and covenant; embracing the self-same theme; cast in the same mould; directed to the same aim; prompted by the same Spirit of the Son crying, Abba Father; and risked upon the same destiny and issue; thy prayer with his; bound up and identified with his; cannot but be heard, as his was heard in that he feared. Be thou separated from Christ, standing apart in thine own right-eousnesses, which are filthy rags; leaning on thine own

strength, or following the dictates of thine own understanding. And there is no acceptance for thy prayer at
all. The proud and self-sufficient he seeth afar off. But
be thou one with the suffering suppliant in Gethsemane.
By faith, fall thou into the strain and concert and fellowship of that very prayer whereby he prevailed with God
—the true Israel and Prince with God—the Prince of life,
the Prince of peace, the Prince of prayer; and thou shalt
never miss the blessing. The King will crown thee with
his love.

Yes, believer; your prayer of faith may well be linked
on by faith and identified with Christ's prayer, for is it
not very closely bound up with it already and from the
first? Is not every prayer of faith allied to Christ's
prayer by this most singular and interesting bond, that it
is in part the very answer of that prayer of Christ? Is it
not in answer to his very prayer that you have been taught
and led, by the Spirit of faith and of adoption, to pray?
Was not this, in part, what Jesus sought, when he prayed
that his Father's will might be done—by the which will
we are sanctified, set apart to God, set apart to that life
of which prayer is the vital breath and element? Why!
what is your prayer of faith but the fruit of what Jesus
in his prayer sowed? He sowed his prayer in tears; and
he watered it in blood; and he pressed it down into the
ground by his death and in his grave. "For except a
corn of wheat fall into the ground and die, it abideth
alone; but if it die, it bringeth forth much fruit." Thus
spake Jesus of his person, which by death should become
the living root of innumerable redeemed ones, rising in
him to newness of life. The principle is true of his prayer
as well as of his person. The prayers of faith are the
fruit of his prayer, even as the children of faith are the
travail of his soul. And as the persons of the redeemed
are united to the person of Christ, the prayers of the
redeemed are one with his prayer. Realise, then, your

fellowship in Gethsemane in prayer with Jesus, for this is no fancy but an animating spiritual truth. Realise the union of your prayer with his prayer, even as also of your person with his person. Abide in him and he in you; with your prayer also abiding in his, and identified therewith; and his words and his prayers abiding in you. And you shall ask what ye will, and it shall be done unto you.

Thus will you learn to wield with growing spiritual power and wisdom your liberty of praying in the name of Jesus. You pray not only in the merit, but in the strength and the fellowship and the succession of his own prayer. And then your answer is secure. For as Jesus in his own risen person is the first fruits of them that slept, assuring the resurrection in due time of all his own; so the answer of his prayer is the first fruits of all answers whatsoever. For his prayer, in a high sense, is in reality the first answered prayer among the sons of men; and all others have received, or shall receive, an answer, only by falling into the concert of *this*, into the succession and series of which *this* is the leading type and forerunner— the series of which this prayer, like Jesus himself, is the first-born and the beginning, in all things having the pre-eminence. True, in mere point of time others had been answered before it: just as in mere point of time Lazarus, and the widow's son of Nain, and the man whose body touched the dead prophet's bones, and others were raised before—some of them long before—the Lord died and rose and was revived. Yet in reality he is " the first that should rise from the dead " (Acts xxvi. 23): he is the first fruits from the dead, and every one in his own order. And so his answered prayer of Gethsemane was the first fruits of all answers to prayer. It takes the lead. It gloriously leads on the prayers of faith in all climes and ages. Oh! follow thou here where Jesus leads. Pray thou in Gethsemane where Jesus prays. Be thou with him here, though it should be with strong crying and tears.

Be thou with him here, where the kingdom of heaven suffereth violence, and the violent take it by force. Be thou with him here, agonizing to enter in at the strait gate; taking the kingdom of heaven by force, as he did; and do it, in and with him. Be thou one with him in his faithfulness and importunity; and thou shalt be one with him in his high success.

And now, if you disdain not to associate with Christ in prayer amidst the tears and cries and blood of Gethsemane, thou shalt be with him also by faith, and that even now, in the unutterable glory of the Most Holy Place, sitting with him already by faith in the heavenly places. For the principle is that if we suffer with him we shall also reign with him. And if you fall into the concert of his humiliation prayer, you shall partake with him in the glorious fruit of his sovereign and authoritative intercession at the right hand of the majesty on high. For in this respect will God fulfil to you the promise that he that humbleth himself shall be exalted. He fulfilled this promise to Jesus. And not a single point in which he was abased, but correspondingly was he glorified. Was his person, in this garden, rolled in blood, stained with the dust of battle and the soil of earth? Ah! who can comprehend the glory of his humanity now as, possessing the power of an endless life, and inheriting incorruption, he stands in the midst of the throne, radiant in the glory which he had with the Father before the world was? But his prayers also are glorified. Yes; they are as free from strong crying and tears as his blessed person is purged from the blood of his conflict and the soil of his prostration on the ground. And what difference there is between his person as then and now; the same difference there is between his supplications in the days of his flesh and his mighty and majestic intercessions at his Father's right hand. For whereinsoever he was abased, the Lord also hath highly exalted him; and his person and his pleadings, which were alike in humiliation, are now glorified together. Dost thou, O believer, join thyself in the prayer of humiliation with Jesus in the garden? The Lord exalts thee in his own estimation by seeing thee in Christ in the Holy Place not made with hands. Oh! how grand the reward! How precious the inducement to prayer! Thy prayers, as they come up for a memorial before God, are purged from all imperfection, and glorified in the High Priest's censer. Thy many painful wanderings of heart; thy manifold infirmities; thy distressing conflicts with unbelief and temptation, which in prayer are thine own burden and thy constant cause of humiliation and of shame; are all—if thou dost only pray in faith and in fellowship with Jesus—all intercepted and disentangled and annihilated by the intercessory advocacy of thy glorified head. All thy supplications are cleansed and purified and glorified, and fragrant with added incense; free from all stain of sin and of the soil and blood and dust of battle as surely as the person of the Advocate himself is glorious in the eyes of the Lord, and his intercession free from crying and from tears. And wilt thou barter this privilege of prayer, O my soul, for any mess of pottage or any pleasure this world can give, or any bribe with which the powers of hell can tempt thee? Be ashamed and confounded, for thy little valuation of it in the time that is past; and henceforth abide thou with Christ, though it be in Gethsemane; and thou shalt ask what thou wilt and it shall be given thee. What though, to thine own sense and feeling, thou art still in the garden of wrestling, where strong crying and tears can often be by no means dispensed with? The Father seeth thee already spiritually raised up together with the Son and made to sit together with him in the heavenly places. By faith and hope thou enterest within the veil, where Jesus hath already entered as the forerunner. And what by faith and hope is already thine shall be thine in the glory that cometh, when the Lord himself shall come and bid thee enter into the joy of thy Lord, where Gethsemane's strong crying and tears and bloody sweat shall no more come into remembrance, save as the purchase price of the blood-washed and white-robed throng to whom Gethsemane hath been, through grace, a vestibule to that glory in which God shall wipe away all tears from all faces.

VI.

THE ARREST—I.

SECRET PRAYER ANSWERED OPENLY.

"Judas, then, having received a band of men and officers from the chief priests and Pharisees, cometh thither with lanterns, and torches, and weapons. Jesus therefore, knowing all things that should come upon him, went forth, and said unto them, Whom seek ye? They answered him, Jesus of Nazareth. Jesus saith unto them, I am he. And Judas also, which betrayed him, stood with them. As soon then as he had said unto them, I am he, they went backward and fell to the ground. Then asked he them again, Whom seek ye? And they said, Jesus of Nazareth. Jesus answered, I have told you that I am he. If therefore ye seek me, let these go their way: That the saying might be fulfilled which he spake, Of them which thou gavest me have I lost none" (John xviii. 3-9).

THE arrest and capture of God's Messiah, as a criminal, is a procedure so replete with scandal and offence as loudly to demand an explanation.

It is not the part which man enacted in this matter which needs to be explained; or if it does, the explanation is very obvious, and was furnished some time before by Jesus himself when contending with his persecutors: "If ye were Abraham's children, ye would do the works of Abraham. But now ye seek to kill me, a man that hath told you the truth, which I have heard of God: this did not Abraham. Ye are of your father the devil, and the lusts of your father ye will do. He was a murderer from the beginning" (John viii. 39-44).

But admitting all this, the real difficulty and the deep offence still remain. For all the shame to which Jesus was thus subjected was controlled " by the determinate counsel and foreknowledge of God " (Acts ii. 23). And the explanation so urgently required, the scandal or stumbling-block to be taken out of the way, is *this:* In view of the personal innocence of Jesus, how can it possibly comport with the righteousness of God that he should load his Messiah with the accurately-sustained reproach and the systematic destiny and retribution of guilt? Is it not, at the first blush, a very grievous scandal —soon to be spread all through Jerusalem and thereafter all through the world, till the end of time, wheresoever this gospel shall be preached, that this Jesus, through whom mighty works of God had shown themselves, is under arrest as if he were a thief or a robber? And is not the rock of scandal or offence mightily increased in magnitude and dangerousness when it is understood that such is the will of God concerning him?

For this is no random or riotous mob that overpowers the Son of Man. His position is very different from what it would have been had the members of the synagogue of Nazareth made him prisoner on the occasion of his first discourse among them, " when, being filled with wrath, they rose up and thrust him out of the city, and led him to the brow of the hill whereon their city was built, that they might cast him down headlong " (Luke iv. 29). And it requires another explanation. For here we have the forms of justice gone through, and the rights of authority put forth for his apprehension. The determinate counsel of God operates its own profound will through the deliberate counsels of men in high places. Civil and ecclesiastical powers combine to place Jesus, by every legal form, in the position of a criminal, under the charge of having broken laws civil and sacred alike—human and divine. The great multitude, with staves and swords, with lanterns and torches, were acting as men under commission to do what they did.   They had all the authority with which they could possibly have been armed.   They were the "chief priests and elders and Pharisees" (John xviii. 3; Matt. xxvi. 47), who had procured the band of men and officers.   This "band," with their officers or captains, were undoubtedly a detachment of Roman soldiers obtained from Pilate.   Already, therefore, the rulers took counsel against the Lord's anointed.   Onwards from this ominous commencement of the dreadful game on hand, Jew and Gentile were playing it in consultation; and whatever authority the Synagogue could wield, or the Governor's hall put forth, were combined to give official force and validity to the warrant that now went forth against the Son of Man.

For it was a thoroughly official warrant which was now out for his arrest, thoroughly competent, however unrighteous.   Barabbas himself could not have been more duly apprehended than Jesus now was, and that by the determinate counsel of God.   Now, what is the explanation?   Why did the righteous God place his holy Messiah in such an attitude and destiny?   Why did his determinate counsel arrange that the innocent Jesus should depart this life under all the forms of a criminal's punishment, preceded by all the steps of a criminal process or prosecution?

The Socinian doctrine of Jesus dying as a holy martyr, sealing his doctrine with his blood—will *that* remove the scandal?   Nay; it blasphemes the character of God and shocks the conscience of man.   Was the righteous overruling God, the judge of all, evoking merely a martyr's testimony, when he awoke all legal and official powers in Jerusalem to serve the ends of his "determinate counsel," and put the case against Jesus into legal shape and follow it out from first to last in all due legal form?   God forbid.

Or will the Arminian notion of Jesus dying in some sense, and in the same sense, for all men—that is, when rightly sifted and examined, merely in some sense for the good of men, so that now all men can make better terms with God or have another chance of escaping hell—an opportunity, through a relaxed or softened covenant, to save themselves. That also is very far from removing this grievous scandal or explaining this most offensive exhibition.

There must be an explanation that will gloriously vindicate the justice of God in so pursuing and prosecuting legally the man of sorrows. There must be an explanation which will not merely vindicate the character of God, in the sense of showing that this process or prosecution which the divine "determinate counsel" carried on, is no impeachment of the divine justice, but that it involves an illustrious instance and forthgoing of this divine justice. There must be an explanation which will even swallow up the scandal in glory and make the very offence of the cross a fountain and a revelation of high moral excellence and triumph—not only not the eclipse, but the victory of righteousness.

The doctrine which thus at once vindicates the personal innocence of Jesus and the public righteousness of God, and transforms the scandal into glory, and the shame into moral loveliness, is the suretyship and substitution of Jesus in the room of his people, with the imputation to him, thereon, of his people's transgressions. Accordingly, for this very reason—the Holy Ghost signifying this very truth—both at the commencement and at the close of this criminal process, the imputation of sin to Jesus is announced as the satisfactory and sufficient explanation of the whole.

1. Thus, in the first place, when warning the disciples of the shock which their feelings, and their faith, would sustain that night when these things should come to pass,

Jesus furnished them with the true principle that would guide them safely: " For I say unto you that this which is written must yet be accomplished in me, *And he was reckoned among the transgressors:* for the things concerning me have an end " (Luke xxii. 37). This is the end which the things concerning me must have; namely, that I must be reckoned among the transgressors. This is the issue and the outgoing that my destiny must have. To this end all things are now pointing with me, even that I should be made sin, and bear the sins of many, having their iniquities made to meet upon me, being by imputation a transgressor and dealt with as such—yea, bearing the sins of a multitude whom no man can number, and through federal unity with them and as their legal representative and surety, responsible for all their transgressions and liable to be righteously and relentlessly pursued in their name even unto death. Grasp ye this principle: see me as in the eye of the righteous God standing in this position; and behold how the determinate counsel of God gives palpable revelation of the hidden realities of this marvellous case as it stands at his bar in righteousness by overruling and employing what of official power and authority are existing in the land, so that on the platform of obvious events there may be represented in symbolical or dramatic exhibition the infinitely righteous but invisible quarrel of the divine sword against the soul of the sin-laden substitute of sinners.

2. And then, secondly, the Scriptures formally and expressly announce this principle again, when the process is closed and the sword is quenched in the blood of Jesus. For when the evangelist Mark records the final act of this legal process, namely, the crucifixion itself, " And with him they crucify two thieves, one on the right hand and the other on his left," struck with the literal event as forming a marvellous and forcible commentary on the prophecy, he adds: " And the Scripture was fulfilled,

which saith, *And he was numbered with the transgressors* " (Mark xv. 27, 28).

That Scripture, in all the fulness of its doctrinal meaning, might have been fulfilled although many of the outward circumstances of Christ's final sufferings had been ordered otherwise.   Substantially it received its fulfilment in the fact that Jesus died the cursed death in the room and stead of the guilty.   And Jesus might have so died, unto the satisfaction of divine justice, though he had not been arrested as a criminal by the hand of man or subjected to a judicial trial at the tribunals of the Jewish Sanhedrim and the Roman Governor, or crucified in company with malefactors.   But then the palpable and blessedly abounding evidence that he so died as a surety for the guilty, himself laden with guilt, the guilt of imputed sin, would have been marvellously diminished. The anger of the invisible God against the invisible soul of the man Christ Jesus could not be beheld by mortal eye.   But the world might be constrained to behold it as in a glass.   And hence, to set it forth as if in unmistakable and terrible sacramental signs and seals, in and with which to the experience of the soul of Emmanuel the unseen process of his Father's wrath was being carried on, the Father wielded at his pleasure, in infinite holiness, the official authority of those in high places of the land; put in requisition all forms of competent and legal order in criminal procedure; sacramentally, as it were, prosecuted the surety by awaking and employing against him all the constituted functions of " the powers that be " and which are " ordained of God," every one in his place " the minister of God, a revenger to execute wrath." Hence the oracle which we hear resounding both at the commencement and the close of this process we ought to accept as justifying and explaining all that takes place between.   " He was numbered with the transgressors, for he bare the sins of many " (Isa. liii. 13).   And it was to

exhibit this hidden, spiritual fact that from the initial
process of arrestment to the final execution on the cross
God exhibited his own Son, a spectacle to angels and to
men, in all the successive stages of a prosecuted criminal's
position; while thus, also, it comes to pass that what were
otherwise invincibly scandalous, becomes a brilliant
mirror in which to the eye of faith there shines forth with
dazzling splendour the unmistakable evidence of that
glorious covenant whereby Jesus the Holy One and the
Just made sin for us, makes an end of sin, makes reconciliation for iniquity and brings in everlasting righteousness.

It is a strange midnight scene, this at the gate of Gethsemane. The rich flood of silver moonbeams, for it is
full moon at the passover, fills the quiet vale, and here
and there breaks in shivered gleams upon the little brook
that murmurs among the olives. A grief-worn figure
stands among some others, sleep-worn and fatigued, whom
he is addressing in the mingled vein of rebuke and
tenderness, when lo, a rush and hurried tread of many
footsteps, the sudden gleam of lamps and torches, the
clash of weapons; and immediately a great multitude, a
band of soldiers, led on by one who knows the ground
and where the object of their search must be, confront
the Lord and his disciples. And now the conduct of
Jesus—full of immediate majesty and unbroken self-
possession—demands our notice. Setting aside the
traitor's kiss and salutation, he presents himself at once
as he whom they seek and surrenders in due order to
their commission and their warrant.

It is to this part of the transaction that we confine our
attention at present. It is detailed by John alone, being
entirely supplementary to the information of the other
Evangelists; and we can hardly help feeling that John
recorded it with peculiar pleasure and as a very study in
illustration of his master's glorious character and conduct.

For this procedure on the part of Jesus is, as we have said, full of majesty, and it is full of spiritual import. In fact the key to it is to be found by tracing in it the answer to the prayer in the garden: and viewing it in this light, the accordance is more complete than might at first be supposed, while the interest of the passage is greatly enhanced.

We must bear in mind that the ultimate agony of Christ's prayer consisted of a burning and unquenchable desire that the will of God might be done. " O my Father, thy will be done." And this will of God embraced immediately and directly these two objects: *first,* that Jesus should offer himself a sacrifice of a sweet-smelling savour to God; and, *secondly,* that herein he should be an effectual and accepted ransom securing the redemption of those whom the Father hath given to him. The first part of this will of God, namely, the offering of the body of Christ once for all, is asserted in the well-known passage: " Sacrifice and offering thou wouldst not, but a body hast thou prepared me; in burnt offerings and sacrifices for sin thou hast had no pleasure. Then said I, lo! I come to *do thy will,* O God " (Heb. x. 5-7). And the second part of God's will, namely, our separation and consecration to God, and thereby also our salvation, as the fruit of Christ's death and sacrifice, is set forth in close connection with this in a subsequent verse, when the apostle says, " By the which will we are sanctified through the offering of the body of Christ once for all " (Heb. x. 10). Hence when the apostle describes his prayer of anguish in Gethsemane in these terms, " In the days of his flesh, he offered up supplications with strong crying and tears unto him that was able to save him from death," and when he assures us that his prayer was heard and answered " in that he feared " (Heb. v. 7); he proceeds to show that it was precisely in these two points that the answer to his prayer consisted; *first,* that he might receive all needed grace to be " obedient unto death," positively offering himself a sacrifice; for this was that will of God which he came to do: and, *secondly,* that all his sheep, his children, the travail of his soul, might be secured unto eternal salvation. For unquestionably in these respects would the apostle have us to understand that he was " heard in that he feared "; namely, *first,* inasmuch as " though he were a Son he learned obedience by the things which he suffered " (verse 8), being made perfect in his function as a high priest, not by mere passive suffering, which is the destiny of the victim, but by active obedience, which is the duty of the priest, and especially of such a priest as Jesus, to whom it appertained, through the eternal Spirit, to offer himself without spot unto God. And then, *secondly,* the will of God being thus performed by Jesus, the sanctification or salvation of his people is also given to him; for being thus " made perfect he became the author of eternal salvation to all them that obey him " (verse 9).

Such are the two objects of God's will, the two corresponding elements of Christ's prayer, and the two-fold and complete answer. They embrace indeed, and briefly represent, the grand will and purpose of God in the everlasting covenant, consisting, as they really do, of the mutual pledge between the Father and the Son; *first,* on the part of the Son to the Father, that he should be obedient unto death, the ransom and the righteousness of the Church; and, *secondly,* on the Father's part to the Son, that he should indeed see the travail of his soul, and that the Church in all her members should be ransomed and made the righteousness of God in him for ever.

Now, it is precisely these two elements of God's will, of Christ's prayer, and its answer, which reappear in this scene of the arrest and surrender of the Surety. For in the intercourse which he conducts with his pursuers before they lead him away captive there is, you will observe, a double series of inquiry and response; and the special character and aim of each is opened up by the key which we have suggested. Thus:

I. " Jesus therefore knowing all things that should come upon him, went forth and said unto them, Whom seek ye? They answered him, Jesus of Nazareth. Jesus saith unto them, I am he. And Judas also which betrayed him stood with them. And as soon as he said unto them, I am he, they went backward and fell to the ground " (verses 4-6).

Now it is obvious that the whole point of this first series of questions and replies turns on the fact that Jesus means, positively and distinctly, by his own will unmistakably expressed, and his own deed unconstrainedly performed, to surrender himself into their hands. It is not enough to say that " he is led as a lamb to the slaughter, and as a sheep before her shearers is dumb, so he openeth not his mouth." That is truth, most blessed truth; and regarding Christ as the victim, the Lamb slain from the foundation of the world, it was very necessary that there should be realised in him the conditions requisite in the ancient and symbolic offerings, that he should go not unwillingly to the altar, even as also that he should be without spot or blemish. Hence there is very special attention directed to the fact that he was " led as a lamb to the slaughter." But this is not the whole truth concerning him; for he is not only the Lamb, but the High Priest also whose duty it is to present the Lamb, to present himself an atonement and a sacrifice, to go forward not merely in uncomplaining submission, but in the active discharge of duty, learning not only to suffer meekly, but " learning obedience " in his sufferings; himself, in unutterable majesty, even in the midst of all his shame, conducting the glorious service at the unseen altar of God, and positively there offering up himself by his own intensely active will and deed. He is now come more immediately to that portion of the destiny assigned him where Eternal Justice prosecutes him as responsible for the guilty. The cup put into his hand in the garden was, doubtless, the final assignment to him of the position of a Surety and the consequent imputation of sin. Immediately thereafter his destiny and position became obviously those of a criminal. However unrighteously assigned to him by the malice of men, his position in all its steps, from his apprehension to his execution, had sacramental significance and truth in it terribly, as assigned to him by God; and from the very first stage of it in which the warrant went out for his arrest, it behoved him to feel that the time was specially come for him to adopt the oracle of the fortieth Psalm concerning him— Sacrifice and offering thou wouldst not, a body hast thou prepared me: Lo, I come to do thy will, O my God; Father, thy will be done; and now when the commissioned agents of lawful authority, moved by thy holy and determinate counsel, are here to lead me to the death of shame, they are to me, as by a holy sacrament of thy holy wrath, the agents of thy will, pursuing against me the quarrel of thy sword, O righteous Father: and there-fore to them—yea, rather to Thee in them—I yield. " Whom seek ye?" " Jesus of Nazareth." Then " I that speak unto you am he."

Now this was the first part of Gethsemane's prayer answered, in so far as the arrest or apprehension of the Surety was concerned. He agonised for grace and strength to be obedient unto the will of God. And now, by express will and act of his own, he offers himself to be apprehended.

This is the point or substance of the passage, and the separate circumstances all find their due significance, and are seen to be introduced with much precision, when the aim and scope of the whole is thus viewed.

1. Thus, in the first place, the Evangelist introduces the circumstances of Christ's perfect knowledge of what should happen to him. " Jesus therefore, knowing all things that should come upon him, went forth and said unto them, Whom seek ye?" (ver. 4). It is not merely that Jesus, though he foresaw the consequences, was willing to surrender himself, so that we may be sure that in love to his people he knowingly placed himself in the very way of the sufferings which on their account awaited him. All that is true: and it greatly commends the love of Jesus. But it is something more immediately to the point which the Evangelist has in view. Jesus " knew all things that should come upon him "; and that they might not come upon him as a mere passive sufferer or victim, he went forth to meet them and actively present himself. He did not do so before; for that would have been ultroneously provoking, eliciting against himself and unduly hastening the destiny that was awaiting him: *that* therefore he did not do. The things that should " come upon him " he was not in any sense to *bring* upon himself. He did not go forth to seek, or court, or call forth danger. But now that the danger and the destiny were " coming upon him " he " went forth " now! Earlier, he would have been eliciting and producing evil against himself, the author of his own sorrows. Later, he would have been caught by them as their victim, the mere passive sufferer—not the positively active—the " *obedient* unto death." Here, then, was the precise moment for Jesus to offer himself; neither the author, nor the passive victim, of " the things that should come upon him," but meeting them in the moment when by active duty he could so suffer as to vanquish them. Hence Jesus, in the very moment and manner requisite, " knowing the things that should come upon him, went forth and said unto them, Whom seek ye?"

2. Hence also, in the second place, the significance of the fact that Jesus extorted from them an acknowledgment that it was him they sought. " He went forth and said unto them, Whom seek ye? And they answered him, Jesus of Nazareth." For he will not be captured incognito. It shall be thoroughly understood on all sides who it is that is sought, and who it is that is taken. He will answer only to his own name and surrender with all things explained and understood. It shall be done with all quietness, but it shall be done with no room for mistake. It is Jesus that is surrendering. It is no nameless wanderer—no unknown adventurer. It is he of whose mighty works and gracious doctrines Jerusalem has heard abundantly, and these very captors themselves have heard. This whole work is at their peril; and it touches their responsibility that they should be constrained to confess that it is Jesus whom they seek, and constrained to know that it is Jesus who puts himself at their disposal. Yes! it is at the name of Jesus that he surrenders; it is in that capacity that he offers himself a sacrifice—as one who " saves his people from their sins."

3. Then a third circumstance noted by the Evangelist is the fact that Judas stood by, a spectator to this intercourse of inquiry and reply which now went forward. Then " Jesus saith unto them, I am he. And Judas also, which betrayed him, stood with them " (ver. 5). He stood with them. He saw the whole transaction. He heard all the conversation. And he was confounded and amazed. This was what he had never expected. This positive obedience on Christ's part, in absolutely and freely surrendering himself, he had not looked for. It renders all his own treachery and planning in a sense ridiculous. It sets aside, as null and useless, all his scheme to indicate his master by a kiss, and all his excited conjuring to the soldiers to " hold him fast "—" to take him and lead him away safely " (Matt. xxvi. 48; Mark xiv. 44). It

pours contempt upon the whole part the traitor took in this scene. It renders his procedure utterly superfluous, utterly abortive. His kiss, his clever secret sign or token previously arranged and agreed upon, is altogether unnecessary, for Jesus announces and acknowledges himself. His admonition to "hold him fast" is as unnecessary for Jesus surrenders himself. His fraud and force —his concerted fraud and his advised force are rendered all useless together. It is a shocking and a galling attitude in which the traitor is placed by this positive obedience of Jesus. For thus Jesus "makes a show of him openly" as immersed in a "superfluity of naughtiness"—unnecessarily wicked, wicked overmuch!

Yes; do thou the will of thy God, O believer, as Jesus did, and thy faithfulness shall reveal an eternal confusion and abortion in all that the enemies of thy soul can undertake against thee.

4. And now, in the fourth place, the last circumstance mentioned by John in this part of the scene finds its interesting explanation also. "As soon then as he said unto them I am he, they went backward and fell to the ground" (ver. 6). For while concerning that positive obedience to the will of God which is the key to this transaction, the Apostle says, "Though he were a Son yet learned he obedience by the things which he suffered" we must also remember that though he learned obedience by the things which he suffered, yet still he was the Son, the Eternal Son, the effulgence of the Father's glory; the true and very God, "by the blast of whom men perish, and by the breath of his nostrils they are consumed" (Job. iv. 9). And it was not without its significance that his obedience, as the Son of Man, God's faithful servant, should carry with it on the minds of men some terrifying stamp and witness of his glory as the Son of God. Thus his voice seems in this instance to have conveyed some impression of majesty and terror: and his enemies fell

before him as if driven by a flash of fire to the ground. "For the voice of the Lord is powerful; the voice of the Lord is full of majesty; the voice of the Lord is upon the waters; the God of glory thundereth." "And the Word was made flesh and dwelt among us, and we beheld his glory—the glory as of the only begotten of the Father."

Was the voice of Jesus, when he thus spoke gently, surrendering himself a prisoner, so terrible that a great multitude with swords and weapons rushed back as if blinded by the lightning? And when he sits, the Eternal upon his throne, that same arrested prisoner the judge of all the earth, what power will his words of retribution carry!

But with regard to this incident in its bearing on Christ's procedure as manifesting the answer of his prayers; observe in conclusion, that it puts the copestone on the evidence that Jesus was in reality and in good faith surrendering himself by an act of positive and meritorious activity. It was not because he could not do anything better in the circumstances; not because he was already in their power and he would make a virtue of a necessity, claiming credit for an act of self-surrender which the overwhelming force of the adversary counselled as the most advisable step that now remained. No. He had but gently to announce himself to these men as the object of their search, and immediately, like the keepers of his grave, when the dazzling glory of angelic beings falls upon their eyeballs, they tremble and become as dead men. And thus the whole fulness of will and merit in his positive obedience in yielding himself to them or, rather, to God, announcing his hidden will through them, is gloriously vindicated as the doctrine which this passage is designed to teach and which every circumstance which the Spirit of God thought right to record is fitted to confirm. Thus, as far as this portion of Gethsemane's prayer in reference to the will of God is concerned, we see it fully and gloriously answered; and in this noble instance may we see, in the case of our great High Priest himself, his own blessed word fulfilled, " Thou, when thou prayest, enter into thy closet, and when thou hast shut thy door, pray to thy Father which is in secret, and thy Father which seeth in secret shall reward thee openly."

But there was a second element in the will of God and in the prayer of Jesus, having reference to the fruit of his obedience unto death—the deliverance, namely, and salvation of the Church.   Accordingly it is on it that the second series of question and reply is fitted to throw an interesting light.

II.   " Then asked he them again, Whom seek ye? And they said, Jesus of Nazareth.   Jesus answered, I have told you that I am he.   If therefore ye seek me, let these go their way : that the saying might be fulfilled which he spake, Of them which thou gavest me, I have lost none " (verses 7-9).

The special feature of this resumption of the strange work of interrogation lies manifestly in the fulfilment here described of the word which Jesus had formerly spoken. This is the point and scope of this second half of the conference.   The first turned upon the absolute perfection of Christ's positive obedience in surrendering himself. The language of it is : " Lo, I come to do thy will."   The language of the second part is : " By the which will we are sanctified, through the offering of the body of Christ once for all."   For Jesus has no intention whatever to surrender in any other character or capacity than as the surety of his people, the shepherd of the sheep, the good shepherd giving his life for the sheep; by death redeeming the transgressions of the guilty; by death ransoming many sons unto life and glory who were all " as dead men."   As to himself, personally considered, his captors have no right to seize him, even as they have no power but what he gives them; for behold, they are " gone backward and fallen to the ground." And if he yield himself at all, it is to his Father and not to them—to his Father, as announcing his will in and through them. And he does so as the representative and substitute of his flock, called to be so by his Father's will, called of God an high priest after the order of Melchisedeck. But his Father's will also is that none of his little ones should perish; that they should be emancipated from the curse of the law, by the surrender of their surety in their stead. Jesus knew this portion also of his Father's will, and his heart was set upon it. It was indeed the joy that was set before him—the purchase of his pain—the pledge and promise made to his obedience unto death. Hence Jesus is resolved to guard and defend this element of his Father's will as much as he is prepared to acknowledge and fulfil the former.

But a distinction must here be premised. We may regard these pursuers of our Lord in two lights; either, first, personally and in their responsibility as consciously fulfilling their own wicked passions; or, secondly, as unconsciously fulfilling the holy purpose of God—not witting that they are the agents of the Most High accomplishing the determinate counsel of his will and prosecuting the righteous cause of his justice.

1. Viewing them in the former light, we see in their conduct a terrible violation of divine restraint. For though baffled at first and thrown back—overthrown marvellously by a word—it is clear they never seek to quit the ground or lay aside their purpose. Had they done so, certain it is that Jesus would never have challenged or provoked them to resume it. It was not with this view, or for this reason, that he resumed his interrogations. He saw them still resolved, so soon as they recovered, to continue and prosecute their design; and undoubtedly he gave them a renewed opportunity of

apprehending him, only because they desired and sought it. Now, mark in this the grievous hardness of their hearts: for, to prosecute a guilty purpose after the grace of God interposes obstacles and restraints, whether on the conscience secretly, or by obvious providences, argues that hardening of the heart, and that following of an evil course greedily and with resolution, which points in the direction of judicial blindness and abandonment, and which approaches fast towards the sin which is unto death. Beware how you deal with such restraints; for the manner in which you deal with them discloses very much of your moral and spiritual state, and deeply and solemnly and very dangerously affects it.

You design some evil course or end. You covet the wages of unrighteousness, or you resolve on such a deed of wrath as worketh not the righteousness of God. You are tempted to go and curse Israel, or to go and avenge yourself on Nabal. But on your way the Lord's restraint interposes. Abigail waylays you, or rather God in his mercy waylays you, seeking to turn you from your purpose. And this dispensation of restraining influence distinctly says: Oh, do not this wickedness which I hate, and it shall be no grief unto thee nor offence of heart another day. You listen. You see the Lord's hand. You hear the Lord's voice. You stop short. You are reproved. You are snatched from evil. You breathe freely and thank God. " Blessed be the Lord God of Israel, which sent thee this day to meet me, and blessed be thy advice which hath kept me this day from evil." Yes! bless God who hath thus interposed to warn; and bless God again who hath given thee grace to take the warning and to turn from thine evil purpose. Follow up such gracious dealing. For surely the Lord would seem in all this to have towards thy soul a purpose of life and of love; and thy soul, if thou art faithful, shall be bound up in the bundle of life with the Lord thy God. For such restrainings upon his part, when met by humble submission and docility on thine, would seem to prove that there is the grace of God in thine heart and the fear of God before thine eyes; and if thus thy gracious state be revealed, its graciousness shall hereby also be confirmed and be strengthened too.

But dost thou despise, and burst, and break through the restrainings of the Lord? Then fear lest this demonstrate gracelessness and confirm unchangeably and finally thy graceless state. What! You will curse Israel for the wages of unrighteousness! You will go with the men! But in the way the Lord interposes. He sends the angel with a drawn sword. He opens the dumb beast's mouth to speak with man's voice. He interferes at least sufficiently to show that you are rushing violently against his will and righteousness. But still you go with the men: you go as soon as the angel's sword is withdrawn. You rise from your sick-bed and return once more to love the world as before, and serve mammon with the best of your heart, as really your master and your god. The voice of trembling that spake on that sick-bed and cried, " Let me die the death of the righteous and let my latter end be like his," is silent now; and the restraining angel being thus gone, you resume your journey and your course of sin. Then, know that your latter end shall not be peace, but calamity and desolation at which the Lord shall mock! Or, if it be not so, the Lord being marvellously merciful unto you, your salvation shall be accomplished only by marvellous mercy on his part, and through the depths of terrible repentance on thy part— as it was doubtless in the case of some of these very men who forgot the voice which felled them to the ground and resumed their evil work notwithstanding; but who were brought to repentance, if they were among the penitent, only under that sore charge and conviction: " Jesus of Nazareth, a man approved of God among you

by miracles and wonders and signs which God did by
him in the midst of you, as ye yourselves also know "—
even as when his gentle voice, like a thunderbolt, threw
you to the ground—" him ye have taken, and by wicked
hands have crucified and slain: and when they heard
these things they were pricked to the heart, and said,
Men and brethren, what shall we do?" (Acts ii. 22, 23, 37).

Ah! it had been better for them that they had accepted
the restraint which the Lord placed upon them: better far
that they had returned, as a previous band of agents had,
without their prisoner. And had the chief priests and
Pharisees asked them, Why have ye not brought him?
—remembering his word which, as a whirlwind, drove
back an armed band of men, they might have said, surely
with even more force than their predecessors said, " Never
man spake like this man!"

Still in his gospel Jesus speaks, and speaks as never
man spake, even in the foolishness of preaching, as it
touches and tells upon the trembling consciences of men.
There is something far more than man's voice—a proof of
Christ speaking to us through our fellow men. Alas! it
is still too largely true that the restraint of Christ's voice
still goes for nothing: and men, overthrown by it for the
moment, rise and resume their sins!

2. But, secondly, losing sight of the individual
responsibility and wicked wills of these men, and regarding them as the unwitting instruments by which the will
and purpose of eternal justice is indicated, the lesson
which their terrified resile and strange return to their
purpose reads, is a different one. It is to this effect, that
even Divine Justice—thus secretly pursuing Jesus, and
giving obvious and sacramental representation of her
secret pursuit of his soul even unto death, by wielding
against him all the authority of the land—even Divine
Justice could not consent to accept of Christ's surrender;
yea would have shrunk back as affrighted from the

proposal; except on the condition and proviso that he was surrendering on his part, and accepted on hers, as the ransom and the price for a multitude who should thus " go free." Jesus, as an independent king, demands these terms from his pursuers. He demands, as one able to enforce what he demands; as one who has his very captors in his power, having altogether changed places with them; and able to appal and paralyse them by his gentle speech. " If ye seek me, let these go their way." It is the King of Israel commanding deliverances for Jacob. He demands this as the condition on which he surrenders. But far more may we say that Divine Justice demands this also, as the only condition on which she will consent to accept his surrender. Till this is clearly brought out, her unconscious agents fall back in amazement and terror at the very offer of himself which Jesus makes. It is not till the safety of the sheep is on all hands guaranteed and secured that the Justice of God will allow her agents to place their rude hand upon the shepherd. The determinate counsel of God drives them back in dismay till it be understood by all concerned that the arrest of Jesus shall purchase the freedom of his children. It is, you say, Jesus whom ye seek—Jesus who saves his people from their sins. If ye seek me, let these go their way: " And hereby was fulfilled the word that he spake, Of those whom thou hast given me I have lost none."

But is not this straining the event too far and dragging out of it an inference which it is not fitted to yield? How can the plain fact of Jesus demanding the liberty of the eleven be taken as a proof of the profound truth that the salvation of those for whom he died is secure; a fulfilment of his own saying, " Of those whom thou hast given me I have lost none "?

Let it be borne in mind that this whole scene is dramatic, symbolic, sacramental, in the sense in which we have already explained. The substantial fact of Christ, the surety, guilty by imputation in his people's sins, being therefore summoned and arrested by Divine Justice to appear before the tribunal of his Father and the incensed face of an angry God, is an invisible fact. But at the time when it was in reality accomplished—invisibly accomplished, as of course its nature implied—it was also symbolically represented, while its reality and terrors were also as it were sacramentally sealed, by the accompanying formalities of a criminal prosecution, visibly conducted by human agents accomplishing the counsel of God. And thus in symbol, as well as in secret and in infinitely more terrible reality, " He was numbered with the transgressors."

Over against this invisible arraignment of Jesus at God's tribunal must be placed the emancipation of the Church and the letters patent of her liberty, which as the fruit of Christ's surrender passed under the great seals of heaven at the very same time—a glorious transaction in the court of the Most High God; glorifying the arrest of Christ as infinitely holy, wise and righteous—itself also an invisble transaction. But then it might be, it ought to be, symbolically and sacramentally set forth also on earth, by some visible sign and seal, or drama, simultaneously with the substitute's arrest, transacted on the same spot and at the same time, secured by the surety himself as the fruit and condition of his surrender. Hence, just as his capture by the hands of men obviously shadowed forth and surely sealed his arrest under the hand of the King invisible, so this escape of the eleven equally represents as in a mirror—and, be it observed, seals with all sensible proof and conviction—the eternal salvation which Christ's offering and sacrifice secured for his people. So that we see, in this very humble fact of the eleven being exempted from apprehension or arrest with Jesus by the Roman soldiers, a sacramental or symbolic and confirming evidence—a dramatic representation, and thereby and therewith also a real fulfilment of the saying, " Of those whom thou hast given me I have lost none."

Oh! Jesus did not die—why should he die?—how indeed could he die?—ignorant of the fruits which his death should bear. That man indeed saw little of the truth and glory of the everlasting covenant who said that " the work and death of Jesus would have been very glorious though no individual of the human race had ever come and reposed living faith in the surety." How dishonouring to the work of Jesus! How dishonouring to the righteousness of God! To what straits are men reduced when at all hazards they will have it that the death of Jesus was accomplished alike for the saved and the lost! For if he died for the lost, and yet his death did not secure them from being lost, it must be something else than his death that secured the saved unto salvation. So that if Jesus died for all alike, it is not his death that secures the salvation of any; it only secures, it seems, the possibility of salvation to all! That is the whole fruit of it, and it is this which has tempted to the terrible and blasphemous assertion that " his death would have been a glorious work though none had been saved by it at all." That is to say, though he had never earned the name of Jesus, who *saves* his people from their sins! We have not so learned the covenant or gospel of our salvation. And very clearly our blessed Lord did not so understand the case in which he himself has so glorious an interest. " If ye seek me, let these go their way, that the saying might be fulfilled, Of those whom thou hast given me I have lost none."

Now this was his Father's will: these were his Father's gift. Concerning this gift and this will of his Father, his soul in Gethsemane had agonized in prayer. And now his prayer is answered. His Father's will on this most vital point is done. " All whom the Father giveth me shall come to me; and him that cometh I will in no wise cast out. For I came down from heaven, not to do mine own will, but the will of him that sent me. And this is the Father's will that sent me, that of all which he hath given me, I should lose nothing." "Even so, Father, for so it hath seemed good in thy sight; be it unto me according to thy word. O my Father, thy will be done." And even so it is done indeed. "If ye seek me, let these go their way. And the saying is fulfilled which he spake, Of those whom thou hast given me I have lost none."

It appears then, on a review of this whole transaction, that in so far as this first and initial process admitted of it, the whole is conducted as in precise answer to the prayer of Gethsemane; and the answer in reward is given openly. *First;* the surety prays for grace to do the will of God—to be obedient unto death. And he shows that in answer to his prayer the Lord has taught him, and that he has "learned *obedience.*" He is not arrested in the imperfect and incomplete capacity of a passive victim; he surrenders in the duty and the action of an High Priest made perfect. And it is openly transacted. A great multitude look on and behold the majesty in which he acts. *Secondly;* the surety prays that by this will of God his sheep may be sanctified and set apart in safety and unto holiness by the offering of his body once for all. And it is done unto him, and done also openly. They go free in the presence of their foes; there doth not an hair of their head fall to the ground; none of them is lost. And a great multitude looks on and sees their salvation. Thus all that Jesus prayed for is granted, and granted openly before the world. And now, "Thou also, when thou prayest, enter into thy closet, and when thou hast shut thy door, pray to thy Father which is in secret, and thy Father which seeth in secret shall reward thee openly" (Matt. vi. 6).

Pause then, O my soul, and contemplate and improve this great sight of the Substitute and Saviour of sinners arrested and surrendering to the hands of justice. It is sin that makes him liable to this arrest; and it is the wages of sin, it is death, that pursues him relentlessly unto the end. And how, O sinful soul, shalt thou escape? If these things be done in the green tree, what shall be done in the dry? If this judgment and arrest begin on the Son of God, how shalt thou be allowed to go at large? Thy sins are many: they are legion. Each one of them has power to awaken a relentless prosecutor, who will never slumber till he hail thee to the bar and judgment seat of God. All may be smooth and quiet with thee now; but be sure thy sin will find thee out. And then, whither wilt thou flee? Whither shall I go from thy Spirit, or whither shall I flee from thy presence? If I ascend into heaven thou art there; if I make my bed in hell, behold thou art there. If I take the wings of the morning and dwell in the uttermost parts of the sea, even there thy right hand shall hold me. If I say, surely the darkness shall cover me, even the night shall be light about me. For there is not a word upon my tongue, but lo, O Lord, thou knowest it altogether. Thou hast beset me behind and before, and laid thine hand upon me.

And now, O my trembling soul, thou hast no escape from this warrant that is gone out from the Judge of all against thee. Though thou dig into hell thence will his hand take thee; though thou climb up to heaven thence will he take thee down; though thou hide thyself on the top of Carmel, he will search and take thee out thence; and though thou be hid from his sight in the bottom of the sea, thence would he command the serpent to arrest and bring thee forth into his sight. Yea, in vain, even in the awful end, wouldst thou call upon the mountains and the rocks to fall on thee and hide thee from the face of the Lamb.

Men and brethren, what shall we do? Agree with thine adversary quickly, whiles thou art in the way with him, lest at any time the adversary deliver thee to the judge, and the judge deliver thee to the officer, and thou be cast into prison.

But thou art guilty. Thy conscience tells thee so; and tells thee that thou oughtest to be arrested and hailed to the bar of God. Yea verily. But is there not a shield? Is there not a plea? Might it not be well to arrest thyself and surrender? Oh! that I could but get the counsel of the Wonderful, the Counsellor, you say. Oh! that I might live in the redemption and freedom purchased by the arrested, the self-surrendered Substitute. Oh! that I were verily among the number whom Jesus shields with that omnipotent demand, " Let these go their way." And wherefore mayest thou not? There was not one vile and wretched slave of sin among these Roman soldiers, had he only arrested himself instead of arresting the Lord, and thrown away the weapons of his rebellion, and self-surrendered and self-disarmed passed over to the little band of disciples, but—on the spot where he had shown his guilty will to kill the Prince of Life, but shown his will also to turn to him and live—would have shared at once in the shield which Jesus cast around his own, in the exemption and salvation which with a great price he was procuring for them, and with a prevailing voice pronouncing over them.

And what remains then, O my sinful and troubled soul, but that with all weapons of self-defence and all pleas of self-justification for ever thrown away, thou too, like those pursuers, but in a very different spirit, must " seek Jesus of Nazareth "; and, when thou hast found him, thou too, like them, must " hold him fast," but after a very different fashion, even with bands of faith and love. Art thou begun to seek him? And has he never asked thee,

" Whom seekest thou?"   He still conducts such confer-
ences of interrogation.   To those that seek him in this
other spirit, he is still known to say, in another manner
than he doth unto the world, in another voice than he
spake to his pursuers, " I am he."

Ah! when in his word, in his sanctuary, by his pleading Spirit, he draws near, do not put the Lord away. " If
thou knewest the gift of God, and who it is that speaketh
unto thee, thou wouldst ask of him and he would give
thee " all the safety and salvation thou canst need. Say
not, " When Messiah is come " he will put all my guilty
fears to flight and give me liberty to " go my way " when
he hath enlarged my heart. For " I say unto thee that
Messiah is come already," and you see how " they have
done unto him whatsoever they listed!" And he is come
again, he is always coming again in the power of his
Spirit, to divide the spoil with the strong and gather up
the fruits of what they listed to do unto him. Hark! his
voice!   " Behold, I stand at the door and knock." O
seeking soul!   " Messias is come already."   Hear him,
Oh! hear him saying, " I that speak unto thee am he."
Fall not back affrighted. Fall down rather at his feet,
self-surrendered to thy Lord. Surrender thyself into the
hands of justice in the virtue of thy Lord's own surrender.
Arrested, with thine own full consent, by the word of
God, by the ambassadors of peace, by the Spirit of truth
and holiness—self-arrested before a God of grace, and
self-surrendered in the faith and fellowship of Christ's
vicarious surrender to a God of justice—the same God,
his God and your God—a just God and a Saviour; in
union with Christ, and in the communion of his law-
magnifying obedience unto death and finished work of
priestly presentation of himself a sacrifice of a sweet-
smelling savour unto God; thou yieldest thyself now to
God, in Christ and with Christ; and thy life is held sacred
and secure indeed. Thou yieldest thyself, not as a dead

man, but as one alive from the dead. Thou dost arrest thyself, and art not arrested but released. Thou dost judge thysel: id thou art not judged but acquitted. Thou dost humble thyself, and the Lord exalts thee in due time. For thou art arrested with Christ; nevertheless, yea thereby, thou art acquitted. Thou surrenderest with Christ; nevertheless, yea thereby, thou art gloriously emancipated and made free indeed. No more dost thou flee to hide thee from thy God. Rather thou dost flee unto him to cover thee. He himself is thy hiding-place now, and under his wings shalt thou trust; for he will keep thee from trouble and compass thee about with songs of deliverance. The warrant to arrest thee, to bind thee hand and foot, and cast thee into outer darkness, has been gloriously answered—the warrant that went forth against thy Lord is its answer. Any handwriting demanding *thee* also is seen to be void, obliterated, nailed to the gate of Gethsemane: and over thee and all thy fellows in the fellowship of faith in Jesus there is heard the prevailing voice, securing that no weapon formed and no prosecution raised against thee shall prosper, the pass-word and watchword of the Lord's blood-bought and embannered host, in the power of which they pass and re-pass, " going out and in and finding pasture " ever safe, ever free—the voice of their Lord, which the gates of hell must ever hear with trembling: " Ye sought me, but let these go their way."

Yes! Go thy way: thy substituted Lord hath saved thee, and thou hast faith in him, hast thou not, as well thou mayest? Go thy way in peace; hunted no more in terror, as by any broken bond of law divine, for thy substituted Lord hath magnified the law and made it honourable; nor as by any lawful warrant of guilty conscience, for the blood of thy substituted Lord cleanseth the conscience from dead works to serve the living God. Go, as the free child of the Highest, an heir of his house

and of his heavenly land for ever. Go; and the shield of
thy Saviour's defence be ever round thee! Go thy way,
and walk in it undefiled. Go, and sin no more. Go on
thy way rejoicing.

VII.

THE ARREST—II.

The Prisoner Judging All Parties.

"And while he yet spake, lo, Judas, one of the twelve, came, and with him a great multitude with swords and staves, from the chief priests and elders of the people. Now he that betrayed him gave them a sign, saying, Whomsoever I shall kiss, that same is he; hold him fast. And forthwith he came to Jesus, and said, Hail, Master; and kissed him. And Jesus said unto him, Friend, wherefore art thou come? Then came they, and laid hands on Jesus, and took him. And behold, one of them which were with Jesus stretched out his hand, and drew his sword, and struck a servant of the high priest's, and smote off his ear. Then Jesus said unto him, Put up again thy sword into his place; for all they that take the sword shall perish with the sword. Thinkest thou that I cannot now pray to my Father, and he shall presently give me more than twelve legions of angels? But how then shall the scriptures be fulfilled, that thus it must be? In that same hour said Jesus to the multitudes, Are ye come out, as against a thief, with swords and staves for to take me? I sat daily with you teaching in the temple, and ye laid no hand on me" (Matt. xxvi. 47-55).

GLEAMS of glory may be seen ever and anon flashing through the dark shadows of Calvary. Strange transitions —marvellous contrasts—that take us by surprise! An argument for the divine authorship of the narrative might be perilled on them.

The grandest instance was on Calvary itself. The last was the grandest, when Jesus, hanging on the cross, turned that shameful cross into a throne and, himself in the hour and article of death—death with all its curse and woe—dispensed from that strange throne, divine forgiveness and eternal life to a dying malefactor, his fellow sufferer at his side.

We have an illustrious and somewhat similar case in the narrative of the arrest in Gethsemane. For while "numbered with the transgressors" and captured as a criminal, he does, nevertheless, in reality, himself ascend the tribunal, and bringing all the parties on the scene in turn to his bar, he pronounces judgment on the conduct of each. And it may give unity to our reflections on this amazing drama if we examine it from this point of view.

The arrested prisoner has turned judge, and his sentence goes forth and takes range over all around him. He has a cunning traitor; a little band of true but weak and erring friends; and the host of open foes to deal with. These are on the stage before him, and there are no more. They all act their different parts. Jesus has his opinion concerning each of them. And with ineffable discrimination and dignity, he constrains them in their order to hear it.

I. And first he sets aside the traitor. " Friend, wherefore art thou come?" " Judas! betrayest thou the Son of man with a kiss?" (Matt. xxvi. 50; Luke xxii. 48).

We all know the fearful part which he enacted, and on which Jesus animadverted in these emphatic questions. It was he who had projected the scheme of this arrest, and procured the warlike band of agents who were now putting it in execution. It was under his direction that the soldiers, and their officers—men of an honourable profession and usually making a strong point of their honour—had basely consented to act. It was the man who had sold his friend for thirty pieces of silver by whom they had agreed to be guided. And not thinking his past treachery enough, nor leaving it entirely to himself as his own matter, they join with him in a new exhibition of it as calculated to save them perhaps a little trouble and enable them to put through the business more quietly, they consent to a secret sign by which the traitor purposes to guide them to their object; for Judas " had given them a token, saying, Whomsoever I shall kiss that same is he," " hold him fast "—" take him and lead him away safely " (Matt. xxvi. 48; Mark xiv. 44). And then, when it is all arranged, see how the traitor draws near, as if shocked by the threatened danger to his master's person and, affecting at once total ignorance, surprise, and sorrow in reference to it, offers the last salutation of faithful love, and pathetically laments his master! For he " goeth straightway to him and saith, Master, master, and kissed him " (Mark xiv. 45).

But Jesus quietly and quickly despatches his case. " Friend, wherefore art thou come?" (Matt. xxvi. 50). " Judas, betrayest thou the Son of man with a kiss?" (Luke xxii. 48).

Why indeed should Jesus dwell at any length on such a case? There is no hope of bringing such a one to penitence. The Son of perdition has already sealed himself as lost. Already he has passed his day of grace. The dealings which infinite compassion had taken with him to turn him from his purpose, he had resisted and rendered unavailing. Infinite righteousness and infinite wisdom have resolved to leave him now alone. Why should Jesus dwell on *his* case? It is already ripe for the Eternal Judgment, when the Son of man shall sit on the throne of his glory and all nations shall be gathered before him. It can stand over till then. The very briefest mention of it may be sufficient now!

Hence the curtness with which Jesus deals with him. He does not at all expostulate. He does not show him the source of his sin, as when he deals with Peter: Peter is true at heart and shall be restored. He does not tell him that the power of darkness and of Satan has swept over him, as he tells the rude soldiery: the rude soldiery do it very much ignorantly in unbelief. He does not even demand him to abstain. He does not even command him to depart. He says enough to reveal his knowledge of the traitor's treachery, and has nothing more to say to Judas—till the great white throne shall be set!

Yes, it is the very brevity that is the lesson here: the terrifically short and easy method with the sealed for hell! Mark you this: that if you put away the discipline of Christ in grace and providence, in forbearance and affliction, as he seeks to probe your evil heart and show you all its treachery to him and its love for the world and the sin which crucified him—if you set your face against his efforts to emancipate you from the carnal mind which is treachery and enmity to God—then these efforts will become more and more brief, till at last the Saviour, who once yearned to pluck you as a brand from the burning, shall treat you with the utmost brevity and most perfect coolness, scarce even condescending to express in this life his indignation at your crimes. Ah! how many, by resisting the Spirit of the Lord, bring themselves to this dread experience! The time was when God's dealings with them in providence and on their consciences exhibited on his part a prolonged and warm interest in their spiritual condition: such manifestations of his gracious disposition towards them have been slighted and perverted; till gradually diminishing they are at length withdrawn, and the final expression of his mind towards them—terrifically brief, scarcely indicating either wrath or compassion —seems designed for little more than to remit the case to the eternal tribunal. Ah! what fresh force and meaning this gives to that blessed sentence, so full of mingled tenderness and terror, but so often heard in vain—"Seek ye the Lord *while he may be found; call ye upon him while he is near.*"

And especially when you see the one design of such a final and brief and unimpassioned utterance to the traitor.

What is it, in the essense of it, but just a disclosure of his guilt? It serves this one purpose, and is intended to serve no more—to paint the crime as with the blaze of a lightning flash upon the dark cloud. " Friend!" professed friendship and its opportunities now turned by thee to serve the devil! Treachery! " Betrayest thou?" " The Son of man," who came to call sinners to repentance and save the lost, whom thou hast known well for years as going about doing good and nothing else. " With a kiss "?—the last token of affection! And this lightning flash, bursting in upon his black soul, unlike the lightning of the skies, which the darkness devours immediately, dwells there in permanence, making his guilt to glare on his conscience for ever! Ah! that is the object of the Lord's last dealing with the impenitent: brief in other respects, it shall be long enough and full enough for *that* His sin shall be forced upon his view, and burned in upon his soul in letters of fire that cannot be quenched. And with this terrible engraving on his soul, the man disappears, remitted to the throne of judgment—to the left hand, among the lost!

Are there any whose ungodliness, amidst a life of Christian profession, of apparent friendship, is ripening them for this?—as it ever must be ripening them, till the heart be changed and made true. Ah! better be anything than a church-going, communicating, professing " friend," ripening for the judgment of the lost. Better be a rude Roman soldier, in heathen baseness and blindness. Awake and flee. Flee to Jesus himself in truth. Confess thy sins and want of love. Seek forgiveness in his blood: ask if he will still be reconciled. If thou do this in truth, he will be found of thee. Thy converse with him shall not be cool and brief, but full, and long, and loving. Repent truly of all thy wickedness, and turn to him as all thy desire: confess to him fully, even all the treachery and enmity that are in thine heart: deplore it as thy grief and burden—and appeal to him at once to ransom and renew thee. Then will he put the best robe on thee as his child that was dead and is alive again; he will kiss thee with the sweet kiss of reconciliation complete and irreversible; and suffer thee to kiss him with that of true faithfulness and love. Yea, do thou thus " kiss the Son, lest he be angry, and," like the Son of perdition, " ye perish from the way, when once his wrath is kindled but a little " (Ps. ii. 12).

II. Jesus judges the conduct of the disciples. And there is great need for the expression of his opinion here, for the eleven by their violence have well nigh banished from this wondrous scene all its moral grandeur and turned it into an unseemly broil. " For when they saw what would follow," even that their beloved master, made prisoner, should be separated from them, " they said unto him, Lord, shall we smite with the sword?" (Luke xxii. 49). And not waiting for their Lord's reply, they rush forward to oppose his apprehension, under the hot and hasty championship of Peter—of Peter, of course, as usual. " And Simon Peter, having a sword, drew it, and smote the high priest's servant and cut off his right ear " (John xviii. 10). Now this looks friendly, zealous, noble, daring. On Peter's part this looks very like redeeming his animated promise of faithful and devoted constancy: " Though I should die with thee, yet will I not deny thee." Is it not hard that Peter should be blamed? Would you have him to stand aside, and quietly and basely see his beloved Lord fall into the hands of his unfeeling foes? And when Peter sees Judas, one of the twelve, betraying him —when that infinitely scandalous fact bursts on his view —above all, when he thinks how he himself failed to watch as his Lord had bidden him, and how if he had done so, he might have given timely warning as he saw the many gleams of torchlight indicating the approach of a multitude striking down into the valley and nearing the fated garden; burning with true love to Jesus, with speechless indignation against Judas, and torturing reproach of himself, what wonder if he throws discretion and wisdom and calmness to the winds, and drawing his sword rushes forward to the rescue? But then he *does* throw everything like judgment and prudence to the winds and interposes in a manner fitted to increase and complicate the evil. And it is thus also that you will do, if you fail in commanded duty as he had failed, and attempt to resume the work of serving the Lord without a due humiliation and forgiveness. Conscious disobedience, or neglect of duty, has involved the name or cause of Christ in your hands in difficulties from which you long to extricate it. You see the bitter fruits of negligence. Oh, that you had watched and prayed! You might have given, you might have taken, warning in time, before the band of the enemy had got such advantage against you. But now, they are at hand that will betray your master's name, or your own Christian character or peace. You have entered into temptation. You are almost in the grasp of spiritual wickedness in high places, if not of the rulers of the darkness of this world. You make a convulsive rush against them. You stretch out a rash hand to save the ark. The sword flies from its scabbard, or the hot flashing temper pours out its indignation. Or you call down fire from heaven. Your self-reproach hurries you to do something, if by any means yet the threatened evil may be averted or the evil done be reversed.

Ah! but there is no meekness, and no wisdom, and no life divine in your purpose, and no strength divine in your execution of it. What you do in this spirit only complicates the difficulty: you do not walk safely in the midst of trouble. Nor will you ever do so till there be true repentance and true restoration, till you go and weep bitterly, till in secret you confess your sin and be forgiven. Till before the Lord you feel that you are a fool and a weakling. *Then* will you reappear before men, wise in the light of the Lord and strong in the glory of his power. Yes, and this course had better be taken at once, else the past unwatchfulness will work onward unto greater sin, till you deny the Lord as Peter did and your weeping be the more bitter in the end.

But let us listen to the judgment and opinion of Jesus. It is given with instant promptitude, and is supported by rich and overflowing reason. " Put up thy sword into his place: for they that take the sword shall perish with the sword. Thinkest thou that I cannot now pray to my Father, and he shall presently give me twelve legions of angels? But how then shall the Scripture be fulfilled that so it must be? Then said Jesus unto Peter, Put up thy sword into the sheath; the cup that my Father hath given me to drink shall I not drink it?" (Matt. xxvi. 52-54; John xviii. 11).

Now this throws a flood of light upon the subject. For in these words Jesus presents the question of Peter's conduct in four convincing aspects; placing it in its true relation to four different parties: the authorities of earth; the angels of heaven; the Scriptures of God; and the will of the Father. He introduces as parties variously interested in the case this splendid gradation: the powers that be; the angels; the Scripture; the Father. And he shows that the various relations in which they stand to the presently enacting scene Peter's conduct violates.

1. And first, " the powers that be which are ordained of God," are interested parties in this case. It is by their authority, by their warrant, most unrighteously extorted, or put forth, but still in itself competent and inviolable, that he is now arrested; and resistance in such a case by a private party is simply rebellion.

For such is undoubtedly our Lord's meaning when he says, " Put up thy sword into his place, for they that take the sword shall perish with the sword." It is ridiculous to profess to find in this a decision of Christ on the subject of war; far more so to find in it a decision against even defensive war as sinful or against the profession of a soldier as in itself unlawful. It is equally absurd to plead this text in support of what used to be called the divine right of kings, in virtue of which it was held that they might be guilty of extortion and oppression towards their subjects to any extent, while their victims were forbidden by Scripture to rise and resent the tyranny, or rise and throw off the tyrant. The words of Jesus give no countenance to the notion that all war is sinful; and as little to the equally unfounded idea that all revolutions must be rebellions. We live, as Britons, under a constitution guaranteed to us by a revolution settlement, which was righteous and good, and which banished from the throne a dynasty whom the nation declared, most justly, had forfeited its love and its submission, and whom the judgment of God upon their wickedness has since pursued into extinction. And as we live in internal tranquillity under God, in virtue of a settlement secured by a just revolution, we ought to be prepared in like manner to guard our external relations by readiness, when necessary, for defensive war. The righteousness, in certain cases, of revolution within; and the righteousness, in certain cases also, of war without, are principles indeed absolutely necessary to the maintenance of peace within the nation itself and of peace with those around us. And these are principles sanctioned in many passages of Scripture, and certainly not condemned by the words before us.

We venture also very strongly to assert that the admirable historian of the Reformation has done deep injustice to one of the finest portraits in his noble picture gallery —we mean Zwingle—whom, simply because he died in the field, sword in hand, he represents as having forgotten that the " weapons of our warfare are not carnal," and as having violated the command which Jesus here gives to Peter. We are persuaded that the lawfulness of the battle in which the great Swiss reformer fell is not to be settled by the offhand quotation of this or any other text. The fact that they were religious men in Switzerland was no reason why they should see, without a struggle, their fatherland overrun and devastated by the wild troops of their allied persecuting foes. Apart from their love to the gospel, it will be no easy matter for any historian to show that the Swiss did wrong in risking their liberties on the issue of battle; and most certainly the introduction into the question of their religious rights as Christians, which they loved and sought to guard even more than their liberties as men, will not make it any easier to prove that they sinned in fighting to defend and retain them. We feel interested in the question, for the memory of our covenanted forefathers in one period of their history stands in the same position, and must share the same fate, as the memory of Zwingle.

But passing from this: observe the extremely limited judgment which Jesus really gives in the text and which cannot properly be applied save to circumstances similar to those which called it forth. A thoroughly competent warrant for his apprehension had been issued by the civil authorities of Jerusalem, and was now being served upon him, very rudely, no doubt, but still by the competent and appointed agents. What is duty in such a case? Manifestly to yield obedience to the powers which be, and which are ordained of God; for " whosoever resisteth the power, resisteth the ordinance of God; and they that resist shall receive to themselves condemnation. We must needs, therefore, be subject, not only for wrath, but for conscience sake " (Rom. xiii. 3-5). The duty manifestly is to respect the authoritative warrant; to yield and permit the case to go to proof and judgment. It is not the case of a whole capital or kingdom put under arrest, or in a state of siege, by a bloodthirsty and ambitious tyrant.

But it is a competent warrant executed on a private party. For such, in relation to the state or civil power, Jesus was simply a private person, " made under the law," refusing most properly to be accounted " a judge or a divider." Hence the duty of the blessed Saviour was clear: it was submission. And the resistance which he could not consistently with duty offer himself, he could not permit his friend to offer in his defence: he commanded him to " put his sword into his sheath"; for any loss of life he might cause in such circumstances would be, not manslaughter, as in lawful war or righteous self-defence, but murder, an iniquity to be punished by the judge according to the primeval sentence, " Whoso sheddeth man's blood by man shall his blood be shed." Hence both the meaning and the strict applicability of the Saviour's words in the circumstances: *" They that take the sword shall perish with the sword."* Peter then was forgetting his calling and position as a private man and as a subject, when he rushed forward sword in hand to defend his master.

It was far otherwise when Abraham took up arms to rescue his friend Lot from captivity. Abraham was in reality, and by the word of God, no private person, but the very king and heir of Canaan, though his inheritance was held in reversion. And what is even more in point than that: it was not by competent and lawful authority that Lot had been made a prisoner, but by a wild marauding band of robber border chieftains, to whom neither Lot nor Abraham owed the least allegiance or submission. Very different is the position of Peter when Jesus, his friend, is arrested. Peter is no prince in disguise as Abraham was; no heir by covenant of the land in which he is a sojourner. And Jesus is not exempted from allegiance, as Lot was, to the parties concerned in arresting him. To draw the sword therefore in these circumstances is rebellion, and the bloodshed which Peter might cause would be murder.

This is the first light in which Jesus puts the case, and though it stood alone, it is a very serious one.

2. But, secondly: Jesus introduced a far nobler party in the case when he refers to the spectatorship and possible interposition of the angels. " Thinkest thou that I cannot now pray to my Father, and he shall presently give me more than twelve legions of angels?" There is great beauty and sublimity in this. The military legion was of Roman origin and peculiar to the Roman army, and the introduction of the idea at this moment when Jesus is confronted by a band of Roman soldiers is singularly apposite and happy. And then the number twelve is that of the disciples, including alike the eleven rash and unhelpful friends and the false-hearted and exposed betrayer. Jesus gathers up, as it were from all sides, the references suggested by the scene before him, and embodies them in one of the most exalted utterances of which the case was susceptible: " Thinkest thou that I cannot now pray to my Father, and he should presently give me more than twelve legions of angels?"

Thus was Peter rebuked for his sin and folly in fleeing to an unlawful method of defence. This Jesus, whom he would defend by his rash sword, is the head of all principality and power. When God bringeth in his only begotten Son into the world he saith, Let all the angels of God worship him. Even Satan knew that God had given his angels charge over him lest he should dash his foot against a stone. Jesus reminds Peter of this. He tells him he could at once obtain a resistless phalanx— more than seventy thousand strong—of heavenly angelic beings; that he has only to call upon his Father, " who maketh his angels spirits and his ministers a flame of fire," and presently this Peter, this New Testament Elisha, looking up after the blinding glory of the chariots of fire and horses of fire, might mourn his safely ascended Lord crying, " My Father, my Father, the chariots of Israel and the horsemen thereof!" But it is not thus that Jesus shall ascend, without tasting death. He must "taste death" for Peter himself, and "for every one" who like him loveth the appearing of the Lord the second time. And hence if the Father sends not such an angelical guard of honour and of safety to the Son, and if indeed the Son abstains from asking it, ought not Peter to see that it is because the united will of the Father and the Son is otherwise; and how vain, therefore, and fruitless, must be the interposition of Peter's sword!

Is the Christian at any time in great distress and danger? And is he tempted to flee to an unlawful mode of relief from the distress, or of averting the danger? Remember this consolation concerning the angels, and possess your soul in patience. "You are complete in Christ, who is the head of all principality and power." You are complete in him because he is so. He is exalted above all principalities and powers, both good and evil, that he may guard you safely from the evil; that he may minister to your salvation by the good. Are they not all ministering spirits sent forth to minister to them that shall be heirs of salvation? Never flee to sinful schemes of self-protection and defence while there are legions of angels at your Father's disposal to entrust with the charge of your safety and deliverance. If it be for your good, they will surround you invisibly, and suffer not a hair of your head to fall. Ah! how often may these holy beings act as a wall of fire round about a child of God. Have faith in God. Take not one step aside from the path of strict integrity and truth to procure a quicker return of peace and comfort. And suffer no friend of yours to aid you by any scheme in which unrighteousness enters even by an hairsbreadth. If thy Father in heaven, who consults thy good, and could give thee twelve legions of angels immediately to free thee from all that troubles thee, is pleased still to leave thee for a while wrestling with spiritual evils or exposed to temporal danger, then how vain must thine own unauthorised remedies prove! Buy not exemption from danger at the price of sin: that is a bargain which Satan often counsels, but which never really stands. Wait till the angels bring it thee, a free donation from thy Father, without money and without price: thine, then, by high authority that can never be questioned, by safe deed of gift which can never be reversed.

Wait patiently and do not fret. If the vision tarry wait for it: it will come and will not tarry; and in the meantime the just shall live by faith. Have faith in thy Father, and it will emancipate thee from the bondage of carnal policy. It is never time to cease your faith in him and flee to sinful or unauthorised methods of your own. His angels are innumerable; his resources are inexhaustible: it is better to trust in the Lord than to put confidence in princes; it is better to trust in the Lord than put confidence in any fleshly wisdom or any arm of flesh. For while you do this, nothing, absolutely nothing, can do you any real evil. " Because thou hast made the Lord which is my refuge, even the Most High, thy habitation, there shall no evil befall thee, neither shall any plague come nigh thy dwelling. For he shall give his angels charge over thee to keep thee in all thy ways " (Ps. xci. 9-11).

3. But, thirdly: in judging Peter, Jesus brings in another, a still nobler party, to this singularly interesting case. He introduces now the Scriptures of God. They, too, have interest in this matter: all their truth and faithfulness, all their divine origin and accuracy, are at stake. For says Jesus, " How then shall the Scriptures be fulfilled, that so it must be?" If I evade this warrant of arrest, which shall now lead me as a lamb to the slaughter; if this their purpose so to lead me away be defeated, whether by thy sword or by legions of angels, in either case " How shall the Scriptures be fulfilled?"

Here is the honour due to Scripture—a party in the case, higher, we have said, even than the angels, since to the living oracles of God's written word even *they* must defer, for by the Scriptures their office must be guided, by the Scriptures must their visits be controlled or restrained. It is the Scriptures that withhold them now from pouring forth in thousands to defend their arrested Lord. We may well be in subjection to the Scriptures, when we see them taking rank as higher than the angels.

Yes! but there is a higher honour put upon these Scriptures still, when we see Jesus in subjection to them. It is he that pleads their authority—it is he that yields himself up to that which they require. " Lo, I come to do thy will, O my God: thy law also is within my heart; in the volume of the book it is written of me: yea, also, thy word have I hid in my heart that I might not sin against thee." How grand and exalted the position of the Scriptures! They must control the zeal of Peter. They must withhold the visit of the angels. They inspire the soul of Jesus, the Son of God.

1. Are you in the position of Jesus? Your cause, or person, or character, or comfort is attacked and endangered? Defend it scripturally; in the spirit of the Scripture. Defend it so that the Scriptures may be honoured and fulfilled. Though you walk in the midst of trouble, you shall walk in safety while you walk in the leadings and in the line of the Scriptures. It is there that Jesus walks; and there you walk therefore humbly with him—in the participation both of his company and safety. " Tell me, O thou whom my soul loveth, where thou feedest; where thou causest thy flocks to rest at noon?" Under the burning sun, where do thy flock seek the shade and the safety? Follow the Scripture which is the Shepherd's voice, and thou shalt find rest unto thy soul. How readest thou? Let the Scripture be fulfilled.

2. Are you in the position of Peter? It is not your own, but your friend's person, or character, or comfort that is imperilled. Defend him scripturally—in the spirit of the Scriptures: as one who considers well the question, How must I act that the Scripture may be fulfilled? If you do not so; if you act on the hot impulse of mere passionate sentiment, and not on the calm, clear judgment of Christian principle, you may give him cause full soon to long to be saved from his friends. Your good will to help him may only complicate his danger. Ah! it is the service of Christian friendship that is truly valuable; the interposition of him who aids me, invisibly, by the effectual fervent prayer which availeth much; who aids me, outwardly, by movements in my cause prompted not by mere natural affection, but by spiritual love, and guided by, not the rash impulse of his own mind, but the wisdom of God which he hath received liberally from him who upbraideth not. Would you really help your friend? Let the Scriptures of the Lord be your councillors. As in the friendship of Jonathan and David, these loving ones exclaimed mutually, " The Lord be between thee and me," the Lord as indicating his will by the oracle anent the throne of Israel, so let the Lord as speaking in his own written word be between you and your friend. And this will be the source and secret of effective aid rendered on your part, and of the highest possible enjoyment in receiving it on his.

3. Or, again, is it still more exactly the position of Peter that you occupy, in that the friend you are called to defend is actually the same, Peter's Lord and yours? The name of Jesus is dishonoured among those in whose company you are often thrown, or his cause reviled, or his servants abused. Ah! let this friend, if any friend, be defended scripturally. Seek the meekness and wisdom which the Scriptures enjoin: avoid the wrath of man which the Scriptures forbid, and which never worketh the

righteousness of God.   Inquire at the living oracle, " Lord, what wilt thou have me to do?"   Lord, how wilt thou have me to confess and defend thy name?   Labour to live so blameless and without offence that if Christ in you be hated, or you for the sake of Christ, the Scripture may be seen to be fulfilled which saith, " They hated me without a cause."

4. But, fourthly; Jesus ultimately carries the matter to the highest court of all.   " The cup that my Father hath given me to drink, shall I not drink it?"   He now makes his Father a party in the case.   Hence this noble series of gradations by which Jesus brings this matter into relation with successive rights and agencies: the authorities on earth; the angels of heaven; the Scriptures of God, till he place it in immediate connection with the will of the Holy One of Israel—is like that mystic ladder which the pilgrim father saw, which was " set upon the earth and the top of it reached to heaven, and behold the angels of God ascending and descending on it; and, behold! Jehovah stood above it."

Thus ultimately the case in hand is carried up to Jehovah, submitted to the Father's will.   This brings out the chiefest aggravation of Peter's sin.   He would have interposed to frustrate the will of God; yea, the will of God for the redemption of the Church.   Strange that this should have been so often the temptation under which Peter fell, the temptation also which he so often brought to bear, though in vain, upon his master!   What else was it than an undisguised attempt to bring to nought the whole scheme of salvation when, Jesus having " begun to show them how he must go to Jerusalem and suffer many things of the elders and chief priests and scribes, and be killed, and be raised again the third day, Peter took him and began to rebuke him and say unto him, This be far from thee, Lord: this shall not be unto thee " (Matt. xvi. 21-23)?   What was this but an effort to undo the whole plan of redemption and forbid the work of the Redeemer? "Jesus turned and said unto Peter, Get thee behind me, Satan; thou art an offence unto me: thou savourest not the things that be of God but those that be of men." Did Peter learn wisdom? How read we? "After six days Jesus taketh Peter, and James, and John his brother, and bringeth them up into a high mountain apart, and was transfigured before them: and his face did shine as the sun, and his raiment was white as the light. And, behold, there appeared unto them Moses and Elias talking with him; they spake of the decease which he should accomplish at Jerusalem. Then answered Peter, and said, Lord, it is good for us to be here: if thou wilt let us make here three tabernacles: one for thee, one for Moses, and one for Elias." What! Simon Peter; no more shame; no cross; no sacrifice for sin; no death; not even the decease thou hast heard the visitants from heaven talking of? Still savouring not the things which be of God but those which be of men?

And now again the third time; when the Father's sword of awful righteousness awakes against the shepherd, must thy puny sword be ready to dispute it? Oh! thine infinite folly! What! in thy blindness measuring swords with the supreme God! And all to prevent the salvation of the elect and thine own! Go thy way. We shall never call thee, nor thy successor, the Father of the Church; thou canst not even feed one lamb till thy Master's death which thou wouldst again forbid has taken place; yea, till the crucified One shall rise again and forgive thee, and restore thee from thy sin. Thou art a loving and an earnest man; and worthy in much of our esteem and imitation; but in this thou art walking by the wisdom which is from beneath. Thou shalt be in no sense the Church's head. Her salvation is far from safe in thy hands. It is not thy fault that she is saved at all. Yet thou art truly loved by all the faithful, for Jesus hath prayed for thee that thy faith may not fail.

How gloriously does Christ's constancy shine forth in the contrast! How safe is our salvation in his hands! How unsafe would it be in Peter's or our own!

Now this is the very essence of the contest between faith and unbelief. Unbelief shrinks from being contented with having my eternal salvation entirely in the hands of another. Unbelief searches diligently for somewhat to trust to in myself, and would look upon it with complacency, and rest upon it with peace and delight, could it but succeed in the search. The search is vain. In me, that is in my flesh, dwelleth no good thing. But faith looks out. Faith looks to Jesus. Faith says, Jesus is sufficient; Jesus is infallible and true. Faith sees salvation safe in his hand and says, " My Lord and my God," I am thine: and we *so* are one, that thy will to save me is as good to me as my own willingness to be saved; yea, better, brighter, steadier, unslumbering, unflagging, changeless. And then thy power is all-sufficient. Thou art all my salvation; thou art all my desire. None but Christ: none but Christ.

Hearken, then, to the great Councillor as he sets his erring follower right, pointing out to him the true aspects of the case in all its glorious breadth: telling Peter his sin, and showing him his Master's duty and his own. Behold how safely Jesus walks: surrendering to the powers that be; believing in the guardianship of angels, but forbearing for the time their aid; fulfilling the Scriptures of God; yielding submission and obedience to his Father's will. Thus also would he have Peter to walk; and thus also thee, O believer, as thou takest up thy cross and followest Jesus. Abide in thy calling and observe every ordinance of God. Pray in faith to thy Father, refusing the aid of fleshly wisdom and sinful policy; for multitudes of angels at the last moment can rescue thee;

and at the worst even, as thou thinkest, it shall be the best, when they carry thee to Abraham's bosom. Fulfil the Scriptures, being not a forgetful hearer but a doer of the word, and blessed in thy deed. And finally receive all appointments of God as from your Father's hand; that hand in which you must be for ever safe. So shalt thou walk in safety, amidst all adversaries whatsoever, thine eye being single and thy whole body full of light.

III. But there is another party standing at the bar of this singular arrested judge. He judges not the traitor only and his own rash friends, but his captors even must hear his judgment concerning themselves. " Then said Jesus to the chief priests and captains of the temple and the elders which were come to him, Be ye come out as against a thief with swords and staves? When I was daily with you in the temple, ye stretched forth no hands against me. But this is your hour and the power of darkness."

Now the point of this address turns on the fact that Jesus complains of their attempt to place him in a false position, and raise against him a groundless prejudice. They come against him with swords and staves as if he were a thief, a malefactor, a felon. No doubt this was done that the Scripture might be fulfilled which saith, " And he was numbered with the transgressors "; and in this light Jesus willingly submitted. But then it was not with the will and the view to fulfil the Scriptures that his captors acted; neither came it into their heart. And on this ground, in addressing them, Jesus was entitled to complain. This was an act of low cunning, and discreditable trickery, on their part. They might have taken him at any time in the temple, but they feared the people. They must affect to regard him as a felon before they dare to arrest him. But they get the length even of doing that For it is " their hour and the power of darkness."

Now here is the principle on which all persecution against the godly is conducted. It is not for being godly that the world professedly persecutes them. The world feels that decency forbids to touch them till a semblance of some other charge is raised to cover and, if possible, conceal the real ground of hatred. It is not as a holy and benevolent teacher, winning the esteem of the nation, that Jesus is arrested: it is as a felon. It is not as holy and heavenly minded men that primitive Christians are persecuted. It is as disturbers of the peace of the Roman empire; as setters forth of strange gods; enemies of the imperial authority, as it prescribes the imperial religion. It is in that character they are given to the wild beasts at Ephesus or at Rome.

It is the same principle and policy in all cases, great or small. Look into the family, the field, the workshop, where the ungodly scorn and ridicule the righteous. It is not under the character of righteous that they persecute him. That would be too obviously and visibly the very spirit of hell. It must be a little masked and hidden from the view of others; ay, they seek even to hide it from themselves. It is not because he is a Christian, righteous, godly man they hate him. They cannot condemn him under that which is the true aspect of his character. They must misrepresent him first.

Did you ever thus ridicule the strictly godly? And do you not remember that you first called him hypocrite and tried to make yourself believe him a hypocrite before you spoke against him? Who is among you that dislikes the prayerful, bible-reading, righteous child of God? You dare not do it till you have attempted to believe him hypocritically and uselessly precise. It is under that false aspect you feel at liberty to ridicule the godly, and ridicule them accordingly you do. Then know that you have entered on an " hour of the power of darkness "; for this is a very special device of Satan to seal your

impenitence and harden your heart. What! this godly
man whom you despise is a hypocrite, is he? You come
out strong against him as a poor hypocrite? And yet he
is " daily with you in the temple." At least he is weekly
with you in the sanctuary, and you " lay no hands on
him " *there;* you lift not your voice of ridicule against him
there. He and you both are there—both there on the
Lord's day; coming as the Lord's people come; sitting
before him as his people; both, with your lips, showing
much love unto him. And the difference is that when
gone from the temple he prays to his Father in secret and
glorifies his Father in public, while you are prayerless at
home and godless abroad. Who is the hypocrite?

Beware! When you scorn the righteous you may
succeed in injuring, you may succeed in paining them.
But the hour in which you do so coincides with the hour
of the power of the devil. How horrible! if your opportunity and Satan's coincide! How far may they carry
you when thus combined! They carried these men the
length of crucifying the Lord of glory. May they not
carry you the length of crucifying him afresh?

Despise not, then, the children of the Lord: rather join
their ranks. Say to any of them with whom you stand
related, " Entreat me not to leave thee; nor to return from
following after thee: we will go with thee; for we have
heard that God is with thee. Thy people shall be my
people, and thy God my God." The blessed time which
sees this holy resolution, far from being the hour or the
power of darkness, shall be thy day of gracious visitation
and the day of thy Saviour's power; and like his people,
whom you once despised, you also " shall be willing in
the day of his power."

We close by calling your attention once more to the
glory of Christ as a judge, even in the midst of his shame
as an arrested malefactor. With his vesture dipped in
the blood of his agony and stained with the soil of earth,

he still gives pledge and prelude of his victory, when he shall come with dyed garments from Bozrah, glorious in his apparel, travelling in the greatness of his strength. Above all, he gives pledge and prelude of that awful final assize when we must all appear before the judgment seat of Christ.

VIII.

THE ARREST—III.

The Captive Carrying Captivity Captive.

"Then the band and the captain and the officers of the
Jews took Jesus and bound him, and led him away to Annas
first . . . And Annas sent him bound to Caiaphas"
(John xviii. 12, 13, 24).

Among the various aspects under which this singular
drama of Christ's capture and arrest may be viewed, there
are some that almost prevent us from seeing the insult
and shame poured upon him, by concentrating our attention on certain features of countervailing dignity and
glory. The lights in which the subject has been already
presented have partaken very largely of this character.
What could excel the majesty with which Jesus surrenders
himself into their hands, affording as it does a picture
and a representation of the glorious truth that he through
the Eternal Spirit was offering himself without spot to
Gód; while in sovereign authority and covenant right he
was securing and demanding the safety of the elect? Or
what could be more glorious than that sudden change
that passes on the whole scene; startling us by its abrupt
and unlooked for occurrence; when the prisoner becomes
the judge and arrests, as at an invisible tribunal of his
own, every soul around him, and pronounces judgment on
them all, speaking with authority and not as the scribes?

But perhaps we have looked at the scene too exclusively
in this light and not sufficiently contemplated the abyss
of dishonour in which the Son of God was now plunged.

Let us attempt then to remedy this defect before we pass away from this portion of the narrative.

And yet, what can be said in this direction more affecting or impressive than the simple words of the Evangelist: " Then the band and the captain and officers of the Jews took Jesus, and bound him, and led him away to Annas." They took him, and bound him, and led him away bound! And who was it that they were leading back into the city in triumph, under all the guise and treatment of a felon? Hear, O heavens, and give ear, O earth! The captive is the brightness of the Father's glory and the express image of his person; the heir of all things—(" this is the heir, come let us kill him ")—the same who was even then in the bosom of the Father as well as in the hands of murderers—who was even then upholding all things by the word of his power! It was their Maker and their God whom these men had captured; it was their judge whom they shall see face to face when they rise from the dead! Yes, look again, look long and thoughtfully on this marvellous event. It is the Living God—the Lord God Omnipotent—whom these rude men lead off in fetters. " Though he was in the form of God, and thought it not robbery to be equal with God, he made himself of no reputation."

Now, when we have said this, do we not feel as if the subject had gone altogether beyond the power of language—yea, beyond the power of thought? They took HIM, and bound HIM, and led HIM away bound!

Still, there are circumstances noted in the narrative singularly fitted to deepen the impression. For instance, in the first place:

1. We may notice the recklessness and relentlessness of his captors. How mad on the execution of their work! Have these men no knowledge? Will no terrors affright them? Will no tender mercies melt them? Will miracles neither of judgment nor of kindness turn them from their

purpose? Alas! they are proof against every appeal. The terrific power of their prisoner has cast them to the ground as with the force of lightning. His marvellous mercy has shone forth in the work of healing one among them whose ear the rash disciple's sword had cut off. " And one of them smote a servant of the high priest and *cut off* his right ear. And Jesus answered and said, Suffer ye thus far. And he touched his ear and healed him." And yet, in the face of a display of divine power and divine gentleness and kindness such as this, they stagger not, nor swerve from their design. Defying the secret power that prostrated their persons on the earth, stifling the appeal that with such dignity and force Jesus had addressed to their consciences, and trampling under foot the miracle of love of which their comrade had been made the subject and the trophy, they dread not to fetter those hands, fresh though they be from such a demonstration of the tenderness of his heart and the truth of his Messiahship and Godhead. Thus recklessly and relentlessly was Jesus captured.

What aggravation of reproach and shame that he should be the prisoner of men who could carry through the work with such appalling blindness of judgment and baseness of heart! To have been brought to the tribunal by men mourning the destiny that appointed them to make him prisoner would have been a sufficient depth of dishonour, but to own as his captors a band of men so lost to all that could sober or solemnise, that could shame or melt them—men that could rush through all appeals of righteousness, and works of power, and deeds of love divine, who had neither fears nor consciences nor hearts to plead with: to be led captive by such was reproach and dishonour unfathomable.

2. But, secondly, the scene must have been rude and violent in the highest degree. No sooner do they seem to have laid hands on him after he became silent and

suffered them to bind him, than the order which his voice
of majesty had hitherto compelled, seems to have given
way to ruthless tumult. Rioting in brutal joy at their
success, they abandon themselves, especially the younger
men among them, to shameless and unbridled violence,
as if hell itself were loose among them. A single stroke
of Mark's graphic pencil speaks volumes for the wild and
disgraceful features which the scene now assumed.
" And there followed him a certain young man, having a
linen cloth cast about his naked body, and the young
men laid hold on him, and he left the linen cloth and fled
from them naked " (Mark xiv. 51, 52). They had their
warrant to apprehend Jesus, and in doing so might have
pleaded, in a sense their duty. But now, as they lead
him away to the city, like a frantic mob, they rush upon
the innocent against whom they have neither charge, nor
warrant, nor quarrel. Amidst such a scene of shameless
riot was Jesus led away in bonds. What unutterable
reproach and humiliation! And was this the same whom
Isaiah beheld, when he saw his glory and spake of him?
" I saw the Lord, sitting upon a throne high and lifted
up, and his train filled the temple. Above it stood the
seraphim: each one had six wings; with twain he covered
his face, and with twain he covered his feet, and with
twain he did fly. And one cried unto another and said,
Holy, Holy, Holy is the Lord of hosts: the whole earth
is full of his glory." Was it indeed the same person whom
this wild mob of men was leading away a prisoner? O
the depth! He who was rich for our sakes became poor!
He who was the God of glory, dwelling amidst all insignia
of majesty, yet for our sakes submitted to be sunk in
shame! Oh! well might Jesus, in the depths of his soul,
repeat his own prayer and Psalm of mourning, " Draw
nigh unto my soul, O Lord, and redeem it: deliver me
because of mine enemies. Thou hast known my reproach,
and my shame, and my dishonour: mine adversaries are

all before thee. Reproach hath broken my heart, and I am full of heaviness; and I looked for some to take pity, but there was none; and for comforters but I found none " (Ps. lxix. 18-20).

3. And, thirdly, another circumstance of dishonour to which Jesus was now subjected was the loneliness to which he was forsaken. " For now all the disciples forsook him and fled." Peter, we shall see, afterwards rallied somewhat from this panic and returned and followed Jesus afar off, but it was only ultimately to heap more shame on his Lord, while one of the reproached prisoner's favourite companions demeaned himself so basely in denying all knowledge of him. As it was Jesus was left in reality alone. Now was fulfilled the Father's oracle: "Awake, O sword, against my Shepherd, and against the man that is my fellow; smite the Shepherd, and the sheep shall be scattered," while his own prediction that it should be fulfilled this night and fulfilled in this manner was also accomplished: " He is despised and rejected of men, a man of sorrows and acquainted with grief, and we hid as it were our faces from him " (Isa. liii. 3). And as Jesus saw this new indignity, and found himself now at length utterly alone—deserted of all on every side—might he not well adopt, as written already in the Psalms concerning him, such " grievous complaints " as these: " I looked on my right hand and beheld, and there was no man that would know me: refuge failed me, no man cared for my soul. I cried unto thee, O Lord: I said, Thou art my refuge and my portion in the land of the living. Attend unto my cry, for I am brought very low. In the way wherein I walked have they privily laid a snare for me. Bring my soul out of prison, that I may praise thy name: the righteous shall compass me about, for thou shalt deal bountifully with me " (Ps. cxlii. 4-7). " O Lord God, my soul is full of trouble; my life draweth nigh unto the grave. I am

counted with them that go down into the pit. Thou hast laid me in the lowest pit, in darkness, in the deeps. Thy wrath lieth hard upon me, and thou hast afflicted me with all thy waves. Thou hast put away mine acquaintance far from me: thou hast made me an abomination, a stone of scandal to them: I am shut up, and I cannot come forth. Lover and friend hast thou put far from me and mine acquaintance into darkness " (Ps. cii., Ps. lxxxviii).

Now draw near and see this great sight. He to whom the Father saith, " Thy throne, O God, is for ever and ever "; he who is the mighty Lord and unto whom belong the issues from death, is made a prisoner by his own creatures, beings whose life is in his hand and whose destinies obey his will. Recklessly seized and pinioned; rudely borne off in triumph, with every degrading accompaniment of violence and tumult; forsaken by his friends; alone in his reproach and shame—how infinitely marvellous is this sight! Might we not say with Moses, " I do exceedingly fear and quake "? Behold the Lamb of God! He is led like a lamb to the slaughter. He is taken from prison and from judgment, and who shall declare his generation? Behold how he loved them, loved the guilty sons of men! He will be a captive prisoner for their sake! He will wear these fetters of a malefactor, that he may draw them with " bands of love and with cords of a man " even though in doing so he finds them all forsaking him and fleeing, " ashamed of the prisoner " and " ashamed of his chain " (II Tim. i. 8, 16). " Then took they him, and bound him, and led him away to Annas, and Annas sent him bound to Caiaphas." What shall we say to these things? This humiliation of the God of glory passeth all understanding: and the love that reconciled him to it and made it welcome, passeth knowledge and adoration and praise. Praise is silent 'for thee, O God, in Zion. Though in the form of God, thou humbledst thyself!

But " he that humbleth himself shall be exalted." And this great principle of the kingdom of grace finds its seal and noblest illustration in the Head himself. " Because he humbled himself, God also hath highly exalted him " (Phil. ii. 8, 9).

Now we ought to attend to this, in examining together the humiliation and the exaltation of our Lord, namely, that the justice of the Father towards his obedient well-deserving Son is illustriously exhibited in giving him a reward rich and full as his sufferings and shame were deep: a reward contrasting, in every point and element, and circumstance of it, with the various descending steps of his humiliation. There was not one element of that shame which he despised, but there was an answerable and countervailing element in the joy that was set before him, and which enabled him to despise that portion of the shame to which it corresponded. And the glorious contrasts and harmonies which a study of these scenes will more and more reveal, evidence that those Scriptures which attest them are not cunningly-devised fables but a more sure word of prophecy than transfiguration disclosures or any voices from the excellent glory could be. Do we see Jesus for a little made lower than the angels? His reward is that the world to come is put under him, and in his suffering nature he is head of all principality and power. Is he placed as a panel at the bar where Caiaphas the high priest is the judge? The answerable reward to this is, as he testifies to Caiaphas himself, that God hath given him all authority to execute judgment because he is the Son of man, for " I say unto you, hereafter ye shall see the Son of man sitting on the right hand of power and coming in the clouds of heaven." Do his disciples forsake him, scattered every one to his own? The shame and sorrow of this are redeemed when Paul says, " I charge you by our gathering together to Christ at his coming." What portion, then, of his glorious recompense and exaltation shall we set over against the shame of these chains with which he is bound and led away a prisoner to trial? What is the precise element in his reward—the exact counterpart joy set before him—on which his soul may rest in full assurance and complacency, while wending his way an insulted prisoner to the city? What shall be a due solace and recompense for the dark night of his captivity? What but the glorious prediction concerning him: "Thou hast ascended on high; thou hast led captivity captive." Here is the singularly satisfying arrangement which his Father's righteousness hath made for him. The shame of his chains shall be obliterated by the triumph decreed for him. The captive Jesus shall carry captivity captive.

Now this prediction concerning Jesus, quoted and applied by Paul (Eph. iv. 8), occurs originally in the 68th Psalm, and the terms in which it is couched are very magnificent. "The chariots of God are twenty thousand, even thousands of angels: the Lord is among them as in Sinai, in the holy place. Thou hast ascended on high, thou hast led captivity captive: thou hast received gifts for men: yea, for the rebellious also, that the Lord God might dwell among them" (Ps. lxviii. 18).

There is every reason to believe that this glorious piece of psalmody was sung on the occasion of carrying up the ark of God from the house of Obed-edom to its resting place on Mount Zion. The whole structure of the Psalm is that of a triumphal ode, intended to be sung with all the accompaniments of David's minstrelsy, and when the tribes are assembled to the praise of the Lord. "The singers go before, the players on instruments follow after; among them are the damsels playing with timbrels"; while some leader answers them, as Miriam to her sisters in Israel, "Bless ye God in the congregations, even the Lord from the fountain of Israel." "Sing ye to the Lord, for he hath triumphed gloriously." Meanwhile, the tribes

in succession gladly follow. " There is little Benjamin
with their ruler, the princes of Judah and their council, the
princes of Zebulun and the princes of Naphtali," all joyful
because of what God hath wrought for them " because of
Jehovah's temple in Jerusalem " (ver. 25-29). And that
the ark of the Lord is with them this day may be gathered
from the opening note of their glorious hymn, the same
as of old in their marching through the wilderness, when
the ark at any time set forward, and Moses said : " Rise
up, Lord, and let thine enemies be scattered; let them that
hate thee flee before thee " (ver. 1 : Num. x. 35).

Now that ark was the symbol of Jehovah's presence,
and when ascending Mount Zion to its resting place which
God hath chosen for himself to place his name there, the
congregation of Israel glorify God as " ascending on
high," the conqueror of his people's foes, bringing all
fulness of blessing to his Church, and dwelling both in
symbol and reality among them.

But evidently while this hymn of triumph celebrates
the presently transpiring event, as the priests bear up the
ark to the mount of God, its strains are framed on the
remembrance and celebration of the past, and already
contemplate a still nobler future.

I. Thus as to the past: The ascending on high and
carrying captivity captive has reference to the glorious
manifestation of the God of Israel in the giving of the
law on Sinai. They feel that the Lord is among them
as in Sinai (ver. 17) as, " when, O God, thou wentest
forth before thy people, when thou didst march through
the wilderness. The earth shook, the heavens also
dropped at the presence of God; even Sinai itself was
moved at the presence of God, the God of Israel " (ver.
7, 8). Then " the chariots of God were twenty thousand,
thousands of angels, the Lord among them in Sinai,
ascending on high, carrying captivity captive " (ver. 17,
18).

Now, viewing the triumph here celebrated as referring thus to the majestic display of divine glory on Sinai, there can be no doubt that it is Christ, the angel of the covenant, who is addressed as the ascending conqueror. It is the angel, the messenger, of the covenant, as a son over his own house, the Church in the wilderness. It was " the reproach of *Christ*" which Moses, who was with the Church in the wilderness, as a faithful servant, preferred to the treasures of Egypt (Heb. xi. 26). And it was Christ, as Paul testifies, whom the Israelites tempted (I Cor. x. 9), when their sin was avenged by the judgment of the fiery flying serpents.

Then again, to this ascension on Sinai, we must clearly apply the same self-evident principle which Paul educes in speaking of the risen Lord's ascension into heaven. " Now that he ascended, what is it but that he also descended first " (Eph. iv. 9). The glorious God is incapable of ascension in any case or in any sense until he render that ascension possible by some prior voluntary descent, or condescension, in his dealings with men, or his disclosures of himself which he gives them. In this instance the divine condescension, the divine descent which preceded the ascension on Sinai, is expressly declared, even as God testifieth unto Moses at the bush, saying, " I am the God of Abraham, the God of Isaac, and the God of Jacob: I have surely seen the affliction of my people which are in Egypt, and have heard their cry by reason of their taskmasters: for I know their sorrows. And I am *come down* to deliver them out of the hand of the Egyptians. I will send thee that thou mayest bring forth my people, the children of Israel, out of Egypt " (Ex. iii. 7-10). It is in reference to this descent—" I am come down to deliver them "—that the Lord is celebrated as " ascending " on Mount Sinai. How could he have ascended had he not, as Paul unanswerably argues, " first descended "? He that came down to deliver Israel from the captivity of Pharaoh—he that descended into the wilderness of Sinai, and in humble guise set forth the symbol of his presence in the small lambent flame, tabernacling for the time in the humble bush or desert heath—he is the same that hath now ascended on high on Sinai's lofty peak—his symbol of ascension being no more in the solitary flame as when he came down to deliver Israel, but in the wide wasting fire, enshielded in the smoke and cloud, and giving forth the thunder and the lightning as the mountain burns with fire and the sweeping tempest mingles the fire and the darkness, while, amidst the play of nature's mightiest elements, God calls unto the heavens above and to the earth that he may judge his people; and our God doth surely come and not keep silence: a fire devoureth before him and it is very tempestuous round about him (Ex. xix., Heb. xii., Ps. l.). Why should the ascension be in symbols of fire amidst such extensive and terrific elements of grandeur but that it may form the counterpart and countervailing incident to the descent in flame into the bush, that lowly habitation of the glory of the Lord?

And now, what is meant, in this connection, by the triumph ascribed to the ascending King of Israel, Thou hast carried captivity captive? What can it imply but a celebration, in his ascension, of that very work of deliverance from their bondage for which the Lord himself had testified that he descended? "I am come down to deliver them from the hand of the Egyptians: I have seen their groaning, and I am come down to deliver them." And ere he thus ascends again gloriously on Sinai, has he not redeemed his pledge and redeemed his people, having brought them out with an high hand? Yea, "Sing unto the Lord, for he hath triumphed gloriously: the horse and his rider hath he thrown into the sea. The Lord is my strength and song, and he is become our salvation. The Lord is a man of war: the Lord is his name. Pharaoh's chariots and his host hath he cast into the sea: his chosen captains also are drowned in the Red Sea. Thou, in thy mercy, hast led forth thy people which thou hast redeemed: thou hast guided them in thy strength to thy holy habitation. Thy right hand, O Lord, is become glorious in power; thy right hand, O Lord, hath dashed in pieces the enemy" (Ex. xv. 1-6). Yea, "thou hast ascended on high: thou hast carried captivity captive."

There are still other two circumstances to be noticed, namely, the glorious retinue of the ascended king and the practical design of this majestic and solemnising exhibition of his glory.

Attending angels wait upon him; his chariots are twenty thousand, thousands of angels: in the midst of them the Lord appears in Sinai. By the disposition of angels, and as ordained in their hands, or by their ministry, the law is given to Israel (Acts vii. 35; Gal. iii. 19; Heb. ii. 2). "The Lord came from Sinai, and rose up from Seir unto them: he shined forth from Mount Paran, and he came with ten thousands of holy ones: from his right hand went a fiery law for them" (Deut. xxxiii. 2). For the chariot throne of the Lamb, the messenger of the covenant, whether set in heaven as seen by Isaiah (vi. 1) or Daniel (vii. 10), or by the beloved disciple in apocalyptic vision; or moved and pitched as the grand scheme of divine love requires, as on Sinai; is ever waited on by ministering spirits that excel in strength, in numbers without number. "I beheld and I heard the voice of many angels round about the throne, and the number of them was ten thousand times ten thousand, and thousands of thousands" (Rev. v. 11).

Finally, the grand purport or design of this occasion of divine state and dignity was no empty and transient exhibition but a high end worthy of Jehovah's interposition. "The Lord himself now gave the word, and great was the company of them that published it" (ver. 11).

In other words, he gave them now his statutes and his ordinances: he framed them now into a Church visible, compactly built together, his law the charter of their constitution and office-bearers of his own to rule over them in the Lord. Thus did he form them into a household for himself, giving them at the same time " the law of his house," and its stewards also to give them " meat in due season." Beautiful and glorious was Israel then, as taking order at the mouth of the Lord. The defilement and degradation of Egypt vanished, and the rude uncultured mass of erewhile slaves of Pharaoh fell as by the secret virtue of the Lord's own word into the well ordered camp of Jehovah's bannered host—the priestly kingdom of his own inheritance. " Though ye have lien, O Israel, among the pots, yet shall ye be as the wings of a dove, covered with silver and her feathers with yellow gold " (ver. 13). Hereby they became the Lord's congregation, and he confirmed them as his inheritance when it was weary. And then, as their Head and King, as a Son over what was now his own house, he provided of his goodness for the poor of his congregation, having brought out those that were " bound with chains " (verses 6, 10). Thus did he receive gifts for them, yea, for the rebellious, that the Lord God might dwell among them.

Such was the past ascension of the Lord on Sinai and such the principles and circumstances involved in that glorious event.

II. But, secondly, the Psalm has a prospective as well as retrospective reference: it contemplates a future triumph, as well as celebrates a triumph that is past. And it is this prophetic reference which Paul opens up in the fourth chapter of Ephesians.

For there is an ascension and a conquest in Mount Zion, as well as in Mount Sinai, of which indeed the glorious pageant on Mount Sinai in the giving of the law was but the feeble type and preparation. And it is for Mount

Zion, the city of the great King, that the Psalmist claims the honours he records. He will in fact bear no rival to the hill of Zion. He disdainfully sets aside every jealous hill that might emulate the claims of the mountain of the Lord's house. Bashan, especially, with all its noble ranging summits, is set aside indignantly. " The hill of God as the hill of Bashan?" No: " an high hill though the hill of Bashan be " (ver. 15). Not Bashan but " Zion is the perfection of beauty," " the joy of the whole earth." " Why leap ye "; rather, " why look ye askance so jealously, ye high hills? *this* is the hill which the Lord desireth to dwell in: yea, the Lord will dwell in it for ever " (ver. 16). " For the Lord hath chosen Zion: he hath desired it for his habitation. This is my rest for ever, here will I dwell for I have desired it." And now here also, in Zion, as on Sinai, " the chariots of the Lord are twenty thousand, even thousands of angels; the Lord is among them as in Sinai, in his holy place. Thou hast ascended on high; thou hast carried captivity captive." Such are the claims of Zion; vindicated as the ark is borne up to its resting place on the holy hill.

But surely this was but the shadow of the good things to come, and neither the very image nor the body of them. The body is of Christ, as Paul himself teaches us to understand. And the ascension in view is that of our risen Lord as he entered into the holy places not made with hands. And the circumstances are singularly beautiful in their correspondence with those involved in the prior ascension on Sinai.

Thus, first, there is the preceding humiliation, the scandal whereof in all its parts is now to be wiped away. " Now that he ascended, what is it but that he also descended first into the lower parts of the earth?' (Eph. iv. 9). Here was a descent infinitely more lowly than when the divine symbol dwelt for a little in the bush. For here was that type realised, while the fulness of the Godhead tabernacled in flesh with men upon the earth. Truly now it might be said, in no symbol and in no figure: "The Lord hath seen the affliction of his people and is come down to deliver them." He hath come down in the likeness of sinful flesh, and he will descend even to the lower parts of the earth, to the depths of the grave; for in this deliverance he will redeem his people not by power merely but by price, giving his soul a ransom for sin; bearing our sins in his own body on the tree; making his grave with the wicked and with the rich in his death. A descent so profound as that implied in the incarnation and death and entombment of the Prince of Life must call for an ascension proportionally grand. If the condescension of the Shechinah to dwell for a little at the foot of Sinai in the heath of the wilderness, required that the glorious symbol should ascend and expand and flame out so terrifically on Sinai's summit what, when the Divine angel of the covenant in all the fulness of his Godhead dwelt in the humanity of Christ Jesus, and died and was buried— what shall the countervailing glory be in this case? Surely not to Sinai's summit, nor to any region less glorious than one far above all heavens shall our high priest proceed as he passes through the heavens to the throne of his reward. Yea, "he that descended thus into the lower parts of the earth, is the same that ascended far above all heavens that he might fill all things with himself" (Eph. iv. 10).

Farther, the attending retinue of angels are here also as before. Again "the chariots of the Lord are twenty thousand, thousands of angels," and the Lord is once more "among them as in Sinai." For, as the risen Jesus passes beyond the cloud that receives him out of the disciples' sight, the hosts of principalities and powers, of whom in our glorified flesh he is now recognised as head, come forth to grace his entrance into the heaven of heavens; knowing that when he is come into heaven to the right hand of God, angels and authorities and powers are made subject to him, and rejoicing to acknowledge that he is made so much better than the angels as he hath by inheritance obtained a more excellent name than they. Professing loyalty to God manifest in the flesh, they begin their service by an impatient demand that the gates of the celestial Jerusalem admit their king. "Lift up your heads, O ye gates, and be ye lifted up, ye everlasting doors, and the king of glory shall come in." Nor are they slack in announcing his titles of conquest or defending his claim. "Who is this king of glory? The Lord strong and mighty; the Lord mighty in battle; sing unto him, for he hath triumphed gloriously." But while thus his messengers are spirits, and his ministers a flame of fire, unto the Son God saith, while receiving him to the right hand of the majesty on high, "Thy throne, O God, is for ever and ever" (Ps. xxiv.; Heb. i). And then around that mediatorial throne the countless angels worship. "The Lord is among them as in Sinai."

Once more, observe the striking correspondence of the practical design of this ascension in its bearing on the constitution and the confirmation of the Church below. On Sinai the Lord gave the word, and great was the company of them that published it. He gave the law of his house and formed the people into a well-ordered inheritance for himself—a house, a habitation, a temple for himself, as it is said, "I will dwell in you, and I will walk in you, saith the Lord." He gave them ordinances and rulers, and they fell beautifully into the order of a visible Church for the Lord. And does not Paul, according to the wisdom given to him, indicate the like design of the risen Lord's ascension, and the like gifts which he received and gave to the Church, framing the order of a gospel Church for himself to fill and to dwell in, for himself to feed and rule by servants of his own, given by the chief shepherd to the sheep? "But unto every one of us is given grace according to the gift of Christ. Wherefore he saith, when he ascended up on high, he led captivity captive and gave gifts unto men. And he gave some, apostles; and some, prophets; and some, evangelists; and some, pastors and teachers for the perfecting of the saints, for the work of the ministry, for the edifying of the body of Christ, till we all come, in the unity of the faith and of the knowledge of the Son of God, unto a perfect man, unto the measure of the stature of the fulness of Christ" (Eph. iv. 7, 8, 11-13). Thus marvellously do these grand incidents correspond in their great design: the constitution of the Old Testament Church being founded on the ascension on Sinai—that of the New Testament Church on the ascending, far above all heavens. Hence, in the very act of ascending, Jesus gives commandment concerning the charter and the ordinances of his Church visible on earth, saying, "Go ye and disciple all nations, baptising them in the name of the Father, and of the Son, and of the Holy Ghost: teaching them to observe whatsoever I have commanded you." Nor am I removed from you by my ascension— for he ascended rather " that he might fill all things "— " lo! I am with you alway even to the end of the world." " Thou hast ascended up on high that the Lord might dwell among them." And why should we speak of the outpouring of the Spirit which Jesus, having ascended, and having received the promise of the Father, bestowed? Refreshing his inheritance with a plenteous rain, confirming the congregation of the Lord, even as without the Spirit they have neither life, nor beauty, nor order, nor holiness, nor power to lengthen their cords or strengthen their stakes, as the young gospel Church so marvellously did.

And now the only other parallel circumstance, or point of correspondence, is that to which our subject especially draws our attention, namely, that in this case also, the enemy is laid low and a triumph decreed to the conqueror and embodied and enacted in his high ascension: "Thou hast ascended up on high, thou hast again led captivity captive." And who are the adversaries led in triumph at the wheels of the conqueror's chariots? To answer this requires an answer to the question, From whom did the conqueror deliver his people, when for their redemption he came down once more, yea, descended now into the lower parts of the earth? No tyrant of the human kind; no Egyptian king and his captains drowned in the waves of the Red Sea, but the original foe of the family of man, the same in reference to whom this conqueror was promised from the beginning—the serpent whose head he came to bruise. For he descended into the earth in his incarnation and was manifested in the flesh that he might destroy the works of the devil. And he descended into the lower parts of the earth, in his crucifixion and burial, in prosecution of the same purpose of his grace and judgment, when by death he destroyed him that had the power of death; that is, the devil, and delivered them who through fear of death were all their lifetime subject to bondage. He met the strong man armed in his house; and he spoiled him by greater strength than his; yea, by the strength of the weakness of his cross he overcame him. And he spoiled principalities and powers even in the hour of the power of the kingdom of darkness, and made a show of them openly triumphing over them in his cross.

He came down of old in the bush in the wilderness to deliver Israel from Pharaoh's captivity; and he ascended on Sinai having carried their captivity itself captive, his right hand and his holy arm having gotten him the victory. He descended infinitely lower, not abhorring the virgin's womb, nor Bethlehem's manger, nor Calvary's cross, nor Joseph's sepulchre, that he might bruise the serpent's head and proclaim liberty to the captive, announcing a salvation procured over the defeat of all the powers of hell that had

withstood it: and in his ascension he is celebrated as a
triumphing Captain of Salvation, having gotten the neck
of his own and the Church's foes, and now carrying
captivity captive.

Such is the analogy between the two glorious ascensions
—the one on which the Church in the wilderness was
founded, purged from Egyptian bondage and disorder;
the other to which the gospel Church traces her constitution and her office-bearers and her spiritual gifts and
ordinances, obtained and enjoyed by her in the liberty
wherewith Christ hath made her free. For in both cases
the constitution of a Visible Free Church unto the Lord is
the grand aim in view. In both instances, accordingly,
the bondage is destroyed: in both cases captivity must be
carried captive: and in both cases it is the angel of the
covenant, having first descended, who ascends gloriously
amidst the myriads of the heavenly host, receiving and
giving gifts unto his Church under its twofold dispensation—the Church in the wilderness and the Church of the
fulness of times. And yet, while liberty is the grand aim
secured for the Church in both cases, and while according
to the bondage in each case, the corresponding captivity
is carried captive, it is not difficult to decide in which of
them the nature and the amount of liberty procured pre-
ponderates. In fact, although in the first case, captivity
was truly carried captive, and the Church was redeemed
from the bondage of Egypt, yet as compared with the
rights and feelings of liberty enjoyed now by the redeemed
of God in the fulness of times, those of the former dispensation were poor indeed. In reality the comparison when
made becomes a contrast, even as the apostle has drawn it
in his allegory to the Galatians when dissuading them
from the folly and the sin of a return to the ceremonies
of the law. He contrasts Mount Sinai and Mount Zion on
this very point, namely, in reference to the covenants or
Church constitutions which are involved in the ascensions

of which these mountains were the scenes. " These," says he, " are the two covenants, the one from the Mount Sinai which gendereth to bondage, even as Hagar, the servant in the house, begat a son who had not the birthright and could not be accounted the heir, being not freeborn, not the child of the free and honoured spouse: and this Hagar, whose child's birth is neither free nor his abiding in the house secure, is Mount Sinai in Arabia, and answereth to Jerusalem that now is, and is. in bondage with her children. But Jerusalem which is above, Mount Zion, the city of the living God, the heavenly Jerusalem, where still there are the innumerable company of angels, the chariots of the Lord, as of old and as ever, twenty thousand, thousands of angels—Mount Zion, which indeed is the General Assembly of the Church of the first-born whose names are written in heaven—Jerusalem which is from above—the Gospel Church, founded on the everlasting covenant, and constituted on the Lord's ascension triumph, enriched with his ascension gifts, and emancipated and redeemed by the price and the power through which he carried captivity captive; this Mount Zion, this Jerusalem which is from above, is free, and is the mother of us all. For of old, and at Sinai, the heir was a child. " Now the heir, as long as he is a child, differeth nothing from a servant, though he be lord of all; even so we," says Paul, " while we were children, were in bondage, under the elements of the world. But when the fulness of the time was come, God sent forth his own Son, made of a woman, made under the law, to redeem them that were under the law, that we might obtain the adoption of sons; and because ye are sons, God hath sent forth the Spirit of his Son into your hearts, crying, Abba, Father. Wherefore thou art no more a servant, but a son, and an heir of God through Christ (Gal. iv. 1-8).

Well, therefore, may believers now be congratulated on their greater freedom in the house of God: for though liberty was vindicated, and captivity was carried captive, when the Lord ascended on high, and his chariots were the many thousands of angels on Sinai, still vastly more spiritual, more precious and secure is the liberty wherewith Christ now makes his people free; and it is a matter of rejoicing that we are not come unto the mount that might be touched, and that burned with fire, nor unto blackness, and darkness, and tempest, but unto Mount Zion, the city of the living God, unto the heavenly Jerusalem, which is free, and the mother of all them that believe. For the son of the free woman, the child of the covenant of Zion, is the heir, standing fast in the liberty wherewith Christ hath made him free and not entangled in the bondage or the terror of the mount that burned with fire.

But it remains to inquire what had transpired in the interval whereby Christ, the same ascending conqueror in both cases, was enabled to secure and vindicate a liberty to his Church so much greater in the fulness of times than in the ancient days in the wilderness; so vastly higher, indeed, that the other has no glory by reason of the glory that excelleth, and may rather in the contrast be called a yoke of bondage?

Why did the carrying of captivity captive on Zion secure a freedom so much more renowned than the similar triumph on Sinai?

It depended all on the depth of the descent. Corresponding to the depth of the descent in each case was the glory of the ascension, and the value of the liberty secured. And in the interval the liberty secured became infinitely more precious because the conqueror carried this second captivity captive by being himself subjected to captivity. Himself became responsible, and surety, for his Church. Her obligations became his. Her captivity, her bonds, became his. He submitted to her fetters in her name. " Then the band, and the captains, and the officers of the

Jews took him, and *bound* him, and led him away to Annas, and Annas sent him *bound* to Caiaphas." The handwriting of ordinances that doomed the Church to captivity and bondage, under Satan as her jailor and her tyrant, to whom in vengeance that broken bond and its curse abandoned her, Jesus honoured, obeyed, fulfilled, exhausted. He took the handwriting of ordinances, which was contrary to us, out of the way: he answered and made it honourable. " Ye seek me," he said. Be it so. And they bound him. Satan looked and saw the only document whch he could plead a blank, and his plea become a lie. He saw the only chain by which he could detain the captive broken by being used to bind the surety, the only key by which he could imprison his victims, even the curse, vanished and gone, and buried in the depths of the Saviour's woe. He heard the cry unto the prisoners, " Go forth," and to them that sit in darkness, " Show yourselves." In helpless rage he heard the glorious call: " Awake, awake, put on thy strength, O Zion; put on thy beautiful garments, O Jerusalem: shake thyself from the dust, arise and sit down, O Jerusalem; loose thyself from the bands of thy neck, O captive daughter of Zion: for thus saith the Lord, Ye have sold yourselves for nought, but ye shall be redeemed without money." He heard the mighty voice, the same which said, " It is finished," proclaiming liberty to the captive, and the opening of the prison to them that were bound. He heard, and as he heard he ventured to reply, " Shall the prey of the mighty be taken or the lawful captive delivered?" But thus saith the glorious Lord, forth from out the glory of his angel chariots and his ascension triumph: " Even the captives of the mighty shall be taken away, and the prey of the terrible shall be delivered; and I will contend with those that contend with Zion, and I will save her children." And as Satan heard the call to revolt thus given to his victims, and looked to see the issue, he beheld the captive

exile hastening that he might be loosed, that he should not
die in the pit, nor that his bread should fail: he beheld
multitudes recovering themselves from the snare of the
devil who had been carried captive at his will, " multitudes, multitudes in the valley of decision," choosing
rather to flee to a stronghold as prisoners of hope,
inspired, as they had never hoped before to be, by a voice
that spake of liberty and a Spirit who is such that where
that Spirit of the Lord is, *there* is liberty indeed. And as
he looked to see by what right and power the great Counsellor to rebellion amidst his victims prevailed to trans-
late them from the kingdom of darkness and the bondage
of corruption into God's marvellous light and into the
glorious liberty of the children of God, he saw, to his
eternal confusion, that the fetters which in the hour and
power of darkness he had urged his agents to impose on
Jesus when they led him away as a dishonoured prisoner,
had satisfied and so extinguished the only bond by which
he reigned a tyrant over the victims of his temptation:
and the handwriting of ordinances being gone, he was
himself the writhing captive of the meekly captive Jesus,
spoiled and triumphed over for ever.

It is a scene, this captivity of our Lord, over which to
grieve and mourn and weep. But in the fruit of it—in
our own " most glorious liberty of the children of God "
thus achieved, and in Satan's most confounding baffle-
ment and retribution thus inflicted, it is a scene over
which to smile and sing, to sing and smile again. O! to
be clothed with the beauties of holiness, that as the
chariots of a willing people we too may grace the triumph
of the fettered substitute of sinners. Sound the loud
timbrel! Go forth with thy maidens, O Miriam, with
timbrels and with dances; and answer them, saying: Sing
unto the Lord, for he hath triumphed gloriously; the horse
and his rider he hath cast into the deep. And he hath

done it by his bonds. By means of his bonds the Captive Christ hath carried captivity captive!

And now, if we had faith in the Captive Christ carrying captivity captive, might we not, in his name, compel all manner of captivities to go into captivity?

Who among us, then, is fettered by the conscious guilt of sin and the haunting spirit of bondage? Your hearts condemn you and God is greater than your hearts. Conscience tells you that an unsettled account stands over against you in the book of the Lord's remembrance; and countless offences are between you and your God, hiding his face from you, for they are not forgiven nor forgotten in reconciliation. And this sense of guilt is itself a spirit of bondage, for it straitens your heart and seals your lips in prayer; and it keeps you cold and distant and formal in your worship of the Lord: in short, it keeps you alienated and an enemy in your heart. Ah! there will be no relief from this bondage till you come in penitence and faith to Jesus. Embrace and be one with Jesus. Identify yourself with Jesus. Identify your captivity with his; and you will issue and end it in his also. You will find that his captivity, imputed to you, relieves you from captivity; emancipates you from bondage in the virtue of Christ's own bonds. He was in bonds for bond slaves that they might be free; and there is neither condemnation nor captivity to them that are in Christ Jesus.

Who among us is fettered by the power of sin? For he that committeth sin is the slave of sin. Who groans as an unwilling captive under the bondage of corruption? Fain would you break loose from lusts that are too strong for you and evil passions that are become your tyrants. But you are helpless in their hands. You make a truce with them now and again, but they break all terms with you, and are satisfied only when you are their slave. For " know ye not that to whom ye yield yourselves servants to obey, his servants ye are to whom ye obey? if of sin, unto death." Ah! it is Christ, and the grace of Christ at once free and omnipotent that can alone meet your case. If the Son shall make you free, ye shall be free indeed. For he was made under the law to redeem them that were under the law; and only as thus redeemed can ye be free from the power of sin, for the curse you have entailed seals the bondage as your punishment. But come ye to him who by his own bonds procured emancipation. Accept a free pardon and an immediate liberty from him who preaches deliverance to the captive and the opening of the prison to them that are bound. Through him, come with liberty to the throne of grace; you will find mercy there, and grace to help. And sin shall no more have dominion over you when you are not under the law but under grace.

Who among us is caught in the snare of the devil, carried captive by him at his will? Come ye to him who spoiled principalities and powers by giving Satan his will and permitting himself to be carried captive at his instigation. He will give you repentance unto the acknowledgment of the truth. He will give his free Spirit to convince you of sin, of righteousness, and of judgment—of judgment, because the prince of this world is judged. He will spoil the strong man for you and bruise Satan under your feet.

Who among us, " through fear of death, are all their lifetime subject to bondage "? Come ye to him whose death hath destroyed death, even as his captivity carried captivity captive. He will give you to know that your life is hid with himself in God, carried safely up with him when he ascended on high.

Finally, who among us feel painfully " a law in our members warring against the law of our mind, and bringing us into captivity to the law of sin which is in our members," so that we cry, as the Lord is witness, " O wretched man that I am! who shall deliver me from the body of this death?" Let us " thank God through Jesus Christ our Lord. Let us bear in mind that he was bound for us, but was a captive only that he might lead captivity captive. Let us seek grace more and more that being delivered out of the hands of our enemies we may serve God in holiness and in righteousness all the days of our life. Let us wrestle against that law of sin and death that would lead us into bondage. Let us never yield, but vindicate our freedom as freely forgiven and fully justified, and unchangeably adopted children of God through the work and merit of him who was fettered that we might be free : and let us anticipate the time of our full deliverance into the glorious liberty of the sons of God; when Jesus shall come again and verify in its ultimate and grandest form his glorious triumph, as with his risen saints and all his angels he answereth for the last time the call of Israel: "Arise, O Lord, thou and the ark of thy strength: let thine enemies be scattered and let them that hate thee flee before thee," while once more, yea, more gloriously than ever, the chariots of the Lord shall be twenty thousand, thousands of angels, the Lord among them as on Sinai and the host of the redeemed, from all ages and dispensations shall exclaim: " O Lord, thou hast ascended on high; thou hast carried captivity captive."

IX.

THE TRIAL—I.

THE CHARACTER OF THE JUDGE.

"Now Caiaphas was he which gave counsel to the Jews, that it was expedient that one man should die for the people" (John xviii. 14).

"Then gathered the chief priests and the Pharisees a council, and said, What do we? for this man doeth many miracles. If we let him thus alone, all men will believe on him; and the Romans shall come and take away both our place and nation. And one of them, named Caiaphas, being the high priest that same year, said unto them, Ye know nothing at all, nor consider that it is expedient for us, that one man should die for the people, and that the whole nation perish not. And this spake he not of himself: but being high priest that year, he prophesied that Jesus should die for that nation; and not for that nation only, but that also he should gather together in one the children of God that were scattered abroad. Then, from that day forth, they took counsel together for to put him to death" (John xi. 47-53).

WE have seen the Lord Jesus led away a prisoner to await his trial at the bar of the Jewish Sanhedrim. Accordingly we shall soon see the Great High Priest, the Son of God, consecrated to his office by the word of the oath, and made an high priest for ever after the order of Melchizedeck, confronted with the present representative of the Levitical priesthood. The time was when that Levitical priesthood paid tithes and gave reverence to the priesthood of Melchizedeck. For Levi, being yet in the loins of Abraham, when that father of the faithful was met by the priest of the Most High God, the king of Salem, received Melchizedeck's blessing and without all contradiction acknowledged his superiority. Now, however, Levi exalts himself against Melchizedeck, or rather against him whom Melchizedeck typified, and scruples not to sit in judgment over him.

But before we review the proceedings of the Sanhedrim, it is desirable if possible to have some idea of the character of the chief member of the court, whose influence and decision must so greatly overrule the issue. The Evangelist, indeed, invites us to this inquiry, for, on mentioning the name of Caiaphas, and indicating that it is at his bar that the captive Jesus must stand, he is careful to give us a sufficient hint of what may be expected from the bench by presenting us with a brief sketch of the judge. " Now Caiaphas was he which gave counsel to the Jews, that it was expedient that one man should die for the people." This is a brief sentence, but it will be found to carry in it all the elements necessary to a right view of the high priest's character. We see by it at once that as a judge he is unjust, a fearful and a summary sentence of condemnation to pass upon him, yet an inevitable one, for he scruples not to prejudicate a very solemn case, a case even of life and death and brings the prisoner to his bar to hear a foregone sentence. Caiaphas had made up his mind, before the case was tried, that the prisoner must die.

But the council chamber where this foregone decision was first agreed upon and announced presents a painfully interesting scene, and one from which we may learn not a few solemn moral principles of perpetual application, as well as gain a fuller insight into the moral character of this particular man.

The scene is drawn and the discussion is reported by this same Evangelist in the eleventh chapter, to which indeed he must be understood as referring us back when

he identifies the man at whose bar Jesus is to stand with
him who had already given counsel to the Jews that one
man should die for the people. Let us turn, then, at John's
invitation to the account he has given us of that conference or conspiracy.

And it is well worth contemplating.   It is no dull
affair; no commonplace meeting; it is not called for the
transaction of mere routine business. On the contrary, it
has been summoned eagerly and earnestly, and on the
spur of a great and immediate necessity. In short the
grandest of all Christ's miracles has just taken place. He
has raised Lazarus from the dead—a notable miracle and
undeniable, being performed in the presence of many,
both friends and foes. It was never seen after this fashion
in Israel, and neither the people of God nor the children
of the devil can help their spirit being deeply moved.

The officials in Jerusalem are especially startled. Spies
of their own come and tell them what Jesus has done
(ver. 46). They have always hated him, contested his
authority, and sought to destroy his interest and reputation with the people. Jealously trembling for their own
influence, and all the more as an evil conscience witnesses
to their selfishness, rapacity, and unfaithfulness as
guardians of the people or office-bearers in the church,
they have hitherto heard with increasing dismay of the
doings of one who claims to be the Messiah, and freely
denounces wrath upon the " Scribes and Pharisees hypocrites."   They have attempted to make him out to be a
Sabbath breaker—to be in league with Beelzebub, the
prince of the devils; but his replies have confounded them.
They have sent Saducees and lawyers and Pharisees to
question him and ensnare him in his replies, but a wisdom
deeper than their subtleties has always broken their toils.
They have questioned him by what authority he did these
things, but a pointed question anent the baptism of John
has revealed their hypocrisy and silenced them.   And

every plan they have adopted has failed or recoiled upon themselves. When told now that Jesus has raised from the dead one who had been four days in the grave, and that many of the Jews had seen the things which Jesus did and believed, they are at their wit's end, and their enmity being still unquelled, the council that they hold in such a crisis of affairs must inevitably be distinguished by a peculiar and painful intensity or animation—presenting a very gem or study to those who take pleasure in scanning the motives of men, because affording, as it does, a favourable theatre for developing the passions and displaying the characters of the actors. For they are among themselves. It is a private meeting; there is no check upon their freedom of speech. How the Evangelist came to be able to put the substance of their discussion on record we do not know. It may have been impossible to keep the secret where so many were possessed of it; or some of the parties present, being perhaps brought to another mind after the outpouring of the Spirit on the day of Pentecost, being convicted of having crucified and slain the Just One, and being converted to the faith of him whom once they persecuted, may have subsequently detailed the scenes in which they held so unprincipled a part. And in any event, believing as we do in the full inspiration of the narrative before us, we can have no difficulty in understanding how the all-seeing Spirit of God should have moved his servant to record any portion of the proceedings of any council however secret, all of which had been naked and open before him with whom the speakers have to do. Little did they think that a divinely accurate report of their conspiracy would descend from generation to generation till the end of time. But let us bear in mind that what is spoken in the ear may be proclaimed upon the house tops, and that there is nothing hid that shall not be revealed. What a power is there in this single thought, if habitually realised, to promote our moral purity! Thou, God, seest me.

But the Pharisees and chief priests forgot that and thought they were safe among themselves. Accordingly they speak out plainly and reveal, without mask or concealment, of what manner of spirit they are.

Their discussion takes this shape: *first,* the precise position of the case as they mutually understand it, is stated; the object of the meeting, in short, is announced, and the question to be submitted to them. " They said, What do we? For this man doeth many miracles. If we let him thus alone, all men will believe on him, and the Romans shall come and take away both our place and nation." Then, *secondly,* a remedy or solution is offered, and it is here that Caiaphas comes out as the master spirit of this wickedness, more advanced in iniquity than the others. " Ye know nothing at all," says he, " nor consider that it is expedient for us that one man should die for the people, and that the whole nation should perish not."

Let us consider these two portions of the discussion in their order.

I. The case is stated. The aspect of affairs, it is agreed on all hands, is dangerous and critical in the last degree. Something must be done, and that without delay. They chide themselves, indeed, for having dallied with this danger so long. " What do we?" What are we about? This man doeth many miracles; there is no questioning and no denying that. If we let him thus alone much longer, the whole nation will believe on him, make him a king, provoke the Romans, and ensure the destruction of the temple, of our national worship, and our national existence.

1. Now, in the first place, and at the first glance, we see their dishonesty in the very form in which the case is stated. In fact, this is not the case at all, in the form

in which it ought to be brought into court. Is there no member of council honest enough to move the previous question? That previous and most momentous question is not, What must we do to prevent the Jews believing on this man, or to prevent the Romans destroying the nation? but, Is this, or is this not, the Christ? That is the question which, as honest men, were they such, they would feel themselves bound in the first instance to raise and face and settle. Settle *that,* and it may fairly be expected to carry in its train an adjustment of all their difficulties, scattering those that are imaginary, guiding them safely through those that are real. Leave that question unsettled and danger and evil must thicken.

It is a question they are bound to settle, for their own consciences and their own conduct they are bound to settle it. As public men and judges of the people, they are bound to settle it in order that they may cast all their official influence on the side of the Lord and his anointed, and lest they be found plotting and fighting against God. Moreover, they have the means of settling it in their hands —the Scriptures of God, those lively oracles, the possession of which is the peculiar honour of their nation. Nay, the individual himself, so directly concerned, demands nothing more than that his claim be tried by Scripture; and this he has again and again demanded. " Search the Scriptures, for they testify of me. If ye believe Moses, ye will believe on me, for he wrote of me." Nor can they have a moment's hesitation that the search, if sincere and sustained, will be satisfactory and conclusive. A hasty glance, indeed, may tell them nothing: the miserably short and offhand style of spirit that could say, " Search and look: for out of Galilee ariseth no prophet," is little likely to come to the knowledge of the truth, and rather satisfied than otherwise to remain in ignorance, is far from being in the way to learn that this man was really born in Bethlehem Ephratah, and is indeed the same

whose " goings forth have been of old, from everlasting."
It is an honest and unprejudiced and sustained examination which they are bound to prosecute. And the question
is worth such examination, while the promise of their law
is that the Lord will show them the truth. For of old it
had been written for them that sit in judgment: "The
judgment is God's, and the case that is too hard for you,
bring it unto me, and I will hear it." A promise, how
sure to be specially fulfilled, if sincerely pleaded, in
relation to the one grand end towards which all their
Scriptures and all their offices and ordinances pointed!

Mark how it concerned them to settle this question. Yea,
on whatever side of the question their ultimate decision
should fall, it must very greatly affect all their procedure.
Jesus is either the Christ, or he is not. Take the alternatives.

1. Say, first, that he is not the Christ. They have
examined and seen that his claims are false. By all means
let them come to this conclusion if they can. It must be
greatly to the comfort of their consciences in silencing
him. In that case it is an impostor whose claims they
have set aside, a blasphemer whose crimes they have
punished. And if still the Romans *do* come and take
away their place and nation, they will have the consolation of having done their duty.

Still, it will be a difficult case to bring in all points to a
satisfactory close. It will be hard, for instance, to
explain why their God should give such power to a blasphemer to work " those many miracles which this man,"
on their own admission, " doeth." For, if this man is a
sinner, it was at least shrewdly argued by the blind man
whom he had cured: " Why, herein is a marvellous thing,
that ye know not from whence he is, and yet he hath
opened mine eyes." These miracles must cost them some
anxiety. Still, if he be not the Christ, it must be very
satisfactory to know it.

Even so with the infidel, both professed and practical, who lives as if the Bible were a fable. Let him by all means prove that the Scriptures are not the word of God. He will have emancipated the best portion of the human race from a very cunningly devised fable. And though death has to come and take away his place among the living, yet he will have the consolation of having set aside a great imposture, and of having done his duty.

Still, he will have those miracles to explain. Always those miracles—both for ancient Jews and modern sceptics to digest!

2. But take the other alternative. What if this be the Christ? Ah! then, every difficulty vanishes at once. The Christ can vindicate both himself and his people. He can make an highway in the desert and prepare his own way, either by his forerunner or by his presence. " Every valley shall be exalted, and every mountain and hill shall be made low: and the crooked shall be made straight, and the rough places made plain. And the glory of the Lord shall be revealed, and all flesh shall see it together, for the mouth of the Lord hath spoken it." And as for the Romans, let them know themselves to be men. " The voice said, Cry. And he said, What shall I cry? All flesh is grass, · and all the goodliness thereof is as the flower of the field. But thou, O Zion, that bringest good tidings, get thee up into the high mountains: O Jerusalem, that bringest good tidings, lift up thy voice with strength; lift it up, be not afraid; say unto the cities of Judah, Behold your God! Behold, the Lord God will come with strong hand, his arm shall rule for him " (Isa. xl. 3-10). Yes, if this be indeed the Christ, there is no need to fear the Romans. If Christ be with you, who can be against you? Nor is there any need to fear the scattering of the people. For the sceptre shall not depart from Judah, nor a lawgiver from between his feet until Shiloh come, and unto him shall the gathering of the

people be. Meantime ye may accept the blessed invitation to cast away all fear of man. " Fear not, daughter of Zion; behold, thy king cometh, meek and lowly." And ye may well sound his praise and raise Hosannahs. " Blessed is he that cometh in the name of the Lord to save you."

How joyfully would this emancipate them from all servile fear and all painful forebodings! Why do they not seek this clear, straightforward, honest, blessed settlement of all their difficulties, and then proceed like free and fearless honest men. If this be not the Christ, by all means proceed against him; and let them do so, not because they fear the Romans, but because he is not the Christ, and because it is their duty to punish and silence his imposture. But if he be, they need still less dread the Romans: the only thing then to dread would be lest they themselves should be tempted to fight against God.

Why, then, do they not consider whether Jesus is the Christ? Alas! the terrible truth must come out that they fear he is. They cannot face the inquiry. They are not prepared for an unprejudiced investigation, because they are not prepared to accept either alternative as the issue. And from which alternative do they shrink? Are they afraid of proving him to be not the Christ? Ah, no. They would gladly accept of that solution. It falls in with all their prejudices and all their passions. It would be to them a great relief—a valuable set-off against these perplexing miracles—enabling them to proceed with still more freedom to conclude their purpose. It must be the other alternative they are afraid of. For they shrewdly suspect the demonstration would turn all the other way. They fear being confronted with a sufficient proof that he whom they hate is the Messiah. Hence they will not even raise the question. They have painful forebodings that he *is,* yet from the beginning they hasten indecently to state the question precisely as if he were *not* the Christ.

Ah! how exactly is this paralleled in the conduct of thousands every day! They will not carry their proposed schemes to the tribunal of the Scriptures, because they shrewdly dread a decision adverse to their worldly and carnal desires.

Thus we see not a little of these men's state of mind from the form in which they bring forward the matter from the first. They set aside, dishonestly, the one grand question which it behoves them to consider and substitute another in its room. Prompt action, they say, must be taken with this man. Nay, rather, a scriptural decision ought to be given concerning him. For what if he should be the Christ?

With the bare possibility of his being the Christ (if they would not search and see) the time was at least come for that absolute neutrality which under Gamaliel's counsel they were compelled to observe at a later stage of this same drama, as the old question reappeared in the persons of this Man's followers. If they will not settle whether he be the Christ, they might at least let him alone, believing that if he be not of God, he and all his movement will come to nought, but if he be, as his miracles would seem to prove, then they cannot overthrow it, for they would be fighting against God. But neutrality is the very thing for which they chide themselves. The evil, as they say, is that they are doing nothing, whereas " this man doeth many miracles!" And their resolution is that they will let him alone no longer. And they persuade themselves the case is such as justifies their resolution.

2. Accepting the case, then, as they have stated it— as one demanding action and not investigation—let us see on what ground they plead that action is required. " If we let him alone the Romans will come and take away both our place and nation."

Now here the question may be asked: Were they
honest in setting forth this plea?   Did they really feel
that this afforded sufficient reason for the adoption of
prompt measures such as they desired to set in motion?
Were they really satisfied that serious danger was to be
apprehended from this quarter?   Was it an honestly felt
fear of the Romans which they now expressed?   We must
again take the alternatives.

1.   There is not a little reason to suspect that even in
this they were insincere, and that they were conscious to
themselves of duplicity in affecting to dread any serious
rupture with the Romans in connection with the ministry
or miracles of Jesus of Nazareth.   Nothing, certainly, had
occurred to show that the attention of the Romans was in
the least degree awakened to the matter.   And probably
affairs might have long gone on as they were without the
Romans heeding them if they had not themselves—these
high priests and elders—been the first to call for the aid
and the action of the Romans against him.   We know
how great aversion the Roman Governor had to deal with
the case at all, and how much of the special kind of
influence and argument which only wicked men can wield,
they needed to bring to bear on Pilate before he could
be persuaded to comply with their demands.   But if this
reference to what the Romans might be expected to do is
insincerely pleaded by them, then behold in what a light
they now stand forth!   Understanding one another thoroughly—quite committed among themselves to a policy
that contemplates the destruction of an innocent man—
they yet shrink from realising their sin in its baseness and
nakedness.   It is not as if they were pleading the case
before others who would thwart them if they saw
unmasked their wicked design.   It is not as if they were
striving to gain the concurrence of others before whom
they must be very wary not to let out the secret of their
pure and simple hatred to their victim.   In that case we

might naturally enough expect them to put some colour on
their crime and, masking its true nature and enormities,
labour to secure, under false pretences, the acquiescence
of those to whom they dare not state the case in its
simplicity. It is not in circumstances like these that we
find them enforcing false pleas and arguments. It is
when they are assembled privately, when they can speak
as plainly as they please and have nothing to fear, at
least from man: it is when they are by themselves, with
none to overhear and judge. But even then, such is the
native character of sin, such its revolting nature, that they
labour to throw a cloak of concealment over the real
aspect of their crime, if by any means they can hide it
from one another and themselves. They must affect a
great deal of anxiety about " this place "—that is, the
temple and its sacred worship; and " this nation " with
its stability and liberties! They must come forth in this
affair under the garb of patriotism! Had they been
labouring to spread a panic among the people, this would
have only indicated a hypocrisy for which Christ's denun-
ciations of them as hypocrites would have quite prepared
us. But here they come under our review, not so much
in the light of hypocrites, as in that of self-deceivers, when
at the bar of even their own seared consciences they feel
compelled to put their iniquity upon the plea of the public
good. Men never do care to see their sin remorselessly
stript bare and held up in its nakedness, in its unmingled
exceeding sinfulness. As to past sin, Satan, the father of
lies, willingly labours to supply them with many pallia-
tions and excuses. And as to sin still proposed and contemplated, he can serve them in that matter too with many
blinds and masks and can occupy their attention and keep
up their courage by engaging them in trying on these
masks and pleading these arguments to themselves and
one another, even while they all thoroughly understand
that these masks will never fit and all these arguments

will never do. It is a strange and painful thing to see how men will even hand themselves over expressly to be supplied with the means of self-deception, with some poor and pitiful plea of self-justification, where the project that conscience condemns is nevertheless resolved on, and some rag is sought to clothe its nakedness, some varnish to conceal its criminality. For what else were these men doing?

Ah! be assured sin is a mysterious thing. Beware lest you be hardened by the deceitfulness of sin. Sin is so deceitful that it leads the sinner to seek the means of deceiving himself.

This, on the supposition that they were consciously insincere in pleading any danger that might arise from the Romans. But suppose:

2. That they honestly held that there were great apprehensions to be entertained from this quarter—that they really dreaded the advancing fame of Jesus as likely to induce the people to proclaim him king, to revolt from under the Roman sway, and thus bring down upon them the Imperial power to their destruction. And suppose that in this fear there was more than the selfish dread of all their own comforts and emoluments being lost in the breaking up of their national existence and the loss of their official positions. Put the matter in the light most favourable for their integrity. They had, we shall say, an unaffected regard for the public good and a genuine apprehension of a great public danger. But what then?

Will it mend the matter that they slay the innocent? Will they propitiate the Romans at the expense of incurring the wrath of God? What kind of policy will this be? Yet in the spirit and drift of it, it is very common policy notwithstanding. In fact, it is one of the most general forms into which the contest between good and evil shapes itself; and it reappears in every variety of circumstance and under every variety of phase again and again continually. The fear of man and the fear of God in their opposite requirements come into collision: and the fear of God is set aside. Principle and expediency demand opposite courses of action; and principle is thrown overboard. Interest pulls in one direction, while conscience points in the other; and conscience is silenced. What else is going on throughout the whole frame of worldly society daily?

Such is the course these councillors propose. The fear of man is before them; and having not the fear of God to emancipate them, they fall into the snare. Now herein was their sin whereby they magnify the power of man and treat as a shadow the Almightiness of God. The Romans are to them an object of dread. They can credit *them* with attributes and powers before which they tremble. But the Lord God Omnipotent, who rules supreme above all nations, they regard as such an one as themselves, one whose powers and displeasure they may fearlessly brave. The Romans have power to kill the body, and them they fear; but they fear not him who hath power to destroy both body and soul in hell. In all circumstances this is grievous sin, but especially when permitted to weigh in a case of judgment and to lead to the perversion of the right of the guiltless. For had not the Lord expressly forbidden them when sitting in judgment to allow any circumstances to make them afraid? For, saith the Lord, I charged you, saying: " Ye shall not respect persons in judgment, but ye shall hear the small as well as the great: ye shall not be afraid of the face of man, for the judgment is God's; and the cause that is too hard for you, bring it unto me and I will hear it " (Deut. i. 17). Let them plead that promise: let them act on that precept. Let them judge righteous judgment in the fear of God; and they shall not be afraid for the fear of man. What though the Romans come? If God be among them as they judge righteously—" a Spirit of

judgment to him that sitteth in judgment—He will also be
a strength unto them that turn the battle from the gate."

For this is the first principle of all piety. I have no
personal religion save as I fear God sincerely and
supremely. Neither otherwise have I any safety. If I
fear not God, I am exposed on every side to a thousand
slaveries of men and devils. If I fear him in truth and
abide in his fear, I am before all creatures fearless and
free indeed, and he whose I am and whom I serve will
defend my freedom when threatened.

So ought these Jews to have argued. And their first
question should have been, " Lord, what wilt thou have
us to do?" If they fear God, and if God be for them, as
he ever is for all them that fear him, who then can be
against them? Do they not know of those better days—
those ancestral glories of " their place and their nation "
—when great armies did flee apace because men fearing
God had prayed, saying: " O our God, wilt thou not
judge them? We have no might against this great company that cometh against us, neither know we what to do;
but our eyes are upon thee " (II Chron. xx. 12). And
again, when against a million of foes, another man of God
cried: " Lord, it is nothing for thee to help whether with
many or with them that have no power; help us, O Lord
God, for we rest in thee, and in thy name we go against
this multitude. O Lord, let not man prevail against thee."
And again, when the man after God's own heart sang in
dauntlessness of godly fear, " The Lord is my light and
my salvation; whom shall I fear? the Lord is the strength
of my life; of whom shall I be afraid? Though an host
should encamp against me, my heart shall not fear; though
war should rise against me, in this will I be confident "
(Ps. xxvii. 1-3). And verily in all cases the name of the
Lord is a strong tower, the righteous fleeth into it and is
safe. " Fear not, Abraham: I am thy shield and thy
exceeding great reward " (Gen. xv. 1).

But these councillors despised that shield, for they feared the Romans. They clung to expediency and abjured the demands of principle. They could trust their own views of expediency and the wisdom of their own policy to relieve them from the danger. But they neither so believed God's power as to feel that being against them it would be infinitely worse than the arms of Rome; nor did they trust that power as able to shield and protect them, being on their side, from all adverse power whatever. They braved therefore the divine wrath that by their own hands they might defend the temple and the nation from the Romans.

Did they succeed? Is expediency better than principle? Was it better to lean to their own understanding than to trust and fear the Lord? Nay, the deed they now resolved on, as the price to propitiate Rome, was the very deed that brought Rome upon them in history's most terrific cruelties. " See ye not all these things?" said Jesus to the twelve, as from Olivet they looked upon the goodly buildings of the temple. " Verily, I say unto you, there shall not be left one stone upon another that shall not be thrown down." Nor was that an absolutely new prediction in the Saviour's lips: it was but the repetition and renewal of what Moses so long before had announced as part of the curse for disobeying the word of the Lord. " The Lord shall bring a nation against thee from afar, from the end of the earth, as swift as the eagle flieth, a nation of fierce countenance, that shall not regard the person of the old nor show favour to the young." So spake Jesus to the twelve: and so had Moses spoken to the nation. But then, if they had believed Moses, they would have believed Jesus, for he spake of him. As it was, they betrayed Jesus to make Rome their friend: and the wrath of God, by the hand of Rome, came upon them to the uttermost. " The fear of the wicked, *it* shall come upon them ": yea, their schemes of safety ripen only to make them reap destruction.

Alas! do we not see, in the high places of our own land, a fear of Rome—Rome Papal—as great as ever these Jews had of Rome imperial? And do we not see that in them too expediency is the great rule, and the question of principle is set aside habitually? And is the issue any better? Does Rome become more manageable? more quiet? Quite the contrary. Statesmen confess their disappointment, and acknowledge that the very reverse of their expectations are realised, and the evils they meant by this policy to subdue are gathering strength continually. When will they know that the same principles rule in the destinies of nations now that ruled of old, for the same God governeth high above all people, and that therefore principle is the best policy? Expediency outwits itself.

And the great fear is that a Caiaphas may rise to bring matters much further on to their crisis when once they are advancing in this direction.

II. We have heard the general statement of the case on which all are agreed. We must now hear the remedy proposed. And this is the part of Caiaphas. This honour is reserved for him. Nor have we been in reality putting the high priest out of view. The iniquity we have seen already prevailing in the assembly, he is quite capable of—and more. It is he that carries the matter many steps forward and brings the whole deliberation to a point.

"Ye know nothing at all, nor consider that it is expedient that one man die for the people, and that the whole nation perish not."

Now this is cutting short the discussion and coming boldly to the point. This cuts the Gordian knot and summarily settles all the case. Others may half hint the necessary course, but Caiaphas has no hesitation. No

half measures will do with him: he scorns those that may
think so, and tells them point blank that they know nothing about it. " Ye know nothing at all," says he.   He
pities their ignorance; he makes short work of their
scruples.   This miracle-monger must be despatched: and
why not? he is but " one man."   Better *that* than " the
nation."   Such is the high priest: perfectly unscrupulous
in his wickedness; reckless in the extent to which he is
prepared to carry out his purpose; bold and rude in
propounding and pressing it on others.

1.   For, in the first place, he thoroughly understands
what he is saying.   When the Evangelist says, " This
spake he, not of himself, but being high priest that year
he prophesied," he does not mean that Caiaphas had no
meaning of his own—that he spake unconsciously and
unintentionally.   The prophetic turn which his words are
seen to take was altogether unintentional on his part, and
he was quite unconscious that the words bore any other
meaning than those he meant them to carry.   But that
meaning which he designed them to express, far from
being doubtful, was rather all too plain.   Viewing the
words then in the meaning of Caiaphas, before we review
their prophetic import, let us consider their place in this
discussion and their bearing on the matter on hand.
And,

First: it is obvious that, desperate and accursed though
the high priest's proposal is—to slay the innocent—and
far ahead as he has gone of anything that has yet been
suggested, he proceeds on precisely the same ground as
the others have all taken up already—the ground of
expediency.   " It is expedient," says he, " that one man
die."   And John, in reminding us that this Caiaphas was
the same who had given out the foregone sentence
against the prisoner who was about to appear before him,
is careful to remember and set forth this painful word on
which indeed the whole character and key of the proceed-

ing depends: " Now Caiaphas was he that gave counsel to the Jews that it was *expedient* that one man should die for the people." Hence while he goes a very great deal further than the rest seemed prepared at least to suggest, he is quite at one with them in the motive which is to guide them and the style of procedure which they must adopt. *Expediency,* it is agreed on all hands, must rule the day: that which is *expedient* must be this day decided on. They are all at one on *that.* And Caiaphas has no objection. He says so too. Hence, if he *does* go farther than more scrupulous consciences can go, still there is no gainsaying him. Who is there among them that would fain dissent now as the real villany of this conspiracy breaks out? Is there any among them sensitive enough to feel that matters are at last really going too far, and he hints to Caiaphas that he takes the liberty of thinking so? Alas! how easily he may be answered, and how impertinent his interruption may be shown to be. For he has already granted all on which he could have taken his stand. " You agree, do you not, that there is great danger of the Romans coming and taking away our place and nation? At least you said so this moment. You agree also that that is very undesirable; and that it is expedient that we take means to prevent it? You agree on that, do you not?" " Certainly, that is an evil by all means to be got rid of; anything rather than that. " Exactly so "; then surely " you know nothing at all " if you do not consider that it is expedient that one man die rather than that the whole nation perish. Or are *you* one of his disciples, and ready to back him though the whole nation perish?" So might some sensitive and restive conscience have been bullied and silenced, and taught to feel that it had already resigned all right to object or to protest as soon as the doctrine of *expediency* was granted.

And hence, *secondly,* there was no way open for retreat to any who were now alarmed at the serious turn which the matter was taking, save by taking up at once the ground of *principle,* and demanding a full and fair investigation of the case in the light of Scripture. Where was Nicodemus? He had formerly taken this style of protestation against them when he said, " Doth our law judge any man, before it hear him, and know what he doeth?" In all probability they have learned by this time to dread *his* presence, while he has less sympathy with them and their councils than ever and hates and shuns them. But we feel that had he been present this would have been the style in which he would have at once objected. And so must anyone frame his objection who would escape from the toils in which the snare of expediency has caught him. There is no other help for it but abandon the whole principle in which you are one with those that would lead you farther than your conscience can go. You must raise the question and hold to it: Is this, or is this not, the Christ? Demand the settlement of that and you are safe. Rest the whole on the point of high principle and Scripture. Caiaphas for very shame cannot come out as a denier of the Scriptures, as a professed infidel. Caiaphas! " believest thou the prophets? I know that thou believest them." Press him there and you are safe. But if you yield that, you yield all; for if he goes a little farther than you, or even very much, still it is all in the same style and track, and the argument that is good for you is good for him also against you when silencing your scruples and your fears. Be ye disciples of expediency, and Caiaphas is quite your master. Take up the ground of clear and thorough principle and then you are proof against him. Perhaps you may even convince him and thus gain your brother. At least you will deliver your own soul.

And, then, as to the Romans? " Sufficient for the day is the evil thereof." Nor are glorious promises and precedents awanting. " If a man's ways please the Lord, he can make even his enemies to be at peace with him." " In the fear of the Lord is strong confidence, and the righteous shall have a place of refuge." And in any event, the sublime defiance of the Hebrew children is part of that word which liveth and abideth for ever: " Our God is able to deliver us from the burning fiery furnace, and he will deliver us out of thy hands, O king."

2. The words of Caiaphas are also the words of the Spirit; and in that view they are holy in their import and prophetic in their meaning. And what a startling transition we make from the accursed blasphemy of the man to the holy prediction of the Lord—couched, both of them, in the same words and in the same one utterance of these words!

How wonderful is God's work! Yea, even when it falls into closest contact with the pollution of man's sin, God's work is honourable and glorious, and his righteousness endureth for ever. Verily he maketh the wrath of man to praise him. Nor is this the first time that unwilling lips have been made instrumental in uttering for God the holy and blessed things which He would announce to men. Balaam comes to curse Israel, but his mouth is filled with blessing; yea, and declares that blessing unchangeable, the gift of God and without repentance. " God is not a man that he should lie, nor the son of man that he should repent; hath he said and shall he not do it? or hath he spoken and shall he not make it good? Behold, I have received commandment to bless; and he hath blessed, and I cannot reverse it. He hath not beheld iniquity in Jacob, nor seen perverseness in Israel." Yes, this is the true blessing; the non-imputation of iniquity. " Blessed is the man to whom the Lord imputeth not his sin." But on what grounds can such a blessing be conveyed? Caiaphas will himself supply the ground of the blessing which Balaam uttered. He will tell us that it is the imputation of sin to Christ, the substitute, that relieves and redeems the Israel of God. For in this light and in this view his blasphemous proposal was made not of himself, " but being high priest that year he prophesied that Jesus should die for that nation." Cometh then this blessedness, which Balaam announced upon the circumcision on " that nation " only? Nay, again Caiaphas will teach us: " And not for that nation only, but also that he should gather together in one the children of God that were scattered abroad."

A true substitute and sacrifice and high priest, therefore, Caiaphas in this amazing statement now announces: a statement, as clothing the Spirit's meaning, profoundly grand in proportion to the very baseness and atrocity of the meaning intended by Caiaphas. Nor is it of little moment to observe that it is Caiaphas, the high priest, whose lips the Spirit thus used to speak his prophecy. For evidently the Scripture lays stress on the point that this prophetic sense of his words was in connection with his priestly office as much as on the point that this prophetic sense was not meant by him personally. " This said he, not of himself, but being high priest that year he prophesied." Being high priest that year when Jesus is rejected by Levi's priesthood, it is right that the high priest, if he reject the Eternal Priesthood of Jesus, shall do so in words which the Spirit overrules to announce and confirm that very priesthood. Yes, glorious, we again repeat and honourable is the work of the Lord! The final rejection of Christ's priesthood is in language that accurately describes and predicts and seals it! Nor might this be without an interesting bearing on the moral discipline which the parties present were secretly subjected to and their ultimate responsibility at the bar of judgment. For,

1. Are there any present hesitating about this murderous design, unwilling to commit themselves to a deed so black? And then it *may* be Messiah after all! Hark! the high priest tells " he must die for the nation." So spake the Lord by the mouth of Daniel. " He must be cut off, but not for himself." May it not be He? Good ground has the hesitating councillor to pause, to tremble, to draw back ere it be too late.

2. Are there none that hesitate? Are they all bold in wickedness? Still it is not without a meaning that " a prophet of the Lord has been among them," and he has spoken words which, were they less resolved on sinning and less blinded by the power of sin, might have settled all their difficulties and constrained and taught them to recognise the Christ. They may little think of it now, but they have, nevertheless, the greater sin: and the time will come when they shall know that the spirit of prophecy, in the hour of their dark iniquity, spake words among them by which they and all their house might have been saved. Eternal judgments may be expected to disclose not a few such wonderful conjunctures when God brought some of his most holy and amazing efforts to enlighten and rescue transgressors into the closest connection with the very crisis of their sin! And terrific aggravations of eternal misery may result from revelations that shall show how very strongly great tides of divine light and salvation were beating on the blind sinner's soul. While, in like manner, may not the redeemed expect disclosures that shall carry up their gratitude and admiration to the loftiest heights of rapture as they see in heaven how that all the paths of the Lord were mercy and truth and love and wisdom quite unsearchable?

From among the various important principles that have come under our notice let the two following exhortations be deduced and enforced.

Beware of ungodly fears and beware of ungodly fellowships.

I. Beware of ungodly fears. The fear of man bringeth a snare. Full half of the lies that are uttered on the earth are dictated by ungodly fear; and full half the deeds of unrighteousness are prompted by some ungodly fear. Men will not fear God, and therefore they must frequently be at the mercy of ungodly fear. For men are not self-sufficient gods, quite able to manage themselves; or independent sovereigns that can manage all adverse powers and circumstances: they are but men. And a good lesson it is to learn what this meaneth. Let me learn my weakness and let me fall back upon God as my rock. Let me fear him and inquire, " Lord, what wilt thou have me to do?" Then I need never fear another. " The righteous is bold as a lion, and he that hath clean hands shall wax stronger and stronger." Be ye thus in the fear of the Lord; and there is no want to them that fear him. There is no divination against Israel. Can you not trust the All-mighty, the All-wise, to protect you from all evil? Oh! let the young attend to this. Natural enough it is that you should love life and desire to see good days. But hear the word of the Lord as to how alone this wish can be gratified. " For he that will love life and see good days, let him refrain his tongue from evil and his lips that they speak no guile; let him eschew evil and do good: let him seek peace and ensue it; for the eyes of the Lord are over the righteous and his ears are open to their prayers; but the face of the Lord is against them that do evil. But who is he that will harm you if ye be followers of that which is good?" Yes; who can harm you, if ye do that which is good; if ye speak the truth, and live righteously, and do justly, and love mercy, and keep yourselves unspotted from the world, maintaining a conscience void of offence towards God and man? And then, if danger and a snare should threaten, beware of the temptation to unbelief. The Lord is your refuge, and he is with you while you be with him. Though no man should stand with you, howbeit the Lord will stand with you and strengthen you, and will deliver you out of the mouth of the lion; yea, and he will deliver you from every evil work and preserve you to his heavenly kingdom. But if ye will not believe and fear the Lord, then surely ye shall not be established. The evil that you fear, *it* shall come upon you. The loss that you took sinful measures to prevent shall be the very thing that shall come upon you. God's providence is engaged daily in proving it. The want which you took unrighteous steps to ward off shall fall on you as an armed man. The fellow-creature whose frown you evaded, or whose favour you bought, at the price of sin, shall be he of all others who shall vex and betray you. And you will find in the end that to depart from the fear of God for the fear of creatures, is to be the enemy of the Creator and the slave and victim of the creature all in one. Saul forces himself against his duty to offer sacrifice, and waits not for Samuel because he sees the people departing from him, and he fears the loss of the kingdom: Samuel comes and announces that because of this wickedness the kingdom is taken from him. The Jews betray Christ for fear of the Romans: the Romans drive the ploughshare over Zion and the temple site.

My son, know thou the God of thy fathers, and fear him continually and serve him with a perfect heart. He is no hard taskmaster. " He executes loving kindness and judgment and righteousness in the earth." His own Eternal Son died for sinners to gather together the dispersed of Israel and make them one in the favour and love and fear of the Lord. His blood cleanseth from all sin, and he seeth no iniquity in them that believe. Receive his promise and make that blessedness yours; and be free thereby for ever from the fear that bringeth a snare.

II. For, secondly, ungodly fellowship often brings the very snare by which ungodly fear is punished. Your companion in sin may soon ensnare you and tempt you much farther forward in iniquity. Caiaphas makes his compeers villains; and they have no power to resile. This, of course, you never mean to be. But the question is not what you mean for yourself, but what those sinners may mean for you with whom you are really at one if the fear of God is not before your eyes, or, rather, the question is what the devil means for you: for he is a liar and murderer from the beginning. He will lead you on and on, till you despair of ever retracing your steps. He will flatter first, and then defy you. For it always comes to this, that the friendship of the world tends onward and onward to the thorough proof that it is enmity to God. And there is no safety but in breaking with all its principles. Is this the Christ or no? To the law and to the testimony! Is this conduct you invite me to join you in, such that it will stand the test of Scripture? If you scorn the Scriptures, I see at once with whom I have to do, and I am done with you. "Depart from me, ye evil doers, for I purpose to keep the commandments of my God."

Yes, and then you shall be as a tree planted by the rivers of water that bringeth forth his fruit in his season, and his leaf shall not wither, and all that you do shall prosper. The wicked are not so. Caiaphas was deposed from the priesthood within three years by the Roman Governor! The thing that he feared came upon him. His "place" was "taken away." For "I have seen the wicked in great power, and spreading himself like a green bay tree: yet he passed, and lo! he was not: yea, I sought him, but he could not be found" (Ps. xxxvii. 35, 36).

X.

THE TRIAL—II.

"Given You in that Same Hour."

"The high priest then asked Jesus of his disciples, and of his doctrine. Jesus answered him, I spake openly to the world; I ever taught in the synagogue, and in the temple, whither the Jews always resort; and in secret have I said nothing. Why askest thou me? ask them which heard me, what I have said unto them: behold, they know what I said. And when he had thus spoken, one of the officers which stood by struck Jesus with the palm of his hand, saying, Answerest thou the high priest so? Jesus answered him, If I have spoken evil, bear witness of the evil; but if well, why smitest thou me?" (John xviii. 19-23).

"And as soon as it was day, the elders of the people, and the chief priests, and the scribes, came together, and led him into their council, Saying, Art thou the Christ? tell us. And he said unto them, If I tell you, ye will not believe: and if I also ask you, ye will not answer me, nor let me go" (Luke xxii. 66-68).

AT an early period of his ministry, Jesus, in predicting to his disciples the trials that awaited them as the witness of his truth to the world, comforted them in the prospect of having to maintain their testimony in the presence of kings and rulers by the promise: "It shall be given you in that same hour what ye shall speak. For it is not ye that speak, but the Spirit of your Father that speaketh in you." This promise he seems to have substantially repeated on another occasion, when announcing, namely, the destruction of Jerusalem and the persecutions that should precede that event. "I will give you a mouth and wisdom which all your adversaries shall not be able to gainsay or resist."

In almost literal conformity with this promise, and in evident fulfilment of it, we read of Stephen that his enemies "were not able to resist the wisdom and the spirit by which he spake." In like manner of Peter and John it is recorded that the manner in which they acquitted themselves before their enemies called forth the greatest astonishment, with such precision, wisdom, and courage did they speak. For "when they saw the boldness of Peter and John, and perceived that they were unlearned and ignorant men, they marvelled."

Nor is it an ordinary blessing to be enabled to stand before able and malicious and powerful foes and bear the ark or cause or truth of God through the perils to which in such an hour it is exposed. For aid in such an hour Paul gives special thanks, celebrating the remembrance thereof as a mercy not inferior to the prophet's escape from the den of the lions; for when he stood before Nero, " At my first answer," says he, " no man stood with me, but all men forsook me "—even as with his Master now, for when Jesus was arrested " all the disciples forsook him and fled" (Matt. xxvi. 56): "I pray God," continues the forgiving apostle, similar here in spirit as well as in destiny to the Master, who cried, "Father forgive them for they know not what they do "—" I pray God," says Paul, " that it may not be laid to their charge. Notwithstanding the Lord stood with me and strengthened me; that by me the preaching might be fully known, and that the Gentiles might hear; and I was delivered out of the mouth of the lion " (II Tim. iv. 16, 17).

This blessing was sought from the Lord by holy men of old, as well as promised to apostles. " Lead me, O Lord, in thy righteousness because of mine enemies: make thy way straight before my face " (Ps. v. 8). " Teach me thy way, O Lord, and lead me in a plain path because of mine enemies. Deliver me not over to the will of mine enemies: for false witnesses are risen up against me, and such as breathe out cruelty" (Ps. xxvii. 11, 12).

To be enabled to possess your soul in patience; to give unto every one, even an enemy, a reason of the hope that is in you, with meekness and fear; to walk safely amidst the snares that are set for you, and the efforts made to entangle you in your speech; to bear bravely the contemptuous sneer of rude and worldly men; and withal to rebuke their enmity to God without seeking to revenge their enmity to you; to know when to be silent and when to speak; and to have your speech in all things with grace seasoned with salt—thus to conduct yourself before the enemies of true and vital Christianity, so as to give them no just handle against you, and no ground of triumph over you; yielding to them no hair'sbreadth of truth or righteousness, and carrying Christ's cause in your hands, and bearing it safely through, with no just stain or imputation thrown upon it for your sake—thus to have your way made straight before your face: made plain because of your enemies, is a blessing truly, which when experienced may well confirm you in your confidence in the faithfulness of God and in your joyful belief that the Lord is indeed upon your side.

Be it observed, however, that this, as all blessings, is conferred on you in Christ. You can look for it only as one whom God hath "called into the fellowship of his Son." When you enjoy it, you enjoy it in common with Christ. It is something which you share with him. It is something which he shares with you. Yea, it is something which, in its perfection and pre-eminence as experienced by him, transcends everything you can experience, for "in all things it behoved him to have the pre-eminence."

In his case, therefore, when called before rulers that were taking counsel against the Lord and his anointed, we may look for the pre-eminent and sublime accomplishment of the promise given to the Church—given to the living Head of the Church, as proprietor and possessor in her name of all promises and all blessings: the promise, namely, that in the presence of kings and rulers a mouth and wisdom irresistible should be given them: themselves not speaking, but the Spirit of their Father. For as in all respects and unto all ends the Spirit is given to every believer and servant and witness of Christ according to the measure of the gift of Christ, so to Christ himself was that Spirit given without measure. Now that Spirit, speaking in measure in Peter, in John, in Stephen, in Paul, as a Spirit of wisdom and council against the wiles of enemies, is to be traced in the same forthputting of his light and meekness and wisdom, but in highest manifestation and in the most transcendent illustrious instance, when the Head himself, the elder brother, made in all things like unto his brethren, that he might enter by personal knowledge and sympathy into all their sorrows, stands arrested and arraigned before the tribunals of the wicked.

Surely we may look—may we not?—for a conspicuous display of the Spirit's wisdom in the Saviour's procedure? Yet not such wisdom as forces itself upon our notice: rather that which invites but abundantly repays our search into it; which, however, we appreciate aright only by the teaching of the same Spirit through whom he spake; and who can cause us to set our seal to Christ's own declaration: " All the words of my mouth are in righteousness; there is nothing froward or perverse in them."

Let us trace, then, in this trial before Caiaphas the successive and separate draughts made on the wisdom of Christ as well as his meekness; separate and successive opportunities for Jesus to display, by speech or silence, as the meekness of wisdom might require, his own supreme and immeasurable interest in the promise which he gave to his apostles. His power to give them a mouth and wisdom is to be tested by his own experimental need in the days of his flesh, and his unlimited possession of what he professed his ability and design to confer.

I. It seems evident, or at least probable, that before the formal assembling of the Sanhedrim, Jesus was questioned and examined by Caiaphas in the presence merely of some of the retinue or officers of his household. Captured at midnight and led away bound first to Annas, he seems to have been detained by him but briefly, being speedily sent forward to Caiaphas, his son-in-law. His arrival at the high priest's palace, while it was still dark, was doubtless the signal for transmitting to the scribes and elders and those of the chief priests who had not assisted at our Lord's arrest (Luke xxii. 52) a summons to attend the Sanhedrim immediately. The day, however, had already begun to dawn before, even with all their good will to the evil work, these councillors could be got together, consisting, as the court did, of about seventy members, the original number of elders chosen by Moses in the wilderness (Num. xi. 16). Thus Luke tells us that " as soon as it was day the elders of the people and the chief priests and the scribes came together and led him into the council." It was during this interval between Christ's arrival at the palace and the assembling of the council that the denial on the part of Peter took place—an interval of some considerable time, as is obvious from the fact that an entire hour intervened between Peter's second and his third denial (Luke xxii. 59). In all probability, also, it was during this interval that the high priest, as recorded by John, questioned Jesus " of his disciples and his doctrine." For the three evangelists record what took place after the Sanhedrim had met, and John professes, in what is narrative or historical in his gospel, chiefly to supply additional information. It will accord well with this, therefore, to suppose that while waiting the arrival of his compeers, the high priest attempts a sort of preliminary or semi-official precognition of the case. Thus, also, we may account more easily for the fact that an officer should strike the prisoner, which could scarcely occur in presence of the regularly constituted court.

How passing wonderful the scene! It is yet dark, and messengers are scouring Jerusalem to summon hastily together a tribunal to arraign and condemn the Prince of Life. Meantime the prisoner, with unexampled meekness, forsaken of all his friends, save one who has followed to be no honour, no aid to him, but a disgrace and grief, awaits the assembling of his foes. Seated, probably, or left without the comfort of a seat, standing on the gallery overlooking the court or quadrangle where the soldiers have made a fire—and Peter stands with them warming himself—the blessed Saviour has opportunity to watch the conduct and overhear the words of his faithless and falling disciple; and is prepared immediately to seize the instant of the third denial, and the cock-crowing, to catch that disciple's eye and pierce his heart with the look of righteous reprimand and faithful, injured, yet eternal love.

Here, also, with the underlings of Caiaphas surrounding him, ready to chime in with their master's words and anticipate or outstrip their master's wishes, Jesus is subjected to the beginning of his insulting cross-examinations and his inexpressible indignities.

" The high priest then asked Jesus of his disciples and of his doctrine."

Shall Jesus answer or shall he be silent? There is a time to speak and a time to be silent; and no small part of the divine wisdom exhibited by Jesus on this occasion is seen in his choosing when to speak and when to refuse to speak.

On this occasion Jesus will speak. He will clear at
least his " doctrine " and his public ministry from every
imputation. Of his " disciples," indeed, concerning whom
Caiaphas asks him, he may say little. Alas! at this
moment there is little that he can say on their behalf.
They have forsaken him and fled. One of them, within
earshot, is almost now abjuring him with oaths and
curses. At the bar of Caiaphas, the Jewish high priest,
Jesus prefers being silent concerning his disciples. At
another bar, his Father's throne, himself their high priest
there, he prefers to plead their cause: there he can
announce their excellencies, their graces, their love to
himself, hiding all their faults and procuring forgiveness
for them all (John xvii. 6, 8, 19). But before the bar of
Caiaphas, if he cannot commend them, he will not com-
promise them. Of his disciples he is silent. But of his
doctrine he may speak with all freedom; nay, considering
the insinuations that Caiaphas would throw upon it, he
may speak with some indignation. For the high priest
would evidently insinuate that he had some doctrine to
propagate different from and opposed to the truth and
Scriptures of God as in the hands and keeping of his
nation. Caiaphas speaks of his doctrine with affected
contempt or affected jealousy, or fear, or condemnation:
as if he were some vain babbler or a setter forth of
strange gods, or a vender of secret and seducing
doctrines.

Ought Jesus to suffer any such imputation to lie upon
his teaching and his ministry? It is clear he ought not.
He is bound to vindicate the piety and publicity, the
honour and the holiness of his doctrine. He has never
had any doctrine or any design to conceal. He has never
had any scheme in hand which secrecy could promote.
Nay, while Caiaphas would insinuate a charge of secrecy,
well knows he that it is not secrecy but publicity that has
awakened his own jealousy and hatred. " If we let this

man alone, *all* men will believe on him." It is the publicity of Jesus' doctrine that he dreads. It is its publicity that Jesus had sought, and still desires, and is prepared not merely to avow but to glory in. Jesus answered him, " I spake openly to the world; I ever taught in the synagogue, and in the temple, whither the Jews always resort; and in secret have I said nothing. Why askest thou me? Ask them which heard me what I have said unto them: Behold, they know what I have said."

Such is the warm and almost indignant reply and reproof which Jesus returns when questioned of his disciples and of his doctrine. His doctrine has been the truth. As he subsequently avows to Pilate, he hath come into the world to bear witness of the truth. Now the truth covets the light and shuns concealment. He had spoken the truth freely, boldly, openly. He had not shunned to declare the whole counsel of God. He had kept back nothing that was profitable. To the meek and the poor and the contrite he had preached remission of sins and peace with God. The Spirit of the Lord God being upon him, he had proclaimed liberty to the captive and the opening of the prison to them that were bound. When in other towns he had gone into their synagogues, as at Nazareth and Capernaum, and as indeed his custom was, and had taught publicly, his word being with power, and the people being astonished at his doctrine. When in Jerusalem, the temple itself, even from the beginning, had been the place where he delivered his lessons of mercy to the humble and of wrath and damnation to the proud and lofty-minded Pharisee. There, where the Jews all resorted, and even in the last and great day of the feast, " He stood in the midst and cried aloud, If any man thirst, let him come unto me and drink." For, as to disciples, this was his method of adding to their number. He had, it is true, a small band of more intimate followers—a circle of personal friends. With them, indeed, he spoke oftentimes of his doctrine more freely, with more ease and fulness, than when speaking to the multitude. But even then it was the same doctrines he dwelt upon more fully, the same parables he opened up more fully, the same precepts he enjoined with the greater force and tenderness of a more personal or family affection. But covert disciples, secretly seduced and instigated, he had none. For when on one occasion, while talking to the people, it was announced to him that his mother and brethren stood without, desiring to speak with him, " Who," said he, " is my mother and my brethren?" Who are my most intimate and chosen friends? " And he stretched forth his hands and said, Behold my mother and my brethren! For whosoever shall do the will of my Father which is in heaven, the same is my brother and sister and mother."

Yes, his doctrine had been openly delivered; nor had any man been entrapped or seduced into discipleship. Ask them who heard him what he said unto them. Ask the officers whom you sent to apprehend him, and who returned saying, " Never man spake like this man." They know what he said unto them.

Thus Jesus in this instance speaks out. And rightly so, vindicating his doctrine from every imputation. It was neither secret, nor seductive—neither secretly delivered, nor seductive in its tendency. In itself it courts investigation and the light. Followers he sought only publicly and through conviction. It was right there should be no mistake here—that Jesus should speak out; that he should make this point clear. It was necessary that his condemnation, when it did take place, should be seen to rest on other grounds altogether: that there should not be the shadow of a reason to assert that he suffered as a secret and seductive false teacher. He had not by cunning craftiness lien in wait to deceive his followers or hearers: and the very breath of such suspicion or insinuation must not light upon his name even when he is dishonoured as a captive and a criminal. On other grounds altogether must he be set forth as being condemned. Condemned he is to be, and knows he is to be. But he shall have the right charge brought forth; that for which though false he is willing to suffer, for which he glories to suffer. Therefore the imputation on his doctrine must be repelled. He must go forward to his sufferings, not only clear, but seen to be clear, from this charge. Even when dying a sacrifice and offering, " made sin for us," with our iniquities made to meet upon him, and thereby " innumerable evils compassing him about," even then it is under protest that his ministry of truth has been honourable and glorious. " I have preached righteousness in the great congregation; lo, I have not refrained my lips, O Lord, thou knowest: I have not hid thy righteousness within my heart: I have declared thy faithfulness and thy salvation: I have not concealed thy loving kindness and thy truth from the great congregation " (Ps. xl. 6, 12, 9, 10). " I ever spake openly."

Thus he will allow no shadow to obscure, no stain to alight upon his doctrine or his ministry. And be it observed, his defence is not only satisfactory and sufficient in point of right and truth: it is in point of fact effective. The charge is brought against him no more. It is not as a secret and false teacher that he is put to death. He compels his condemnation to be put on other grounds, such as he chooses to refrain from contesting. Hence the wisdom of Jesus in not allowing this to pass in silence.

II. But soon as he has thus repelled the high priest's insinuation, galled by the truth of this unanswerable and final reply, one of the underlings of the household, with mean subservience to his master and in professed support of his dignity, " struck Jesus with the palm of his hand, saying, Answerest thou the high priest so?"

What is the line of wisdom and the path of duty now? Ought our blessed Lord now to be silent? Ought this blow to be borne with no remark? Or if Jesus shall speak, what shall be the principle or precise object that he will have in view in doing so?

Evidently this blow is to be meekly borne; and so Jesus bears it. " When he was reviled, he reviled not again; when he suffered, he threatened not." But meekness does not always mean silence. The meekness required is the meekness of wisdom; and to be silent is often an easy wisdom compared with the wisdom of speaking precisely the very word, the word in season, whether to him that is weary or to him that is wicked. There is in some circles a demand for a meekness which is not the meekness of wisdom, and for a charity which is not the charity of true love. By all means let injury be borne without wrath; but should injury always be borne without rebuke? Ought not Christian meekness and Godlike charity to be like God's own word, " profitable for reproof, for correction, for instruction in righteousness "? Let there be all long-suffering indeed: yet let the full injunction be remembered: " Reprove, rebuke, exhort with all long-suffering." Ah! the real difficulty is not always to keep silence. One may keep silence and muse in hot revenge, or keep silence in senseless mental indolence or imbecility. Either of these requires little wisdom and little self-restraint. But keenly to feel the injury and quietly to bear it, and yet to this to add the other duty—and perform it well, not wrathfully but righteously, not revengefully but lovingly—the other duty of pointing out the offender's sin and seeking to enlighten his mind, awaken his conscience, and touch and melt his heart in reference to it; here is the difficulty—needing the wisdom of meekness and the charity of love. " Let them alone " is the frequent cry when the invaders of Christ's honour, in respect of his truth and his Church, are exposed, rebuked, reproved by those that are set for the defence of the gospel. Let them alone! Is that charity? Christ did

not mean that for charity when he spake it of the Pharisees
—" Let them alone, they be blind leaders of the blind."
It was not said in love. It was not meant for love. It
was spoken and meant as doom, abandonment, damnation.
" Ephraim is joined to his idols, let him alone." Has not
that the sound of awful wrath? If a man is to be let alone
—if it is right he should be let alone—be it so. Only
let it not be under pretence of charity or meekness: it is
righteous abandonment, relinquishing all effort for his
salvation.

Thus, some might think Jesus would have displayed
greater meekness by bearing this blow in silence. For
himself Jesus could easily have done so. For the
offender's sake he expostulated on his injustice: he
revealed to him his sin. Jesus answered him, " If I have
spoken evil, bear witness of the evil; but if well, why
smitest thou me?" If I have spoken evil, let it come into
judgment against me: I am already a prisoner; you will
have the opportunity immediately of pleading against me,
of securing all the ends and claims of justice. Meantime,
abstain from rude, unrighteous, cowardly violence. This,
even if I have spoken evil. But if I have spoken well, how
much more art thou unrighteous in smiting me!

Thus Jesus testified in meekness and in love to the
understanding and the conscience of his rude assailant.
An inconsiderable and thoughtless subordinate, he might
have been hitherto carried away unthinkingly, in the wake
of his superiors' indignation, against one concerning
whom he had heard many a calumny. An effort, therefore, for his good might yet be tried as far from hopeless.
With this view, far more than to vindicate himself, Jesus
spake. And who shall tell the influence which that calm
and kind rebuke may have had? Who shall say but it
may have lien in the mind till after the whole issues had
transpired, and then germinated in convictions which
may have ended in his conversion to the faith and his

casting in his lot with those who " abode in the apostles' doctrine and fellowship, and in breaking of bread"? And if so, how blessed the result of this meekness of wisdom that was not silent! But, in any event, an effort was made to reprove, correct, and rescue a soul from sin. And the word could not return void. Meantime, Jesus, as he had done his duty by his public doctrine and ministry in vindicating them from misrepresentation, now discharges himself of a solemn responsibility devolving both on public ministers and private servants of God— the duty of rebuke, not suffering sin upon another. " For the servant of the Lord," as Jesus was pre-eminently, " must not strive but be gentle unto all men, apt to teach, patient: in meekness instructing those that oppose themselves if God peradventure will give them repentance to the acknowledging of the truth, and that they may recover themselves out of the snare of the devil, who are taken captive by him at his will" (II Tim. ii. 24-26).

Thus hitherto Jesus has walked in a plain path because of his enemies.

III. We turn now, thirdly, to the account given by Luke, which properly comes in here. For by this time the summoned councillors are assembled, and they lead the way to the council chamber, more regularly and formally sisting the prisoner before them.

" And as soon as it was day the elders of the people and the chief priests and the scribes came together and led him into their council, saying, Art thou the Christ? Tell us."

What is the dictate of wisdom now? Will Jesus answer at this call? or will he be silent? Or if he speak, will he give them the satisfaction they desire? No, he will refuse to answer their question. But he will give them his reason for refusing. " And he said unto them, If I tell you, ye will not believe; and if I also ask you, ye will not answer me nor let me go." What bold resoluteness in sin, what hardenedness of heart does this charge bring home upon them! Jesus refuses to instruct them on the ground of their deep dishonesty of purpose. To the officer who struck him Jesus could reply in terms fitted to enlighten his mind and touch his heart. *He* was not hopelessly given over to a reprobate mind. He was a very secondary and subordinate actor, swept along, probably, in his judgment and feelings by the opinions and sentiments of his superiors, to whom, perhaps, as the authorities in such a case, he resigned the decision, content for his part simply to acquiesce with them. He did it very much in thoughtlessness, deeply misled by those he might naturally think in such a point his rightful guides. For *him,* therefore, Jesus had pity in store. With *him,* Jesus could kindly expostulate and remonstrate to show him his error and his sin. What he did, he did very much like Saul, ignorantly and in unbelief, and Christ's patience and divine mercy might tarry for him and teach him the truth.

But these chief priests and scribes and elders, they are the prime movers in this great evil. They are not carried away by the opinion or example of superiors; nor by the undue influence which a position of servitude might exert, tending to carry them blindly along with their masters. Neither have they any desire to learn the truth by this question which they put. They do not mean to believe Jesus if he confess himself the Christ. If he tell them, they will not believe; and if he ask them, they will not answer. If he question them, they will act as they did anent the baptism of John. They would not say it was from heaven, for then were John a heaven-inspired guide to bear witness of Jesus, and his Messiahship in that case must be acknowledged. Neither would they say his baptism or mission was of men; for they feared the people because all men regarded John as a prophet. If Jesus ask them, they will not answer. Neither will they let

Jesus go. They had seized him in the last resort. They were resolved no more to be delayed in their design of removing him. And their question could not have come from hearts more averse from learning the truth, or more fully set in them to do evil.

With such men, therefore, Jesus refuses to plead his claims; refuses even, at least at this stage, to assert them. He will not so much as tell them that he is the Christ. Thus truth is refused to the deceitful and insincere inquirer, even as prayer is not answered when coming from a heart which regards iniquity. " The secret of the Lord is with them that fear him, and he will show *them* his covenant."

Does the poor guilty woman of Samaria anticipate with pleasure the coming of the Christ because he will give instruction in the worship of God: " When the Messiah, which is called Christ, is come, he will tell us all things "? To *her* Jesus is prepared to reveal himself as the Christ. " Jesus saith unto her, I that speak unto thee am he."

Is the man born blind, whom Jesus hath cured and the authorities have cast out, earnestly desirous of believing on the Son of God? Is he craving an object of faith and confidence and love? so that when the question is put to him, " Dost thou believe on the Son of God?" he is prepared to reply, as one who is ready and longing to believe, " Who is he, Lord, that I might believe on him?" To him also Jesus is prepared to reveal himself. " Jesus said unto him, Thou hast both seen him and it is he that talketh with thee."

Art thou, like him, eagerly craving an object of faith; ready, inclined, desirous to believe? And thou seekest a view of the Son of God in his grace and glory that thou mayest believe on him? Art thou, like that woman at the well, desirous of the instruction which the Christ can give concerning the worship of the Father in spirit and in truth; and desirous of that introduction to the Father in righteousness and peace which the Christ, the advocate, alone can give so that thou mayest really worship Him in confidence and cordiality, and walk with Him humbly and holily as thy God? Then doubt not but Christ will reveal himself to thee. Doubt not but Christ is even now more ready, inclined, and desirous to disclose himself— to remove all veils, all embarrassment, all ignorance, and disclose to thee his person, his presence, his office, his love; more ready, more willing far than thou art to receive the gracious revelation. But art thou an undecided, insincere, formal worshipper of God? not earnestly inquiring anent the Christ and the claims which Christ puts in for all your faith in him as the only priest: your docility to him as the only prophet; your obedience to him as the only king? Do you wait on God's ordinances from mere custom, from regard to character, from motives inconsistent with a supreme fear of God and desire to worship him in spirit and in truth: apparently listening to the claims and truth of Christ; apparently asking instruction in the sanctuary; apparently inquiring Who is the Christ? who is the Saviour? what is the way of salvation and life? and yet with no desire to embrace the Christ who is preached to you and the salvation which he came to preach?

Then to you ordinances shall be useless and worse. From you Jesus will withhold those disclosures of his Messiahship which he gives to the sincere and single-minded, to the poor and contrite in heart. For if he tell you, you will not believe on him any more than hitherto. And if he ask you, ye will not answer him. Ye will neither believe on him as the Christ, claiming to give you a salvation ordered in all things and sure; claiming, there-fore, to receive literally a first and commanding place in your affections. Nor when he demands your submission to him will ye answer. Ye will come to no conclusion, holding, if possible, both with God and Mammon—

serving, if possible, both Christ and the world. Ye will neither believe him when he answers all those questions which the anxious soul must put, as when the cry is, " What must I do to be saved?" or, " How shall man be just with God his maker?" Nor will you answer him when he questions you as when pointing to the unrecompensing character of your worldly career he asks, " Wherefore do ye spend your money for that which is not bread and your labour for that which profiteth not?" or as when pointing to the unprepared for close of that career he asks, " What will ye do in the swellings of Jordan?" If he tell you, ye will not believe; and if he ask you, ye will not answer. Neither will ye let him go. Pilate—heathen Pilate—would let Christ go : not so the members of the Jewish Sanhedrim. Infidels, professed infidels, let Christ and his religion go : not so professing, mere professing, dead members of the Christian Church. If ye still believe not on Jesus and yet seek to hold by his ordinances and his Church and truth, he has cause to complain that you will not let him go. You will neither receive him as the Christ, nor will you let him go. *They* would not let him go till they had crucified him. Ye will not let him go till, by your hypocritical and unholy profession, ye crucify him afresh and put him to an open shame.

Give up this method of torturing Christ in the person of his truth and cause. " Let him go " if you will not honestly and honourably receive him. Have done with him, and with all profession of his name, or else, having named the name of Christ, depart from all iniquity. Let his ordinances alone, or else wait upon them in the fear of God and with solemn desire for his blessing. Attend no more on a preached gospel, or else be ye not hearers only but doers of the word. In one word, choose ye whom ye will serve and halt no more between two opinions. If he whose word is now spoken to you in his name be not the Christ, have done with it, and with *him,* with his house and servants, with his word and ordinances altogether. "*Let him go.*" But if he on whose claims you are called to decide be the Christ; if there really *be* a Christ, a Saviour, a witness of the truth, a messenger from heaven, a priest and king upon his throne in Zion; and if it be in his name, as the name of the Prince of Peace, that you are summoned to surrender that he may save you from all your iniquities and sanctify you for all his service: that he may freely forgive you all trespasses and fully furnish you for all good works, then, as one who has found the indispensable portion, the pearl of great price, the one thing needful, hold him fast and *do not let him go;* for what will you give in exchange for your Saviour? What will you give in exchange for your soul? Once really find Christ, and you *will not let him go.* " I found him whom my soul loveth; and I held him and *would not let him go* " (Song of Sol. iii. 4).

For there are two very diverse senses in which men will not let the Saviour go, carrying with them very different meanings and very different issues. And how marvellous, how startling the extremes which they reveal —extremes of deadliest sin and deepest piety.

Caiaphas! thou priest of the Most High God, thou hypocrite! *Thou* wilt not let the Christ go. Thou wilt not let him go until thou crucify him. Nor thou, O worldling, until thou crucify him afresh.

Jacob! thou prevailing prince with God! *Thou* wilt not let him go. Thou wilt not let him go until he bless thee. Nor thou, O Israelite indeed, until he bless thee too.

In which of these two senses would you have the Christ declare that you *will not let him go?*

XI

THE TRIAL—III.

"DESTROY THIS TEMPLE."

"Now the chief priests, and elders, and all the council, sought false witness against Jesus, to put him to death; but found none; yea, though many false witnesses came, yet found they none. At the last came two false witnesses, and said, This fellow said, I am able to destroy the temple of God, and to build it in three days. And the high priest arose, and said unto him, Answerest thou nothing? what is it which these witness against thee?" (Matt. xxvi. 59-62).

"Then answered the Jews, and said unto him, What sign shewest thou unto us, seeing that thou doest these things? Jesus answered and said unto them, Destroy this temple, and in three days I will raise it up. Then said the Jews, Forty and six years was this temple in building, and wilt thou rear it up in three days? But he spake of the temple of his body. When therefore he was risen from the dead, his disciples remembered that he had said this unto them; and they believed the scripture, and the word which Jesus had said" (John ii. 18-22).

"And they that passed by reviled him, wagging their heads, and saying, Thou that destroyest the temple, and buildest it in three days, save thyself. If thou be the Son of God, come down from the cross" (Matt. xxvii. 39-40).

LET us proceed in tracing the spirit and wisdom with which Jesus spake at the bar of Caiaphas.

Of this we have already seen three remarkable instances —(1) when interrogated by the high priest anent his disciples and his doctrine; (2) when rudely and impiously struck by the officer in waiting; (3) when hurriedly enjoined by the priests and elders, on their assembling in the council chamber, to declare whether he was the Christ. In the *first* instance, he vindicated his doctrine from every insinuation of secrecy, leaving the burden of proving any impeachment of its truth and piety upon those who could easily learn, if they chose to ask any of a thousand witnesses, what was the tenor of his teaching. In the *second* case, compassionating the ignorance and prejudice of the unhappy man, who assuredly knew not what he did, Jesus, patiently bearing the injury, powerfully and faithfully rebuked the author of it. And, in the *third,* he convicts his examiners of dishonesty of purpose, and on that ground declines to answer their question.

Their expectation of inducing Jesus to utter something which they would represent as criminating himself is thus disappointed. Accordingly, they are thrown as a last resort on the shocking scheme of hiring false witness. What a stage of moral debasement had these men reached when not one of them had moral courage to rise and rebuke the accursed proposal! But what do I say? Rebuke it? Nay, not even to dissent from it! There was unbroken harmony among these judges in their unspeakably vile procedure. "Now the chief priests and elders and *all* the council sought false witnesses against Jesus to put him to death." "But they found none." Was it therefore because none among the people could be found base enough to forswear themselves for hire? No: there were at this time, emphatically, "like priest like people." A society ruled by such men could not be destitute of tools and agents, seared and conscienceless as their masters. There will be "wicked" men enough, ready for every evil deed, within call at a moment's warning, "walking on every side when the vilest men are exalted" (Ps. xii. 8).

It was not for want of equal villainy among the people, for "many false witnesses came." Still, "though many false witnesses came, yet found they none," for as Mark says, " Many bare false witness against him, but their witness agreed not together " (xiv. 56). Divine providence presided over and baffled their efforts, filling them with confusion and mutual inconsistency.

At length, however, this method seemed about to succeed, or at least to promise well, for we read " At the last came two false witnesses and said, This fellow said, I am able to destroy the temple of God and to build it in three days " (Matt. xxvi. 60, 61). Or, as given by Mark, " There arose certain and bare false witness against him, saying, We heard him say, I will destroy this temple that is made with hands, and within three days I will build another made without hands. But neither did their witness agree " (xiv. 57-59).

Now, in order to understand the singular turn which the introduction of this topic gave to the procedure, we must recall the original circumstances alluded to. These are given in the close of the second chapter of John. For the incident on which an attempt is now made to ground a criminal charge transpired at an early period of our Lord's ministry.

Jesus had cleared or cleansed the temple. His spirit stirred within him as he beheld them given to their covetousness and filled with zeal for the honour of his Father's house, which a self-seeking generation were transforming into a house of merchandise. Jesus had scourged the sheep and the oxen and those that sold them out of the temple, pouring out the changers' money and overthrowing the tables, lifting at the same time such a voice of holy indignation and authoritative rebuke as was never heard in those degenerate days. It was one speaking with authority and not as the scribes who said: " Take these things hence; make not my Father's house a house of merchandise " (John ii. 16).

Amazed at the claim to be obeyed as an authorised reformer of the house and worship of God which such bold and unshrinking procedure implied, the Jews made the demand with which they so frequently pressed Jesus, and which, made in a right spirit, was in itself nothing more than they might have been expected and were indeed bound to make. They demanded to know his authority for assuming to himself the right of supervision and reproof and reformation which he hereby professed to exercise. " Then answered the Jews and said unto him, What sign shewest thou unto us, seeing thou doest these things?" They will have a sign, a supernatural action or work—a miracle, in short, to show the seal of heaven attesting his claims and right thus to chastise and to correct them, and to constitute a ground or reason of their faith in him. Thus early did they present that demand which, reiterated so frequently at almost every stage and turn of Jesus' ministry, came at last to be emphatically descriptive of the reception which they gave to him, and passed with Paul into a brief characteristic of their whole style and method of dealing with his Messiahship. For according to Paul's concise statement it had become proverbially notorious as their current practice, " The Jews require a sign." It is quite their manner to do so, as much indeed as it is the national tendency and characteristic of " the Greeks " to " seek after wisdom " (I Cor. i. 22).

It is important to observe how Jesus dealt with this practice at its commencement. " Jesus answered and said unto them, Destroy this temple, and in three days I will raise it up."

The explanatory comment is given by the Evangelist immediately, and we have never been left to doubt the import of this reply of our Lord. " He spake of the temple of his body."

But to enter into the spirit of the scene, to understand the singular play of excited thought and feeling that was in progress and that was left to smoulder and break out

again at a later period, as we see, we must evidently
view this response to their demand apart from the inspired
exposition of its meaning which was given subsequently,
and which was not apprehended even by the disciples till
after their Master's resurrection. Not till then did even
they comprehend the precise import of the thought which
Jesus couched under these terms, as we read, " When
therefore he was risen from the dead, his disciples
remembered that he had said this unto them; and they
believed the scripture and the word which Jesus had said "
(John ii. 22).

Now, leaving out of view the light thrown on this
singular reply by explanations subsequently given, and by
the actual resurrection itself, and placing ourselves as
much as possible in the position of those who simply
heard the oracular answer at the time, and had no other
means of judging of its import, what impression would
it convey to us?

Manifestly that Jesus intended to utter a spiritual
mystery or enigma designed, not to flash out all its meaning on the moment to every one who heard it, overbearing
and overpowering their convictions by finally and con-
clusively demonstrating his own claims without any more
possible scope or room for cavil, but, evidently, rather
soliciting and standing in need of additional inquiry, and
fitted emphatically to test and prove the moral disposition
of the inquirer. For, in fact, it was so constructed as to
embody not only a sign, or token, or proof, or seal of his
commission, in the light which it would ultimately throw
upon his claims, but as also to constitute a test or
touchstone of these men's moral character and corruption
in the light in which these would be disclosed in their
present mode of dealing with it.

Thus, in fact, Christ himself, in his whole person and
office, is a sign attracting to himself all hearts whom his
grace has made congenial, while repulsed by, and repell-

ing, the carnal and the unrenewed. To the one he is a "plant of renown"; to the other "a root out of a dry ground." To the one he is "the Branch of the Lord, beautiful and glorious, excellent and comely," under which they repose in peace: to the other he presents "no form nor comeliness." The very proposal, or tender, or forthholding of Christ develops and discloses the character of him to whom that tender or proposal is made. In the proximity of Christ the man's spiritual disposition comes to light. If he be of grace and of God, the nearness of Christ kindles into a flame the erewhile decaying principles and affections of the renewed and regenerated nature, and reveals the urgency and strength of his believing aspirations and desires. If he be of Satan and the world, the nearer Christ is brought—whether in the claims of his kingly rule, or the grace of his priesthood, or the light and doctrine of his prophetic office—the more the man shrinks away, his cold ceremony and indifference passing rapidly into dislike and disdain and enmity, as the truth and grace and righteousness and Spirit of Christ demand the submission of his whole heart and soul: and the Christ can exhibit no stronger sign to that man in demonstration of his divine commission than the powerful and searching testing influence which his person and his office have exerted on the secret substance and staple of his own evil and corrupt nature.

It was this aspect of Christ's person which holy Simeon reverentially admired and celebrated when, holding the promised Child in his arms, he said: "Behold this child is set for the fall and rising again of many in Israel, and for a sign that shall be spoken against, that the thoughts of many hearts may be revealed." Even in being spoken against; nay, in that very specially, he is a sign. He is a sign even in being rejected. He is a sign in his power to reveal the thoughts of many hearts, and that, not by actively reading off in his omniscience the thoughts and

secret character which men's hearts conceal, but in
passively provoking such manifestations of their disposition as make themselves disclose of what spirit they are.
As he passed through the days of his flesh, doing good,
working his Father's work, speaking his Father's truth,
propounding and proffering to guilty miserable men his
Father's grace, he was a powerful touchstone which in its
efficacy brought not to light some of the slighter and
shallower elements of human character merely, but
searchingly penetrated to the depths and brought out into
evidence the essential features and principles of diverse
dispositions.   Wheresoever any groundwork of sincerity
and truth was found, his person and his presence formed
a centre of resistless power, alluring and attracting and
establishing the upright, while conferring light and
permanence and blessedness.   Self-seeking and hypocrisy,
on the other hand, found in him an antagonist that,
awakening them into deeper emotion, forced their existence into obviousness.

What Christ was in his person his preaching still is:
a two-fold sign of mighty efficacy to sift and separate,
thoroughly purging like a fan in the hand of the mighty.
To the Jews, Christ preached is a stumbling block; to
the Greeks foolishness; but to them that believe, whether
Jews or Greeks, he is the wisdom of God and the power
of God unto salvation.   This was predicted from the
beginning.   For it is contained in the Scripture: " Behold
I lay in Zion a chief cornerstone, elect, precious; and he
that buildeth on him shall not be confounded "; and then
follows the testing or discriminating effect which must
always follow: the influence upon, and discoveries of, the
spiritual state of different men: " To you therefore which
believe he is precious, but to them which be disobedient
the stone which the builders disallowed the same is
become the head of the corner and a stone of stumbling

and a rock of offence—to those, namely, which stumble at the word, being disobedient" (I Pet. ii. 6-8).

Who can forget that this same two-fold aspect of Christ's gospel has been so solemnly put before us in the words of Paul: " To the one we are the savour of death unto death; and to the other we are the savour of life unto life "—the same one gospel having these two diverse sides or influences, even as the guiding pillar of old was light to Israel and darkness and a source of terror and death to the Egyptians.

And as Christ's person was this sort of sign, and his gospel still is so, his replies to the reiterated demand for a sign partook of a similar character and proceeded on the same principle. He constructed them, in holy righteous judgment, so as to present two sides: the one to the humble, humbling and instructive, calling for increase of docility and richly rewarding it; the other to the proud, provoking, eliciting and demonstrating their enmity and moral depravity, hardening them in their wilful opposition and punishing them with increase of their self-entailed blindness, and with the wretchedness of their own uncontrolled evil passions.

Thus, when he had fed five thousand with a few loaves and fishes, and the multitude in the face of such a miracle say unto him in answer to his demand for their faith, " What sign shewest thou then that we may see and believe thee? What dost thou work?" he replied that he himself was the bread of life; that he would give his flesh for the life of the world; that his flesh was meat indeed and his blood drink indeed; and that unless they would eat his flesh and drink his blood they could have no life in them. The issue of such a style of response was decisive. The greater multitude had done with him at once and for ever. Seeking literal bread, and hating grace and truth, they went back and walked no more with him. The eleven had their humility deepened, and these very words were to them spirit and life which, as Peter testified, bound them only the more powerfully to him as the fountain of eternal life. " To whom shall we go but unto thee?" (John vi).

At another time the same unbelieving and unreasonable request being preferred, Jesus answered: " A wicked and adulterous generation seeketh after a sign, and there shall no sign be given to it but the sign of the prophet Jonas. For as Jonas was three days and three nights in the whale's belly, so shall the Son of man be three days and three nights in the heart of the earth." In fact, this reply seems to have been given by Jesus oftener than once (Matt. xii. 39, and xvi. 4).

And this is substantially identical with the sign offered at the cleansing of the temple. Jesus here gives substantially the sign of the prophet Jonas. He appeals to his own death and resurrection; and he does so in language extremely enigmatical and obscure. Attempts have been made by commentators to alleviate this obscurity, as, for instance, when they tell us that doubtless Jesus pointed with the finger to his body, saying with marked emphasis and in combination with that action, " Destroy *this* temple." It is a mere supposition. The Scripture itself gives no reason to suppose that Jesus accompanied his words with any explanatory action. On the contrary, the moral import of the transaction implies that we are to regard the obscurity of his words as intentional, as in fact appertaining to the very essence of that test of corrupt character which he was bringing into play in answer to the demand for a sign of his own heavenly commission.

They had already seen enough to have decided them, had they been honestly minded, to give Jesus a just reception, or at least a fair and an honourable trial. Their own consciences witnessed the righteousness of what he had done in the house of God in holy zeal for its purity and honour. The singular authority which his voice and words carried with them must have convinced them that he was very far from an ordinary man; while the dignity, the calmness, the reasonableness that pervaded all his movements must have satisfactorily demonstrated that he was no excited fanatic. Had they honourably yielded their minds and hearts to such impressions, and had they addressed themselves to him respectfully, with that respectfulness which Jesus had already duly earned— soliciting further instruction concerning the claims which he put forward and the work to which he had that day put his hand, who can doubt that Jesus would have guided them in judgment and meekly taught them in his way. Nay, more; received into a good and docile heart, a heart loving the temple, rejoicing in the purity to which it had that day been restored, and grateful that God had raised up one in degenerate days who was not afraid to rebuke iniquity and reform abuse—received into such a heart, this very response which Jesus gave could not but prove, by its very mystery, a provocative to much thoughtfulness and the germ of many a thought; while, stimulated by spiritual earnestness to seek the explanation and exposition of the great teacher himself, such hearers might have been enriched with varied and abundant views of divine truth, developed out of that singular and fascinating oracle which the heavenly-minded stranger, in the hour of holy zeal and hostile arraignment, had with such composure and dignity given to them in answer to the challenge for his authority. And such docile disciples might have lived to know that that single utterance of the teacher's lips implied that the temple on Zion was but the type of a temple made without hands: that the real temple symbolised, true and permanent and eternal, was the fleshly tabernacle or human body of the teacher himself, this spiritual instructor and reformer of the Church; that in that temple dwelt not the symbol of Jehovah's presence but the very fulness of the Godhead bodily; that that temple, so glorious, was designed for an offering and a sacrifice to remove effectually that dread reality of guilt which all the earthly temple's services and sacrifices could never take away; that in offering himself a sacrifice to God's justice he should at the same time fall a victim to man's hatred and hostility, his death being not only voluntarily endured but also brought about by violent and wicked hands; and, finally, that he should vanquish death and in three days arise from the grave—the first fruits of them that slept, a storehouse of a new and a risen life unto all them that should believe upon him. To those that feared the Lord, might so large a portion of his secret or his truth be discovered and disclosed under this one mysterious but fascinating and pregnant announcement. For " the secret of the Lord is with them that fear him."

But not into such hearts did this announcement fall. It was uttered to those that feared not the Lord, and it only elicited and demonstrated more fully their displeasure at the reformation of God's house and worship which they had witnessed. They are not desirous to believe and anxious for a sign to strengthen and confirm their faith, but they are determined to withhold their faith and anxious to justify their refusal to believe. The sign, therefore, is righteously given in the form of a mystery, purposely enigmatical and obscure, that in judgment on their unbelief and perverseness they may stumble and fall and be broken. " To the one we are the savour of life unto life; to the other we are the savour of death unto death."

The Jews took this reply in its literal sense as applying to the temple on Mount Zion, and so they planted themselves more firmly in their unbelief, and blasphemed. " Forty and six years was this temple in building, and wilt thou rear it up in three days?"

But observe, even on the supposition that the reference is to be understood to be to the literal temple; even with their own view of Christ's saying; observe their moral perverseness in replying as they did. They put their own interpretation on the mysterious remark, and then they scorn it. " It took forty-six years to build this temple and you, forsooth, are to rear it in three days!" It is the utter disproportion between the time required in building it and the time they understand Jesus to say he will require in rebuilding it, on which their perverse thoughts fasten. " Will you achieve, alone, in three days that which employed many workmen for forty-six years?" And yet, if Jesus had stated a time in which the disproportion had not been so very glaring and great, would they have been satisfied? They asked a sign. Had Jesus professed to build the temple in a period of time within the range of human probability, that would have been no sign of a commission more than human. It is the utter disproportion implied, it is precisely the brevity of the time indicated, which can alone constitute Christ's offer a sign, even when interpreted after their own fashion. And yet, while it is precisely this which in their view of it could make it to be the sign which they require, it is precisely this also on the ground of which they scorn and scoff at it! So basely false is their whole state of heart.

Such, then, was the sign which they made deadly to themselves and which was destined to be to them the savour of death unto death. For just as it contained the very essence of Messiah's fate, his death and his resurrection, so it bore with like pre-eminent force on their fate. Accordingly it emerges again to play a strange part, and to reveal the ongoing of a mysterious self-acting process of vengeance, under which they are seen hardening themselves more and more unto the end. Not content with drawing deadly mischief from it to their souls at first, and converting it into a theme of blasphemy and scorn against Messiah in the commencement of his ministry, they drag it forward again on his trial to make it serviceable in putting him to death; while in reality the savour of accumulating death upon death is falling from it on their own souls. This strange oracle which once they scorned; this mysterious remark that was food for scoffing, mirth, and laughter! Oh! their very sin in reference to it has given it a strange vitality. It cannot sleep. It cannot pass away and be forgotten. It presents itself once more; yea, and yet again (Mat. xxvii. 39), and each time, through their " disobedience," as malevolently they summon it forward into action, it comes upon them armed with more dreadful and deadly power to judge and harden them and fit them for ruin and for wrath!

Time was when you put away Christ's claims, and there may have been memorable circumstances as, for instance, your joining in the scorning of the scornful rather than be scorned as a reformed or reforming penitent. Are you sure that that event and the circumstances connected with it have spent their evil force? Are you sure that they have no more influence to exert on your heart and character, searing and blinding you against the gracious truth and power of the Lord's salvation? Ah! there may be recurrences of that same event, fitted to reveal and confirm your hatred of the word and the claims of Messiah. When these men scoffed in the temple at Christ's covert allusion to his death and resurrection, ministering to their own moral ruin from his holy words, who could have thought that they would themselves, after nearly three years of interval, revive the recollections of that hour, and revive and deepen on their own polluted souls the accursed influences which, through the god of this world blinding their minds, they were pleased to permit him to exercise over them by an oracle of divine truth that might have proved a reason for their faith and material of reverential admiration of the great mystery of salvation? And who could have thought that yet again, to prove that oracle of truth the savour of accumulating and still increasing spiritual death to their souls, there should have been those who, while Jesus was hanging on the cross, recurred to it once more, and said in the crisis of the power of darkness, and in the climax of this guilty world's blasphemy and enmity to God: "Thou that destroyest the temple, and in three days buildest it again, save thyself"? Ah! when they received not that oracle with reverence; when they received it not with meekness; with ready willingness to have its mysteries disclosed; with the docility of babes to whom God will show his salvation; when, on the contrary, they chose to put their own shallow construction on it, and make their own scornful use of it—from that moment it passed, in one sense, into the hands of Satan, a bright and furbished sword of his to wield upon them; and far will it be from the great enemy to allow his serviceable weapons to slumber and his fitting opportunities to pass. He brought it forth again and again, and ever with deadly effect. They thought they wielded it themselves. No. It was in the hand of a more skilful master. They thought they wielded it against Jesus to his death. No. Satan wielded it against *them*: the savour of death unto death.

It is superfluous to point out the falsehood of these witnesses as they attempted to pervert it into a criminal charge. Jesus did not say, "I will destroy this temple," as they would represent, attempting if possible to make out a hostility on his part to the sacred edifice. Even construed as referring to that temple, he had only said, "Destroy ye this temple, or if ye destroy this temple I will raise it up again in three days." But even on this single point the two witnesses, we are told, could not agree in their testimony. And, in any event, the only thing they could prove by such a course was the injustice and baseness of the cause which they assayed to support.

"And the high priest arose and said unto him, Answerest thou nothing? What is it that these bear witness against thee? But Jesus held his peace" (Matt. xxvi. 62).

"Jesus held his peace." For what reason? "Behold, I lay in Zion a stumbling stone and rock of offence"— and there it must lie! It must not be taken out of the way. Now, for Jesus to answer them, to deprecate their false construction, to explain the import and innocence of his memorable response; to show how utterly harmless it was, how entirely different in its true import from the turn which had been given to it as indicating hostility to the sacred building—all this would have been to expound the spiritual oracle, thereby removing the stumbling stone and rock of offence; while its very mysteriousness constituted it the test and sign which divine wisdom saw meet to afford and continue in the circumstances. To have answered and repelled the accusation would have just destroyed the essential features of that enigma which was given to try their character and elicit their hidden guile. Divine righteousness forbade this mercy towards them and required that the veil should be left upon their minds, that the stumbling block should not be removed. For this reason Jesus is silent. He will neither deprecate nor set aside *their* construction. And as to *his own* meaning, there is still greater reason, in view of *it,* for his keeping silence. When his doctrine was aspersed, and the insinuation of secrecy and seductiveness was thrown out, Jesus warmly replied, vindicating his ministry from all obloquy, and boldly challenging an examination of all that he had said. The honour of his *prophetic* office demanded that he should at once speak out. But now, under this oracle, as Jesus understands and intends it, there is couched and concealed an allusion to the essential service of his *priestly* office, in which he is about to present himself as the slain Lamb, purging sin and procuring favour by the shedding of his blood, yea, by his obedience unto death. It is precisely now that he appears before God as the Lamb, and precisely now therefore that he becomes silent. For it is when brought as a lamb to the slaughter and a sheep before her shearers that he is dumb, opening not his mouth (Isa. liii. 7). Therefore Jesus holds his peace.

Shall we say that Jesus, in his silence, enjoys a comfort which his accusers know not of? For this oracle, anent which they provoke him ineffectually to speak his mind, while it is to them the savour of death unto death, must in other directions and on other minds be the savour of life unto life. If it proved so to the disciples ultimately, why might it not prove so immediately and in the meantime to Jesus himself? Why should we so hesitate to see the conformity between the experience of Jesus and that of his people as to forget that his " having in all things the pre-eminence " implies a transcendent fulfilment in him of all that can transpire in them? If those, therefore, who now wrested his words were dragging out of them repeated influences of death to their own moral nature, ministering to the strength of their own corruption and the fevered violence of their own evil passions, why may we not suppose that the lively oracle which was good but which they made death unto them, was meantime ministering joy and consolation to the silent and abused Divine sufferer at their bar? Yea, were they not holding up before him, as in a mirror, the glory of his own resurrection, his coming vindication, when by the glory of the Father he should rise from the dead, his flesh never having seen corruption? Remembering the finite and dependent nature of our Saviour's created spirit, and the necessity of consolation and hope—great consolation and good hope—to bear him through the fearful anguish of his dying hours, for, according to scriptural assertion, it was "for the joy set before him that he endured the cross, despising the shame," can we help wondering at the beautiful providence which so overruled the malignity of his enemies as to compel them to bring forward, in the crisis of his condemnation, the words spoken by himself long ere the deadly trial and baptism had come, and in which he had expressed his faith that the Christ must not only suffer but must also rise from the dead and enter into his glory? Unknown to themselves, these enemies were vividly presenting to him " the joy set before him " and the promise that " because he made his soul an offering for sin he should prolong his day and the pleasure of the Lord should prosper in his hand."   And when hanging on the cross, he again listened to the voice of malice taunting him with his declaration that the destroyed temple should in three days rise again, would not the blessed Jesus extract from it that sweet theme of consolation which the Holy Ghost had laid up for him in Scripture long ere he came in the flesh: " Therefore my flesh also shall rest in hope, for thou wilt not leave my soul in hell; neither wilt thou suffer thine holy one to see corruption " (Ps. xvi. 9, 10). For even thus did the tender love and infinite wisdom of the Father arrange for him that, in the very scoffs of his malignant foes, he should taste, while dying, of the savour and triumph of his resurrection!

Even so may the memory of former faithfulness and zeal, recalled and forced upon us by an enemy, unlock most sweetly a spring of all-sufficient consolation!

Let us close with some practical remarks.

1.   Beware of the disposition that would seek additional grounds or better opportunities for believing. These you have in sufficient abundance already, and to ask for more indicates, not a desire to believe, but a desire to justify your unbelief.   The voice of authority with

which Christ speaks to you, both in your own conscience and in his ordinances in the temple, is sufficient ground for you to receive and acknowledge him as one having authority and not as the scribes: as one entitled to rule and sway your whole inner man and all your outward life. You feel a strange force in his sacred word: you feel a peculiar striving of his Holy Spirit. It is the great Reformer of the Church seeking to cleanse the temple of your soul for his Father's pure and spiritual worship. Your worldly lusts; your absorbing desires for worldly prosperity; your wanderings of heart in divine ordinances; your cold formality; your ceremonious heartlessness; your dull and dreary bondage of spirit in prayer—to these Jesus points and says: "Take these things hence and worship my Father in spirit and in truth." You know, you feel, that when by his word and Spirit he thus addresses you, as he addresses you now, you have in your own secret misgivings, under the authority and force of such a call, proof sufficient that it is the Christ who is dealing with you. Beware of seeking to delay, waiting for a stronger conviction. You are only waiting till the conviction wear off. You are not desirous of finding ground and reason to believe on him and submit to him more profoundly; you are seeking to justify yourself in not believing at all. In such a frame it is a literal and terrible truth that "neither would you believe though one rose from the dead!"

2. Bring a very humble mind to the interpretation of the mysteries of the word of Christ. "Eye hath not seen, nor ear heard, nor have entered into the heart of man, the things which God hath prepared for them that love him." If any man would be wise, let him become a fool that he may be wise. The grand doctrines of salvation are far beyond the natural powers of the human mind to grasp them. And when proudly you judge them on principles of natural reason, they will only appear to you more and

more foolish and provokingly mysterious. It is this inability of reason to see their loveliness and glory which often irritates the unrenewed mind. " How can this man give us his flesh to eat? And they went back and walked no more with him." It was a hard saying. So also is that other saying: " He shall be for a stone of stumbling and a rock of offence to both the houses of Israel, for a gin and for a snare to the inhabitants of Jerusalem " (Isa. viii. 14). Still, it abides for ever true that " he that believeth shall not be confounded." " Father, I thank thee because thou hast hid these things from the wise and prudent, and hast revealed them unto babes " (Matt. xi. 25).

3. Bear in mind that your rejection of Christ to-day may reappear at a future time in more aggravated form and with more ruinous and destructive effects. The scoff with which you scorn the Christ, whether in himself or in the person of some godly one whose Christian strictness you despise as too much of reformation and religion, while it may be but warrantable zeal for his Father's worship, may be treasured up for you by Satan till another day, brought out again when your heart shall have become still more depraved and made to do service by your mouth in his cause, when he has some still more wicked work for you to do. Beware, therefore, of every feeling that would refuse immediate and absolute obedience to the Lord. Whatever would refuse or question his claim to your immediate faith in him and your immediate acquiescence in his purpose of cleansing the temple of your soul, rejoice that he is saying, " Take these things hence." And in your conscious inability to remove them, call on him to " take away the stony heart out of your flesh and give you an heart of flesh " (Ezek. xxxvi. 26).

4. In acknowledging the claims which Jesus puts forward to your believing confidence, your gratitude and

your cheerful service, let your whole heart rest with appropriating joy on his death and resurrection. Feed upon the mystery and fulness of truth and grace implied in the oracle: "Destroy this temple, and in three days I will raise it up again." In yourself you are a guilty sinner; a criminal doomed to die; a useless, barren fig tree; and the cry is gone out, Destroy it, cut it down. The only hope is in an advocate who shall himself be your substitute. And behold the substitute! Behold his vicarious, sacrificial death! Behold his glorious, federal resurrection! Be thou buried with him by engrafting of faith into his death; and like as he was raised up from the dead by the glory of the Father, even so shall you walk in newness of life. Ah! let the oracle anent the Lord's death and resurrection thus test your spiritual state: let it direct your spiritual aims; let it enlighten and rejoice your weary heart. And if enemies assail your peace and safety, God may overrule their assault to remind you of the foundation of your hopes and enable you thus to reply to those who would lay anything to the charge of God's elect: "It is Christ that died: yea, rather, that is risen again." For when the temple of his body was destroyed, in three days it was gloriously raised up again!

XII.

THE TRIAL—IV.

" NEVERTHELESS . . . HEREAFTER "!

"And the high priest answered and said unto him, I
adjure thee by the living God, that thou tell us whether
thou be the Christ, the Son of God. Jesus saith unto him,
Thou hast said: nevertheless, I say unto you, Hereafter shall
ye see the Son of man sitting on the right hand of power,
and coming in the clouds of heaven" (Matt. xxvi. 63, 64).

THE close of the trial is, on Jesus' part, exceedingly
solemn and sublime. The malicious and paltry charge, in
reference to destroying the temple and raising it up in
three days, has proved not in the least serviceable to his
prosecutors. The witnesses could not agree among
themselves; and Jesus, when questioned on the subject,
maintains a dignified silence. The high priest, therefore,
at last despairing of success by any of the methods
hitherto tried, now appeals with consummate hypocrisy
to God himself, and commands the prisoner, as on his
oath, and as before God, to speak the truth. " The high
priest answered, and said unto him, I adjure thee by the
living God, that thou tell us whether thou be the Christ,
the Son of God."

Thus appealed to by his Father's name and knowing
that his hour is come; willing, also, by his own act, to
surrender himself unto death for " this commandment
received he of his Father," Jesus, with all simplicity and
dignity, admits his personal glory as the Son of God and
his official mission as the Christ, referring the high priest,

however, to a future day for the final and no longer mistakeable demonstration of the truth of his avowal: "Jesus saith unto him, Thou hast said; nevertheless, I say unto you, Hereafter shall ye see the Son of man sitting on the right hand of power and coming in the clouds of heaven."

What a ray of glory this is falling, unlooked for, on the darkness of the scene, contrasting so singularly with the shame and humiliation of Jesus, a prisoner at the bar of man! How startlingly near this brings the two utmost opposites—the depth of abasement of the humbled Son of God, standing before sinners laden with a criminal charge and the climax of his glory when he shall sit a judge upon the throne of his Father, and all nations shall be gathered before him! The case against the prisoner may be closed immediately and carried against him. "Nevertheless," he takes his protest and appeal to a high tribunal, where his murderers must needs appear; where all needful extracts bearing on the decision shall be found safely lodged in the records of Omniscience; and where the throne shall be filled by this prisoner himself, whose protest shall then be justly settled and disposed of, when "every eye shall see him, and they also that pierced him; and all kindreds of the earth shall wail because of him."

Now, the introduction of this sublime allusion to the great day of the Lord may be viewed in reference either to Jesus or Caiaphas.

I. And in reference to Jesus, it is manifestly the fitting comfort in the hour of accusation; the suitable compensation for this special portion of his sufferings. What is the fair counterpoise or reward for Christ's humiliation in consenting thus to stand a criminal at the bar of man, the mark and butt of false accusers? See the shame that covers him, while slander is on every side, reproach and shame and dishonour! See the Son of the Blessed, set forth as son of Belial! standing as a humbled panel at the bar! What shall be the due reward? What but his elevation to the throne—the tribunal of the final, the universal judgment? "The Lord hath said unto my Lord, Sit thou at my right hand, until I make thy foes thy footstool." And all the tribes of the earth "shall see the Son of man coming in the clouds of heaven, with power and great glory."

For it is to be observed that not only is it true as a general principle that "because he humbled himself, therefore God also hath highly exalted him"; but this principle extends and realises itself even into minute particulars and details, so that the component elements, or successive eras and stages, of Christ's deep abasement, have their parallel and corresponding passages of glory in his high reward. The crown of thorns is replaced by the crown of glory; yea "many crowns are on his head." The cross on which he suffered becomes the true car of victory, in which he rides forth conquering and to conquer, subduing the antipathies of his people, renewing their wills, and securing their supreme affection. The chains in which he was led away a captive to Annas and Caiaphas entitled him to have a triumph decreed him, in which he is seen spoiling principalities and powers, making a show of them openly, carrying captivity captive, wresting the prey from the mighty, and breaking off from his people's souls the chains of Satan and sin, of hell and death; thus vindicating for them a glorious liberty which the captive Jesus obtained for them by temporarily surrendering his own. Even so, the shameful bar of Caiaphas is replaced and rewarded by the throne of judgment. For the special shame to which as the panel he has now submitted, the special joy set before him is the glory of sitting on the tribunal of final retribution. And reflecting on *that* joy set before him, he is content to despise *this* shame.

Hence it is observable that he speaks of this splendid prerogative not as an inalienable right belonging to him as the Son of God and in virtue of his Godhead, but as a reward conferred upon him as " the Son of man," and in glorification of his human nature. " Ye shall see the *Son of Man* sitting on the right hand of power." As the Eternal God, in unity of substance with the Father and the Spirit, the Son of God is, and cannot but be, the judge of all the earth. Nor can any but a Divine person possess those qualifications of infallible knowledge and heart-searching omniscience, of infinite wisdom and righteousness, without which the procedures of eternal judgment could not in unerring rectitude be conducted. But the elevation of the human nature, in its indissoluble union with the Godhead, to the tribunal of the final judgment, so that it is the man Christ Jesus who shall judge the quick and the dead, and God " shall judge the world by that *man* of whom he hath given assurance in raising him from the dead "—this it is that presents to us the infinite majesty in which Jesus shall appear on the great day of reckoning as a reward conferred upon him by the appointment of his Father, as well as a prerogative belonging to him by the necessity of his Godhead. And thus we read in his own words that " the Father hath given him authority to execute judgment also because he is the Son of man " (John v. 27).

Who shall enter into the mind of Jesus at this wondrous moment, when despised and rejected as a criminal, his feelings all trampled on and outraged, his good name and reputation loaded with dishonour, his liberty restrained, his person smitten, stricken, and afflicted, and sentence of condemnation about to pass upon him, even unto death? What unspeakable depression! What gloom, what sadness! But he thought of his Father's righteousness and his own sure reward. He thought of the joy set before him. His mind fled for refuge to the recompense of the reward. And from Caiaphas the high priest's bar, he transferred himself, in the anticipation of

faith, to his Father's glory and throne as the judge of all
the earth. " Fret not thyself," O meek and lowly One,
" because of evil-doers." To thee, as the first-born
among many brethren, who shall enter the kingdom of
heaven, like thee, through much tribulation, to thee as
unto them, to thee pre-eminently above them, belongeth
the promise: " Commit thy way unto the Lord, and he
shall bring it to pass; and he shall bring forth thy righteousness like the light, and thy judgment as the noonday."
Thou shalt be seen " at the right hand of power, coming
in the clouds of heaven," and all thy maligned and
afflicted, thy meek and contrite saints, along with thee
(Psalm xxxvii. 1-4).

II.   But it is especially in its bearing on Caiaphas, his
rude interlocutor, that this sublime reply is to be considered. The substance and theme of it, considered as
material for consolation to the afflicted prisoner, might
have served their object, and been, in the joy of them,
sufficiently before him in secret thought and meditation;
and, indeed, how often is the Christian borne through a
trying position by the hidden influence of considerations
that strengthen his action into power or subdue his soul
into patience, without the utterance or any manifestation
to man, of what these considerations are. Thus the
anticipation of his coming glory as the judge might have
been cherished secretly in Jesus' mind, as the sufficiently
counterbalancing consideration to the present shame. But
for the sake of Caiaphas, and with a view to its bearing
upon him and his responsibility, this awful thought must
be expressed.

And as in reference to Jesus himself this prospect held
the place of a counterpoise or compensation, so in reference to Caiaphas the utterance of it ought, in the *first*
place, to have served for an explanation; and, in the
second place, to have been submitted to as an awful
remonstrance; and failing these uses, in the *third* place, it

sufficed as a closing remit, with certification, to the final decision, when the end shall come!

1. And in the first place, as an explanation, this solemn statement contained in it, if Caiaphas would but so have regarded and received it, no small amount of merciful design. For in thus addressing him, Jesus took out of the way a stumbling-block on which the high priest might be apt to fall, and on which, not having had it pointed out to him, he might have been afterwards disposed to rest his vindication. How *can* this be any other, he might be saying to himself, how can this be any other than some wild adventurer, some stray fanatic, practising on the credulity of the people or practising even on his own, in putting forward a claim so great as that of being the Son of God? If he really were so, how would his Father suffer him to be in such lowly guise, in such deep distress and degradation? And would he not himself have called legions of angels from heaven, rather than have fallen into our officers' hands, and suffered himself to be dragged here as a prisoner? What, he might have said, turning to the afflicted humble man before him, What! shall one brought down into the depths so low as *you,* put forward claims so lofty? Are you not ashamed to call yourself the Christ, the King of Israel, the Son of the Blessed, when thus fallen into disgrace, thus destitute of honour, wealth, friends, power, liberty; when thus impoverished, forsaken, sorrowful, a captive moving to and fro, a prisoner, a panel? How can such as *you* claim the sacred honour of Messiah's glorious name?

Jesus said unto him, I *am* the Christ, the Son of the Blessed. It may seem inconsistent with this honour that I should be clothed with reproach and revilings. I may be humbled unto suffering and shame, and such humiliation may seem to prejudice, or even to extinguish, the evidence of my Divine Original and my Divine Commission. Nevertheless, I speak the truth—the truth that shall yet be vindicated from all suspicion, from all semblance of inconsistency; that shall yet be justified before all flesh, for " Hereafter thou shalt see the Son of man at the right hand of power, and coming in the clouds of heaven."

Now, viewed in this light, Christ's sublime reference to the future may be regarded as a very gracious interposition, fitted to save his persecutor from falling on what might naturally enough, in his state and temper of mind, have proved a stumbling-block. Jesus substantially reminds him that a state of suffering, yea, of shame, cannot in itself disprove the sufferer to be the Messiah; that, on the contrary, the Messiah of the prophets is to be identified expressly by sufferings, followed by glory (I Pet. i. 11), and that the adverse hour in which he, this lowly and afflicted sufferer, now stands before his proud accuser, is one that shall be followed and be recompensed by a glory that shall sweep away the shame. Thus warned to judge on a larger basis of particulars, or on a fuller range of view, especially warned to leave room in his imagination for the countervailing facts that might yet occur to prove this lowly one no pretender, though all things do seem to be against him now; and warned above all to admit the light of eternity and eternal judgments on this matter, Caiaphas might have escaped the snare of the devil. If he did not, it was not because an explanation was refused, an explanation that might have been serviceable, and ought to have been sufficient. Nor could he afterwards plead in self-defence the prisoner's shameful and forsaken estate; for he was assured that " nevertheless " he was the Christ, the Son of God, and should " hereafter " be vindicated as such on the throne of universal judgment, on the right hand of power.

2. But not only may this be regarded as a very important explanation set before the high priest's mind, well fitted to guide his judgment and modify his opinion:

it ought to have been felt as a very solemn remonstrance to keep him back from his purposed line of proceeding. For just as Caiaphas might vindicate his own opinion in rejecting the claims of Jesus, on the ground of his evident humiliation and helplessness, so might he be justifying to himself his own conduct in condemning him and compassing his death on the same grounds. Yea, in the bare fact that heaven interfered not to prevent him from executing his evil purpose might Caiaphas perversely read a sort of toleration for what he was about to do, or at least a proof that what he was about to do was nothing so dreadful as the crucifixion of the Lord's anointed. It seems very much to this state of mind, and which, in the essence of it, and in the principle involved, is by no means an uncommon one—that Christ's sublime expostulation addresses itself.

You may think that the very power you have over me at present disproves my claims and allows you, at least, lightly to set them aside and follow your own desires and devices. You may suppose that were my claims really valid, were Messiahship mine, and Sonship to God; my Father, that sent me into the world, would render it impossible for you to injure me; would interpose for my relief; would force you to perceive your error and constrain you to abandon your course and case against me. Nay; but it is not *now* that the irresistible demonstration shall be given. If you are resolved to reject me now, you may: you shall be allowed to do so; yea, to condemn, to crucify, the Lord of glory. It is not yet that unquenchable conviction shall be flashed on the understandings of all men and disbelief rendered an absolute and physical impossibility. Your king cometh unto you *now,* meek and lowly. "He doth not cry nor lift up, nor cause his voice to be heard in the streets." He speaketh in a still small voice, the most powerful of all in convincing the meek and lowly, the humble and contrite in heart—the most effective in filling *them* with the full assurance of understanding and the infallible certainty of divine faith. But pride, and prejudice, and passion, these he will not perforce overrule or overwhelm. The proud shall have scope given them to err, to fall backward and be broken and be snared and taken, for the evidences of his truth and commission shall not be such as to compel and overbear men's convictions; nor are they such as will compel or overbear yours. The time for leaving you without even the semblance of objection, and without even the appearance of excuse, that time is not yet come. But it *will* come. Meantime, it would appear that nothing but irresistible restraint, nothing but overpowering physical control, can keep you from the guilt of imbruing your hands in innocent blood, the blood of the Christ, the Son of God! Be it known that no such restraint shall be exercised. You are allowed another sort of moral scope of action, another sort of moral play to your passions, than such limitation would allow. You may condemn me and crucify me. "Nevertheless, *hereafter* you shall see me at the right hand of power and coming in the clouds of heaven." *Then* there will be no more scope for error: no more freedom of your own will *then*. The overpowering convictions will *then* come, and the impossibility of doing me injustice *then!* Meantime, though I summon not the right hand of power to free me, nor gather round me for concealment, nor for glory, the clouds of heaven now, still I say unto thee, I am the Christ, the Son of God; and though this absence of forceful, physical, unsparing proof may embolden you to take such liberties with me, "Nevertheless, I say unto you, Hereafter"—it shall not be so.

And what but this is the style of remonstrance which the proud sinner needs again and again to have addressed to him? You seem to think sin less sinful because it is left to your own option to sin. You think it cannot be so dreadful an evil or so infinitely hateful to God, else your way would be more effectually and painfully hedged up against it. If God's claims on you were really so strong as the Bible says, he would make it far more impossible for you to mistake or be misled concerning them. If this really were the Christ who is knocking at the door of your heart, the sound would be louder, or he would force an entrance without ceremony and without delay, and leave you not in doubt for a moment of his Messiahship and Sovereignty. But then you see nothing so striking, you hear nothing so overwhelmingly convincing. If a hand seems to be laid upon you to restrain you from iniquity, it is not so strongly laid upon you but you can contrive to shake it off. If you are forbidden to follow your evil courses, you are not so effectually prevented but that many an open door is still left before you. If this holy law of God asserts its prerogatives and claims, it speaks so quietly, it seems to be now in disguise, almost in disgrace. There is so little of the thunder and the lightning of Sinai: and the fence erected seems so easily broken through, that surely it could not be a Divine hand that placed it there. And then this law of God: it stands over you in the aspect of a judge, no doubt, but it seems so neglected; the multitudes around pay so little regard or respect to its demands—it seems almost, like Christ himself, a prisoner at the bar, forsaken on all sides and wholly in your power. And the very option that you have of silencing its requirements and setting aside its honour almost emboldens you to do so with the hope of impunity, if not with the air of innocence itself.

3. Ah! but be it known to you, this is precisely the feature of a state of probation. For in reality it is far more Caiaphas that is on his trial than Christ. It is far more your moral state and temper and character before God that are tried and brought to light than the claims of that law and that God and Saviour whom you refuse

to hear, that Redeemer whom you may be even venturing to reject and crucify afresh. It is far more *your* probation than *his* that is in progress. And the very principle at work is this, that sin and disbelieve you *may:* it is in a sense allowed to you; there is scope and possibility for it. God will not interfere to overwhelm you into obedience or to constrain and compel your repentance and faith. No; you may do the evil, but it is with a drawback and a certification; it is with a " nevertheless " and with a solemn remit to the great " Hereafter." What! Do you think that because God has not made sin impossible, because you have it in your choice and power to sin, because between your purpose to sin and the action of sin he does not interflash his mighty hand, warning you back and keeping you perforce and physical restraint from achieving your designed iniquity; because you simply *can* sin and are not paralysed ere doing so, simply because God leaves it possible for you to sin and allows your sin to pass without immediate retribution, do you think on that account that the sin is less sinful or that you have done with it and it has done with you? Nay; the warnings of conscience may have been feeble; the restraints of providence may have been not insuperable; the strivings of the Spirit may have been quite resistible, and been by you effectually resisted, and so you have gone on your way. " Nevertheless, I say unto you, *Hereafter . . .*"

Ah! how often this takes place! Men would like to be prevented from sinning by sheer force: they will sin and sin and sin because God does not make it impossible for them to sin. Balaam was dealt with so as to make his sin all but literally impossible. The ass turned aside into the field, for she saw the angel's flaming sword, but Balaam smote her, and forced his way forward on his covetous and sinful mission. And again the ass bruised his foot against the wall. But again he urged on against all restraint. And once more the awe-stricken brute falls down beneath her secure, presumptuous master, and in that master's kindled wrath and madness he is wellnigh slain. Then " the dumb ass, speaking with man's voice, forbade the madness of the prophet." Last of all, his eyes being opened to see the angel of the Lord with a drawn sword, and the angel assuring him that he is come out to withstand him because his way is perverse, what saith the wayward and the perverse prophet? " If it displease thee, I will get me back again" (Num. xxii. 22-34).

" If it displease thee "! Can he question that? And this conditional promise of obedience—" I will get me back again if it displease thee." Can he dare to put it in such a form? What does he mean but simply that he will cease from his perverse course only if God will make it utterly impossible for him to pursue it; that he will yet hold on if God will only withdraw his restraints and leave him an open path? Nothing but downright force will he yield to. Nothing but another peremptory command, backed by a freshly threatening wave and flash of the angel's sword before his face will secure his relinquishing the path of sin. No; God will not give him *that*. He has got exceedingly abundantly enough already to demonstrate that the course he has taken " displeases " the Lord. Any loyalty of heart towards Jehovah would have kept him clear and safe from evil from the first. But a heart at enmity to God leads him astray even to the end. For the heart of a child will accept the Father's will, though instructed only by his eye: " I will guide thee with mine eye." The heart of an alien, a stranger, or a foe, will withstand every influence and disobey if disobedience still be possible. Balaam will go because he is not sternly, and to the end, and forcibly prevented. And the angel retires and leaves the way open for him, and

Balaam goes with the princes. " Nevertheless . . .
hereafter!"

Forbearance now and judgment afterwards: *these* are
the elements of a probationary state. There is no probation at all if faith is forced and disobedience rendered
impossible. Men must have scope, amidst a varied play
of interests and motives and temptations, to display what
spirit they are of; and, alas! simply because they have
scope for this they show that their spirit is evil. Because
sentence against an evil work is not speedily executed,
the children of men have their hearts fully set in them
to do evil. " Nevertheless . . . hereafter!"

Yes, this drawback, this certification, this " Nevertheless," always accompanies sin. And well should it be
weighed and pondered. No human eye beholds your
secret wickedness: Nevertheless! Your godly mother's
voice is silenced when she would dissuade; her kind hand,
that never did you harm, is easily shaken off when it
would in love detain you from going out on the evening's
frolic and the folly, and you go: Nevertheless! Your
own conscience speaks a little—at least a little—and you
whistle as you go, to silence it, and brace yourself up to
brush its remonstrances aside or put them down, and so,
onward you go: Nevertheless! The clamour and the
mirth of wild companionship gives you, in a little while,
the victory over every scruple; and as the crackling of
thorns under a pot, your mirthful voice is heard, loudest
among the loud, where God is forgotten and the thought
of living soberly and righteously and godly in this present
evil world would be resented as impertinent if even
mentioned among you, and you are all as joyous as if
there were no " Hereafter." Nevertheless!

What! Is this worldliness—is this wickedness—all?
Does it end here? Have you done with it? Rather, has
it done with you? Nay, it meets you again. It treasures
itself up; secretly, perhaps; steadily, however; growingly,

accumulating; a cup filling up, filling up always, filling up silently; making no noise about it. "Nevertheless, hereafter, ye shall see the Son of man coming in the clouds of heaven, and every eye shall see him, and they also that pierced him shall wail because of him." "Rejoice, O young man, in thy youth, and let thy heart cheer thee in the days of thy youth, and walk in the ways of thine heart, and in the sight of thine eyes; but know thou that for all these things God will bring thee into judgment." Always this "Nevertheless"—always that terrible "Hereafter." "Remember the days of darkness, for they shall be many."

But before the darkness come you have to-day as a day of visitation. Jesus summons you *now* to examine and prove his claims—to search and try his power and willingness to bless you. He consents to put himself, as it were, at the bar; and you are to pronounce on whether he shall have your acquiescence in his mission and his message; your acceptance of his terms and righteousness and grace; your reverence, your gratitude, your love. He will not overflash your whole soul with evidence of his infinite preciousness, and his infinitely perfect power to make you blessed. That style of convincing men pertains not to the dispensation of preliminary probation, but to final judgment. He will give you sufficient proof to satisfy every sincere inquiry. He will sufficiently dispel, or at least disarm, every semblance of a ground or reason for doubt. He will more and more fully advance your conviction to the full assurance of understanding. But if you refuse him because he cometh unto you meek and lowly—not crying nor lifting up his voice—speaking only by his word, which you may silence, if you please, by shutting it and putting it away, or calling you only by his ambassadors, and these men of like passions with yourselves, mere earthen vessels, in which you may refuse to recognise divine treasure of excellency of power from on high, then you must be allowed your own way, even as a wilful man will have his way. Only, in parting with you, Christ, by his word and Spirit and messengers, and vicegerent in your own conscience within —Christ in many ways protests, and remits you to the final judgment bar. He leaves you to your course, but it is with certification that the whole case must be over-hauled again, where there shall be no more remitting of *it*, and no remission of sin; for " Nevertheless, Hereafter " you shall stand before the judgment-seat of Christ!

Ah, Caiaphas! you fancy that if this case were so important, visible beams of glory would glow around that prisoner's head, and flashing swords of wrath from heaven would warn you to lay no rude hand upon him. Nay, but you must be allowed the liberty of sinning even this length, if your carnal mind in enmity against God will have it so; and only " hereafter " will it be suitable to give those vindications of the Son of God which you would demand as preliminary to your letting him alone. But those vindications will come. *He* shall one day be the judge who is now at the bar. "*Hereafter* ye shall see Him coming in the clouds of heaven."

And you, O unfixed and wavering, procrastinating soul! you are waiting for a better season, and a stronger influence, and a clearer demonstration that Jesus is the Christ; or at least for a more powerful conviction that an interest in him is the one thing needful. Ah! you are waiting for the time when by some new and unheard-of instrumentality—some strange and weird influence, as of one rising from the dead—you will find it no more possible to waver or no more possible to wait. Beware! You have all the evidence and all the means you will ever have; and in waiting for something more to make your unbelief impossible, you are waiting for what will never come till the great and irretrievable " Hereafter." Jesus is the Christ, the Son of God, *now;* and his true faith and

holy religion is assuredly the one thing needful, in however gentle strains it commends itself to your acceptance
or however rude the repulses and refusals it consents to
endure at your hands. You may refuse it; you may
neglect the great salvation. You are at liberty, if you
please, to overlook all the considerations whereby it can
abundantly attest its intrinsic excellence, its exact suitableness and rich sufficiency. You *may* set aside the
Messiah's claims. If you think that Baal is God you are not
hindered from serving him; and if sin and the world be
your chosen portion, it is not in the gospel to fray you away
by force. But you must carry with you, as a sting which
can never be plucked out, this distressing drawback on
your pleasures, which will embitter all your enjoyment of
them as often as it is allowed to speak—this strange and
painful and secret protest, which Christ nails on the door
of that heart where he has knocked in vain—this ominous,
this burdensome, this haunting "Nevertheless," this
unsilenceable appeal, this inevitable complaint and remit,
which always hands you onward to a dark "Hereafter."
"Rejoice, O young man, in thy youth, and let thy heart
cheer thee in the days of thy youth, and walk in the ways
of thine heart, and in the sight of thine eyes; but know
that for all these things the Lord shall call thee into
judgment."

You may refuse to repent and believe the gospel. You
may put away from you the call to take your Bible in
your hand, and in your closet cry to Him who seeth in
secret, and there submit yourself to the Saviour's righteousness and surrender yourself to the Saviour's service.
You may, time after time, reject the Christ. "Nevertheless!" "Hereafter!" "Hereafter ye shall see him sitting
on the right hand of power and coming in the clouds of
heaven."

How very different is the style and kind of that
"Hereafter" to which Jesus will point you, if you come

to him as a contrite and sincere believer, as an earnest
soul seeking life and salvation, having done with all
duplicity, desiring no more to deceive yourself, and
resolved no more to be deceived! Are you thus in secret
seeking the Lord? Have you made a point of truly considering Messiah's claims, treating him not as a helpless
prisoner at your bar but as he really is, your Lord and
King? And have you sought an ear to hear and a heart
to understand that gospel of salvation which was sealed
in the depths of his abasement, that office of the priesthood, with all its riches secured for the poor by his
poverty, by his unmurmuring obedience and silent suffering, even as a sheep before her shearers is dumb? Are
you coming to him sincerely, seeking to find him that
Christ to you which he has been to those who have put
their trust in him, who have looked unto him and been
lightened, been unburdened, cleansed, comforted and
blessed? And when invited to taste and see that he is
gracious, do you without duplicity, and without delay,
yield obedience to the call, "Come and see"? (John i.
46-51). Then the heart of Jesus yearns over you.
"Behold," saith he, "an Israelite indeed, in whom is no
guile." Do you say unto him, "Rabbi, whence knowest
thou me?" Ah! long ere they know him, "the Lord
knoweth them that are his." "When thou wast under
the fig tree I saw thee." While thy secret prayer
ascended with groanings that could not be uttered; while
thy burdened soul laboured to throw off its anxious load;
when thy weary wandering spirit first looked abroad,
affrighted, on the ocean of influences and powers of the
world to come on which it is afloat, seeking some pole-
star, seeking some chart, seeking some haven of rest,
seeking some pilot skilled and powerful, gracious and
faithful and true; when struggling with thoughts too
great for you to understand and desires too deep for you
to express; with questions of eternal interests fairly

raised, and none but God now evidently able to solve them to your satisfaction and your salvation; when thus, as a little child, no longer bracing up in pride, or braving it out in presumption, but breaking down in helplessness and contrition, as one by father and by mother and by all forsaken, you fled to the Lord to take you up; then, " under the fig-tree," in that scene of tears, in that agony of thought, in that crisis of awakening, in that birth-place of faith and penitence, in that hour of prayer, " I saw thee," saith Jesus Christ the Lord. My Spirit it was who led thee there and made intercession with those groanings which could not be uttered; and, unbeknown to thee, I made thee mine; and now that thou art taking me as thine, is it not because " I prevented thee in the day of thy calamity," because " I considered thy trouble and knew thy soul in its adversity "—because I anticipated thee secretly with my grace, and girded thy soul in its weakness, and strengthened thy soul in its woe?" Thus does the Saviour reply to you. And now, recognising Christ's kind and gracious eye as having been upon you in all your spiritual anxiety and prayers, and Christ's kind and gracious Spirit as having inspired and secretly guided and controlled them all, you say to him, for a new light has broken over your own heart and history from Messiah's presence with you, and Messiah's glory falls upon all your life and destiny now: " Rabbi, thou art the Son of God, thou art the king of Israel!"

" And Jesus answered and said unto him, Because I said unto thee, I saw thee under the fig-tree, believest thou? Thou shalt see greater things than these. Verily, verily, I say unto thee, *Hereafter* thou shalt see heaven opened, and the angels of God ascending and descending upon the Son of man." Yes, thy " Hereafter " shall be bright and brightening. It shall be like Jacob's, as infefted at Bethel into the Covenant of thy God, into the family of grace, into the fellowship of heaven—that fellowship of the spirits of just men made perfect, and the innumerable company of angels, and the heavenly Jerusalem, and Mount Zion, the city of the living God; in which, living even now by faith as raised up together with Christ and made to sit with him in heavenly places, thou shalt find the Son of God the medium and the mediator of all holy communion with thy God and heavenly privileges with all the brethren, the strong Daysman in whom you have a constant standing in in heaven's favour, and the love and unseen service of heaven's ministering holy ones. " Hereafter " you shall have a growing insight into the intercourse which the Son of man is the medium and the means of maintaining between heaven and earth. " Hereafter " you shall see with growing clearness your own place in the household of faith, and the path of life (your own open path) onward and upward to the household in heaven.

Ah! this is another " Hereafter " such as the believer may delight to anticipate: very different indeed from that which was denounced to Caiaphas—no burdensome, no ominous, no heavy-sounding summons, coming forward as it were from the dark unknown, but a glad and delightsome thought, telling of the darkness as now passed and the true light now shining, and shining more and more unto the perfect day. Viewed in its large and truly comprehensive aspect, the believer's future, the believer's " Hereafter," comes on step by step, bringing with it nothing dreadful, nothing doubtful, nothing really to shrink from. " Thou shalt guide me by thy counsel and afterwards receive me to glory." Even in thy future course on earth, " Hereafter thou shalt see heaven opened and the angels of God ascending and descending on the Son of man." A stone may be your pillow—the cold earth your bed. You may be leaving your father's home and going to the land of the stranger. Nevertheless, in reality, your " Hereafter," in its spiritual essence, in its abiding elements, in its really great and important features, shall be a seeing more and more into heaven, as a home opened for you and kept open by the intervention of the Son of God, the King of Israel, in whom you are an heir of the kingdom and in whom you are truly blessed.

You must either side with Caiaphas in rejecting the Christ or with Nathaniel in receiving him. Each of them has his " Hereafter." And the question is, which of these two " Hereafters " do you prefer? " To-day, while it is called to-day," you have your choice! " Behold, now is the accepted time: behold, now is the day of salvation."

XIII

THE TRIAL—V.

CONDEMNED!

" THERE IS THEREFORE . . . (Rom. viii. 1).

"Then the high priest rent his clothes, saying, He hath spoken blasphemy; what further need have we of witnesses? behold, now ye have heard his blasphemy. What think ye? They answered and said, He is guilty of death" (Matt. xxvi. 65, 66).

"Then the high priest rent his clothes, and saith, What need we any further witnesses? Ye have heard the blasphemy: what think ye? And they all condemned him to be guilty of death" (Mark xiv. 63, 64).

THE protest and appeal which Jesus took against the Sanhedrim, summoning them to his own bar on the day when the great white throne shall be set and the heavens and the earth shall flee away, brought the trial to a crisis and conclusion. He has evidently claimed to be the Son of God. He has made himself equal with God. If he be not in very deed the Messiah, or if the Messiah of the prophets be not held forth in the testimony of the Spirit of Christ which was in them, as a Divine person, the man that is the Father's fellow; then this Jesus who stands before them, and who has ventured in such unsparing terms to remit them with certification to his judgment-seat at the last day, must be a blasphemer. Settling it firmly that he is not the Messiah, and resolved that noth-ing shall induce them to open or consider that question, they have now found him using language which, save on the supposition of what they will not for a moment regard as possible, may and must be denounced as blasphemy. With a sanctimonious and solemn and well-acted pretence of veneration for the name and the glory of God, the high priest dramatically and tragically indicates his abhorrence of the alleged crime; sums up and rests the whole on what has just transpired from the prisoner himself, as sufficient to condemn him out of his own mouth; and, charging the jury so to speak, in the most summary and prejudiced and peremptory manner, demands their verdict. " He rent his clothes, saying, He hath spoken blasphemy; what need have we of further witnesses? Behold, now ye have heard his blasphemy: what think ye?" Nor do they exhibit a moment's hesitation or indicate the least difference of opinion, or take any time for consultation. Summarily, immediately, unanimously, they bring in a verdict of Guilty. " They answered and said, He is guilty of death." " They all condemned him to be guilty of death."

" Of death"! Of nothing less than death! For " the wages of sin is death," and " the soul that sinneth, it shall surely die." " Guilty of death"!

Thus the Lord of glory is in the position of a condemned prisoner, lying under sentence of death! Let us turn aside to see this great sight—our Lord's condemnation.

And this condemnation, supposing his judges were right in refusing to regard him as Messiah, was according to law. So far they spake truly to Pilate when they said, " We have a law, and by our law he ought to die because he made himself the Son of God." For if he were not indeed the Christ, he had undeniably become liable to the penalty which God, by the mouth of Moses, had denounced on the blasphemer: " He that blasphemeth the name of the Lord shall surely be put to death; as well the stranger as he that is born in the land, when he

blasphemeth the name of the Lord, shall be put to death."
It is even provided that he shall be " brought without the
camp " (Lev. xxvi. 14-16) exactly as " Christ also suffered
without the gate " (Heb. xiii. 12, 13).

Thus Jesus appears before us under the condemnation
of the Law; and setting aside the unrighteous action of
human instrumentality, save as bringing about what the
hand and counsel of God determined before should be
done, let us esteem him, in the proper meaning of the
terms, " stricken and smitten of God."   Let us regard him
as " condemned by heaven."

And now, what can this great sight mean?   The Lord
of glory held fast as a criminal, and now a convict,
" condemned," held " guilty of death "!   What reflections should this suggest?   And what emotions?   And
what duties may this scene entail or what demands may
it enforce upon us?   What is the grand and first improvement that we must make of our Lord's condemnation?

Our first improvement of it is to turn it to account,
personally, by faith in a way of grasping, wielding,
pleading it for our own deliverance from all condemnation.

How gloriously we are warranted to do so!   Was
Jesus worthy, O my soul, of this condemnation to death?
Full well thou knowest that he was " holy, harmless,
undefiled, and separate from sinners."   And how then
wilt thou vindicate the great Judge of all the earth in
laying sentence of death, by his own hand and determinate counsel, upon his dear Son, in whom was no
iniquity, and in whose mouth there was no guile; who
was fairer than the children of men, worthy even of the
infinite fulness of the Father's love?   Say not that the
Father can vindicate his own justice and counsel in this
dread drama in the Sanhedrim at Jerusalem, where the
Eternal God, in the person of the Son incarnate, has
decree of death adjudged unto him.   Very true and sure
it is that the Father can justify his own part in this great

mystery. Without thee or thy intervention in any shape or form, the righteousness of God in the cross of Christ shall shine forth with overpowering splendour. And it shall be seen that he bare in his own body the sins of many and died a substitute, the just for the unjust, the living head, responsible, by eternal covenant and voluntary undertaking, for the countless multitudes, his members, whom the Father hath given to him.

But, O my soul, thou hast a duty of thine own to discharge in vindication of the justice of God in condemning the Holy Jesus. And there is a sin of which thou must take heed lest thou be guilty of it—for, alas! many are—whereby, so far as thou art concerned, thou wouldst be doing thy part in concealing and compromising, eclipsing and extinguishing, the justice of God in this condemnation of his Son: even so as that if all men should finally be found guilty with thee of the same grievous sin (though that can never be), the justice of God would be found effectually concealed, compromised, eclipsed indeed; yea, unequivocally extinguished for ever.

What is that sin? It is the sin of unbelief, of proud, impenitent, independent, self-sufficient or despairing unbelief; the sin of standing apart from Christ; of attempting to maintain before God a separate footing of thine own; of offering to deal with God in and by thyself —an attempt and offer which, by their rejection on the part of God, and by dreary sense of failure on thine own part, issue, alas! too often in thy ceasing to attempt to deal in earnestness or truth with God at all.

Shall it be said, O my soul, that having seen the Just One tried and condemned, thou didst leave Jehovah to justify this His " counsel " and procedure as best He might, and leave the Church to justify Him by receiving Jesus as her substitute, acknowledging him the bearer of her sin and sorrow, her condemnation and her death deserved; but that as for thee, when asked to explain the mystery, to add any element of personal demonstration of thine own to show the justice of God herein, thou hadst nothing to say, thou hadst no honest, heartfelt, loyal proof to give? Be that far from thee, O my soul! Come hither into this court of justice as thou art, a sinner worthy of death, for " the wages of sin is death." Come, and as if there were no other possibility of making it righteous for God to suffer this sentence of death to fall on Jesus, do thy part to make it righteous. Say, as if there were no other poor sinner to say it, or needing to say it: " He is here as my substitute and surety, and that is the ground and explanation of the Father's righteousness in condemning him." Say it as if in rivalry with all the saints of God to rescue the Father's justice from the imputation of condemning the innocent. Lay thy sins on the Lamb of God, himself the sinless, that there may be sin for this condemnation righteously to alight upon, for this sentence of death justly to avenge. True, there are others that come along with thee, a people whom no man can number. But the responsibility lies all unbroken on thyself as much as if thou were here alone. For as Christ breaks not up his saving power and love and righteousness into countless shreds and fragments, allocating a share to each of the redeemed, but makes each partaker of all, insomuch that each can say, as if he stood alone, " He loved *me* and gave himself for *me*," so on each, not broken into shreds and elements, minute and numerous as the great multitude of the redeemed, but whole and entire, as if on him alone depended all the issue, responsibility is laid to come by faith, and so, standing at the bar with Jesus—Jesus the holy representative, and thy sinful soul the true and guilty panel—to link on, and merge, and blend and identify thine own case with his; and then to say with all the redeemed (what alone can render Jesus' condemnation just): " Surely he hath borne our griefs, he hath carried our sorrows: he was wounded for our transgressions, he was bruised for our iniquities; the chastisement of our peace was upon him; and with his stripes we are healed. All we like sheep have gone astray: we have turned every one to his own way; and the Lord hath laid on him the iniquity of us all " (Isa. liii. 4-6).

For it is a high and glorious duty to come as a lost, awakened, convinced transgressor, and freely, frankly, boldly, cast myself, with all my heart and soul, into the divine plan and purpose whereof this condemnation of Jehovah's Messiah forms an epoch so astonishing. It is not my privilege merely, as freely invited and earnestly besought of God. That is very wonderful: nor can I really awake from the sleep of worldliness and the deep-drugged slumber of sin, to hear my Maker's voice ringing in my ears in the language of entreaty and compassion, without feeling that to speak thus to one who long amidst His kindness lived dead to His very existence, " without God in the world," must argue a boundlessness of love and pity such that assuredly His thoughts cannot be as my thoughts, nor His ways as my ways. And surprised, indeed, may I be to find that it is my inalienable privilege, as addressed by the embassy of reconcilation, to return and find peace with God and salvation from all my ruin.

But it is not merely as a blessed privilege that this falls happily to my lot. Nor is it merely as one selfishly grasping at a scheme which promises deliverance from the wrath to come, and communication of countless and desirable good things that I am to believe on Jesus. To believe on Jesus: to go and stand at that bar and say, in self-condemnation and abhorrence, " I am the guilty, and I confess it; against thee, thee only have I sinned, madly defying thy threatened wrath, worthy of death and a fearful looking for of judgment," and at that bar, while the determinate sentence of God's counsel is about to go forth even unto death against the Just One, to slip in beneath the falling sentence my sin, my confession, my condemnation, so that there may be a just ground for the sentence, and so that God may be justified when he speaketh, and clear when he judgeth both Jesus of Nazareth and me—that he may be faithful and just in forgiving me (Ps. li. 4; I John i. 9): to do this is to do my part in placing the divine righteousness in a clear and vindicated point of view—to do my part in evidencing that Jesus stood there " the just for the unjust," truly liable in their responsibility, he that knew no sin " made sin for them "; and therefore not unjust, but, on the contrary, very righteous was God the Father in condemning, and in being " pleased " to condemn and to " bruise " the Son of his love. For if I stand apart from Christ, if I manage and contrive to bear in my bosom my evil conscience towards God, my offended Lawgiver, drugging it with more sin, while drinking still from broken cisterns— if thus I go about saying, " Who will show us any good?" refusing to confess my estrangement from God, refusing to end it by returning to Him as a confessed sinner, pleading Christ as my suffering substitute, whose condemnation shall free me from condemnation and whose death shall give me life immortal; if I will not come and, in short, link on my case and destiny with that of Christ; I virtually say that, as far as I am concerned, I do not care though the righteousness of God in condemning the Holy Jesus were never vindicated, and were all to act in like manner, the condemnation of Jesus, as a permission, or appointment, or counsel, or decree of God never could be vindicated, but would be ultimately found to have been in every light groundless and unrighteous, and therefore infinite folly and evil! The salvation of all the sheep, according to the terms of the eternal covenant, must for ever preclude the possibility of such dishonour accruing to the character of God from the death of Jesus. It is absolutely certain that " he shall justify many, for he did bear their iniquities." But the responsibility that lies on me is not by this at all affected. I am bound to do my part that the wisdom and righteousness of God, in appointing condemnation and sentence of death to his dear Son, shall labour under no obscuration. I can have no means, however, of doing so save by saying that whatever others do, if God wants a witness and a vindicator of his honour, behold, here am I. I am under sentence of death already, a child of wrath, and that justly (Eph. ii. 2; Ps. li. 4). I will go and stand beside Jesus. I will say, " Lord, make me one with thee. It is I that am guilty; take my case in hand: be surety for me." Ah! then, full justly may the condemnation fall; full righteous is the sentence of death. And behold, O God, thou art a just God and a Saviour. If none can attest thy justice, I at least shall; for I have so confessed my sin and forsaken it, laying it on Jesus, that thou are just in condemning him; thou art faithful and just in forgiving me! Thus I glorify God by believing on Jesus. Yes; it is not a privilege merely to be a poor and penitent believer after all my sin and with all my sorrow. It is a high point of loyalty to God—the very highest. He is seeking vindications of the justice and righteousness of his procedure in condemning and sentencing his own Son to death. You have it in your power gloriously to answer his appeal—gloriously to serve his glorious purpose. Fear not, O sinner, to bring all thy guilt within the bond and compass of this condemnation that fell on Jesus. Appeal thou, in turn, to thy God to count thee condemned and sentenced; yea, crucified with Christ. Take thy stand beside Christ at the bar. Take up thy position in Christ: he is thy covert, thy refuge, thy hiding-place. Flee into him. It is the righteous sentence of God's law condemning thee to death which then goes out and issues in those words that fell on Jesus' ear: " He is guilty of death." It is a righteous sentence then, though it were only for his partnership with thee and thine in him; righteous, as pro- nounced then on *him;* righteously silenced now as any separate sentence on *thee.* And amazingly there conspire these two glorious issues in one: Thou justifiest God in the condemnation of Jesus; and in the condemnation of Jesus, God exonerates and justifies thee!

Said Paul, "I do not frustrate the grace of God, for if righteousness come by the law, Christ is dead in vain." He felt that in the search for righteousness or justification, to pass by Christ, and turn to any other quarter, were to do what in him lay to make Christ's death meaningless and empty, null and void—in a word, " in vain." It were to "frustrate" or counteract the "grace of God." It were to accumulate all the guilt of reducing God's gracious plan and purpose to folly and failure. Glorious and successful, indeed, that plan and covenant will be. " My sheep hear my voice, and they follow me, and I give unto them eternal life; neither shall any pluck them out of my hand." And they are seen in vision on Mount Zion, all sealed and secured, following the Lamb whithersoever he goeth, his Father's name written in their foreheads— each one made perfect in holiness and without fault before the throne of God. And *this,* the everlasting covenant, with Christ's perfecting and implementing of its terms, perfectly and infallibly secures (Heb. x. 10, 14). Yet, as we say, *no thanks to the unbeliever* if that sealed and irrefragable covenant never fails; and no thanks to him if the blood by which it is sealed is ultimately found not to have been shed in vain. It is not *his* fault if all God's plan is not found a failure and all God's grace frustrated. So far as *he* has it in his choice, he does nothing to prevent it being so, but everything to bring it about, were such an issue possible. And if he never can succeed, his responsibility and guilt are none the less. To justify yourself before God, or attempt to do so, or to attempt to live without justification in the righteousness of

Christ, is to stigmatise the death of Christ as unnecessary and to treat it now as having been " in vain."

Even so, in like manner it is possible to frustrate the whole trial of Christ, the process which divine justice instituted and carried on against him, and to treat the whole as if it were mockery, vanity, and foolishness. What else can it be in your eyes than a mere spectacle of wonder if you come not and enter personally into the divine mind and purpose in the setting forth of God's Christ as the substitute of the guilty, the surety of the condemned? Secretly and in God's sight this Sanhedrim ought to be filled to overflowing, each one of us pressing in to adjoin ourselves to Christ. Rather, the process must be adjourned to the court of conscience and the judgment-seat of God. It is the hour for arresting ourselves and sisting ourselves at our Maker's bar; for it is the hour when a great advocate and interposing victim sums up upon himself the guilt of all who make him their responsible surety and sponsor unto God. It is the hour for anticipating the condemnation of the judgment morning. It is the time for falling into the hands of the living God in conviction, confession, and condemnation of ourselves; for now the hands of the living God are full in dealing as a righteous Judge with him who is pleased to take the place and sin and condemnation and death of the guilty. And here, during the currency, and under covert of this awful transaction—this trial of the Lamb—let our deserved trial be transacted and merged and swallowed up in *it*. This is not only lawful on our part, but dutiful, and loyal, and binding. By the Church coming and transferring her guilt upon her blessed Head, thus only is his condemnation holy or glorifying unto God; while to every one thus repenting, seeking his Maker's presence, believing that his Maker is his Judge, and can by no means clear the guilty, but must ever deal in penal vengeance with all iniquity—to every one seizing a golden oppor-

tunity that never can return (for " there remaineth no
more sacrifice for sin ") an opportunity of placing all his
sin beneath the wrath of God, and the condemnation of
his broken law, where the condemnation has been borne
already, and the wrath has fallen and all past away—to
every one thus coming in penitence and faith to make
Christ his only Head and Surety before the Judge of all,
Christ's trial shall be imputed unto him as his own: its
issues shall be accounted as having already fallen to the
believer's lot.   In Christ's condemnation he shall be held
as having been already condemned; and to him, being in
Christ, there shall be therefore now no condemnation.

Oh! it were a heavenly wisdom, above all things to be
desired and cultivated, to learn in our relation to God, to
use aright the process and the trial, the condemnation and
the cross of Emmanuel.   By nature we are, as sinners
before God, like imprisoned criminals, awaiting gloomily
the day of trial, the day of judgment, and then the eternal
execution of the doom: " Children of wrath," saith the
word which cannot lie, " even as others."   The prison in
which the impenitent and unbelieving are shut up is never
visited by the friendly footsteps of their Maker, nor is it
gladdened by the sunshine of the light of his countenance.
The prisoners live in darkness.   The light of eternal day
streams not in upon them; or if it did, it would affright
them, for they come not unto the light lest their deeds
should be made manifest.   Meantime they contrive to
illumine their prison with sparks of their own kindling,
and decorate their various cells to please their fancy and
their taste.   The night is far spent, and the day is at
hand; but it is a day that shall begin by the great assize,
when the Judge, who is even now at the door, shall sit
upon his great white throne.   Multitudes dislike to think
of it.   The brief interval until the trial they spend in
games called merchandise, and marriage, and mirth, and
such like (Matt. xxiv. 38).   They follow these games

impetuously, but with a dreary sense and dread of something to come, which they desire to exclude and drown
the thought of. Anon, the jailor, death, comes: and by
name he summons this prisoner and that; and as the
summoned soul looks out upon the threshold he meets a
ghastly spectacle—Sin! all his sin in one mass, in one
view. " Sin lieth at the door," as God said to Cain; lieth
at the door, crouching, waiting for him, now dragging
him along and going before to judgment, witnessing
against him, justifying the Judge in consigning the
prisoner to the pit!

Ah! how many have passed forth from their prison into
God's great Court of Justice to find their sin thus
accumulated—waiting for them—witnessing against them
—weighing them down to hell!

Did you never feel that you are a prisoner? that your
soul has no free outlet into the heavenly and spiritual
kingdom of grace and glory, where a reconciled God
smiles on his free-born children, the children of liberty,
the children of the light and of the day? Did you never
feel that you are in prison: that there is and must be a
spiritual region where the soul might walk at large and
free, not struck back and struck down by the bare
attempt to realise its approaching destination and its
eternal destiny? Are you not a poor prisoner, locked up
and shut in from the bright plains of life and immortality?
And ever as thy soul's footsteps would attempt to cross
the threshold and seek a prospect into the eternal state
that lies in waiting for you, a voice of terror—the voice
of conscience—the voice of sin crouching at the door
warns you to retreat, for that region in its blissful realms
is not for you? You dare not meditate in peace and at
ease upon the everlasting state. You are not free to *think*
even of what is beyond the limits of your dwelling-place
upon the earth. All beyond is forbidden to you, as much
as if for you it were the green world lying outside the

convict's cell, beyond the precincts to which justice and his jailor sternly have restricted him.

Did you never feel this? Were you never conscious of a grinding imprisonment whereby your soul is hemmed in within the narrow bounds of the miserable remaining wreck of three-score years and ten; and the wide, glad empire, and holy world beyond is what your conscience of sin, and your forgotten slighted Maker's wrath, warning you back into your dark and dreary cell, forbid you even in thought to enter? And did you never fear that when your prison door at last shall be opened, and you must step forth into court before the Almighty, to hear your own case called, and the process against you prosecuted—did you never fear, yea feel assured, that the Judge has only to remind you of one among a thousand iniquities, and to point to your dreary dread and dislike of Himself, to convict you of rebellion and apostasy and enmity to God? And, O sinner! what wilt thou do in the day when thy case is thus called and tried?

Do you not think that, with such prospects, you really do need something that might be called glad tidings— gospel? Do you not think that, after all, the gospel may be precious—better far than what you have hitherto considered it—a weary tale that hath been three times told?

Art thou, then, this prisoner? " sin lying at the door "; " the judge " also " at the door "; and, ere long, thy case —thine own case, by name—right sure to be called, called by a voice that neither takes denial nor grants delay?

What if there be a strange scheme which some, yea, many, have even tried and proved successful, whereby this dreaded trial may be set aside and cancelled, or rather unstinged and glorified; whereby all process against thee by an angry God may be at once and for ever quenched, and replaced by that wondrous verdict of grace: " Thou art all fair, my love; there is no spot in thee." Would to God you would awake to this matter, the critical and central question, the hinge of your eternal destiny!

In your prison "sin lieth at the door"; and because of sin you dare not come out to look abroad. But there is another than sin at the door. "Behold, I stand at the door and knock," saith Christ: and I preach "deliverance to the captive, and the opening of the prison to them that are bound." Receive him, and he will quench your captivity with his own, and attribute to you all the legal satisfaction which flowed from his own trial all through its various stages, even from the hour of his arrest to his condemnation and his cross—to his loud, heaven-piercing, heaven-opening cry, "It is finished."

Come and hear what the soul can say whom Christ hath taken out of prison, whom Christ hath justified, whom the Son hath made free indeed. Let us question such an one, dwelling now in the heavenly places—not, I mean, as yet in the realm of glory, but in the region of the risen life, free in the risen Jesus, and walking at liberty and in peace with God. "Tell us, O blessed soul, the secret of thy glorious emancipation from prison, thy recall from captivity and bondage, thine absolution in the trial, and thy free fellowship with God—thy full and fearless hope of his glory. Why art thou no more liable to be arrested, carried off a prisoner, placed relentlessly at the bar of justice, witnessed against and condemned for thy sins which thou hast sinned as well as I? Why breaks the eternal future unto thee in thy holy musings as a morning without clouds and as the clear shining after rain? Whence that hope of glory in thy happy heart, that light of heaven in thy glad and kindling eye, that light and hope that have never dawned on me?"

"Wouldst thou know"—that happy soul will say—"wouldst thou know the secret of my escape from condemnation, my fearless freedom, my prospect of no terrifying judgment court when I die, but of my Father's

many-mansioned house?   I have all these privileges
wholly and only *in Christ,* because all that I had to fear I
have learnt to regard as already past and gone in him.   I
was indeed, as a sinner, liable to be suddenly apprehended
and hurried off to judgment; but casting myself on
Jesus, I plead that this is past when Jesus was arrested:
with this I repel all who would lay arrest upon my soul;
and Jesus gives me warrant, for did he not say when
himself arrested, " If ye seek me, let these go their way "?

" I was once a captive and a prisoner, a captive moving
to and fro, at the will of lusts and tyrants, sin and Satan.
But I learnt that Christ had been a captive in chains that
he might carry captivity captive.   I besought him for
liberty to defy my captors and break my chains in the
name and by the might of *his* chains; and I found, as by a
spiritual spell, responsive to my faith, that because of
Christ's captivity, and as its glorious fruit and counterpart, I had the right and the power as his client to be free.

" I was once an outcast, a very forsaken soul, seeing
no fellowship for eternity, and having no communion of
spirit with any one for immortality and the hope beyond
the grave.   A melancholy, solitary, weird strangeness
crept upon my spirit, and I felt the cold dread and chill
of being spiritually and indeed alone—alone—alone! But
I saw that Christ had been " forsaken "; that all his disciples had forsaken him; that Jehovah God had forsaken
him.   And I saw that if this was not to be in vain, it was
appointed and endured in order that such as I, coming to
him, might be, not outcast or forsaken, but " gathered "
with everlasting mercies and added to the roll and fellowship of the brethren of the Lord, the household of faith,
the general assembly and church of the first-born, whose
names are written in heaven, my fellow-citizens now in
Zion and in our Father's house.

" I saw Jesus carried captive to a cruel and faithless
high priest's abode, to be visited with no compassion, to

receive no sympathy in time of need. And I feel that the just fruit of this—the intended import, the gracious design of this—is that I, and such unworthy sinners who are only willing as I am, might have, in the holy place of the Most High, a merciful and faithful high priest, before whom we might appear at the throne of grace, boldly looking for compassion and for grace to help in time of need.

"I saw Jesus denied by a disciple, saying, 'I know not the man.' And Jesus, I am sure, suffered this that he might say of such sinners as I am, 'I know thee by name, and thou hast found grace in my sight.' And the Lord knoweth them that are his and will confess them before his Father and the holy angels.

"I saw him accused; witnesses bribed, produced, and stimulated to accuse him. And if by every part of his poverty I am to be made rich, can I be wrong in thinking that by casting in my lot with Christ and being found in him, one with him in all things, there accrues unto me from *this* the privilege of having no witnesses produced or permitted to appear against me in the judgment: of having that promise fulfilled, 'The iniquities of Judah shall be sought for, but they shall not be found'; and that other promise, 'Every tongue that riseth in judgment against thee thou shalt condemn'; and the challenge found unanswerable, 'Who shall lay anything to the charge of God's elect?' For the destroying of the temple and the rearing of it again in three days answers every challenge, since thus 'it is Christ that died; yea, rather, that is risen again' (Rom. viii. 33, 34).

"I saw Jesus silent: as a sheep before her shearers is dumb, so he opened not his mouth. And am I wrong in therefore 'filling my mouth with arguments'? For he was silent that he might open my lips and cause my mouth to show forth his praise; delivering me, as the God of my salvation, from blood guiltiness, that my tongue might sing aloud of his righteousness (Ps. li. 14, 15).

" I saw his Sonship denied and scouted, the claim of it scorned as blasphemy. And again by his poverty I am made rich, for hereby my sonship is secured and vindicated, and, ' behold, what manner of love the Father hath bestowed upon us that we should be called the sons of God!'

" And finally, consummating all, closing the case and exhausting all the process, that there might be no one element wanting completely to forestall, anticipate, and quench the process that law and justice might have taken against me; that he might stand in my room even to the last, and be able to save me to the uttermost; I saw that he turned not away from condemnation! The Lord of glory turned not away from being condemned! The Prince of Life bowed to the sentence of death! And now, as myself a great transgressor, convicted in my own conscience of sinning grievously, of having continually broken that law, ' Thou shalt love the Lord thy God with all thy heart,' of carrying in my very bosom a fountain of sin, a source of corruption and death, convinced there can be no other escape, seeking no other, marvelling over *this* in that it glorifies God, and suits and saves and comforts me, I become, as by myself, legally quite dead, having no standing in law at all, as the woman on marrying her husband is legally one with and lost in him. I renounce myself : I give my hand and heart to Jesus. I merge and blend my guilt in that responsibility which lay on him when " he who knew no sin was made sin." Mine iniquities when sought for cannot be found save they be found in Christ; I myself when sought for cannot be found save I be found in Christ. I lie down beneath *this* shield, for it is full above this shield that the sentence of death and wrath breaks finally; yea, has broken already, and rolled away for ever; and I know that " unto him that is in Christ Jesus there is now no condemnation."

" Think not," such an one will farther and finally warn us, " think not that this is fanciful or fanatical, that this is unreal or imaginary. It is really the essense of all penitent and believing experience; and for nothing less than to relieve you, by his own trial and condemnation, from the dreadful looking-for of vengeance, is Jesus freely offered to you in the gospel. You tamper with God's blessed gospel, and with the whole wondrous redemption that is in Christ, as a Substitute and Saviour, if you have to do with that gospel for anything less than redemption from judgment and from death, through his blood, even the forgiveness of sins, according to the riches of his grace. It is to bring you at once into all the freedom and all the fearlessness which a full absolution and final cancelling of all penal process against you under the government of your Eternal God must convey that Jesus offers himself to you to be your Advocate and Mediator, promising to bring to bear on your actual acquittal and acceptance all the fulness of his own aton-ing merit in that wondrous work in which He, the High Priest, offered himself the Lamb to God, under curse and condemnation, and thereby quenched for ever for the Church the righteous wrath of heaven. The undefined weight of fear upon the soul; the perplexing sense of guilt and shame in the conscience; the dread terror of the Eternal prospect, and the dark dislike to think of it; by the substitution of himself under the guilt of death he will for ever remove. The deep shadow that loomed so drearily upon your future he will throw back behind you into the past, merging it in the shadow of Calvary and the darkness of his own woe—the hour and the power of darkness, and the future he will unroll and disclose to you, bright with the riches of his grace unsearchable and resplendent in the beauties of holiness."

Oh! it will be as life from the dead, as the falling off of the captive's chains; as the dawning of a propitious sun when you have wandered long on the darksome plains or in the valley of the shadow of death: it will be as the carol of the bird that has broken its little prison and gone forth on its rejoicing element beneath the bright face of smiling heaven; it will be as the calming of a little daughter's sobs and fears on a loving father's breast; when your soul, having learnt to interpret, for its own want and duty, the glorious interposition of Christ as an expiatory substitute, has had the liberty and loyalty, as it has fully the warrant and is deeply under obligation to flee into Christ, the condemned and crucified, and, springing up, as with elastic bound, in the hope of heaven and of home, can say: " I am condemned and crucified with Christ. I am crucified with Christ, nevertheless I live. I am condemned with Christ, nevertheless—yea, therefore —to me in Christ Jesus there is now no condemnation."

" For God, sending his own Son in the likeness of sinful flesh and for sin, CONDEMNED SIN in the flesh: that the righteousness of the law might be fulfilled in us, who walk not after the flesh, but after the Spirit" (Rom. viii. 3, 4).

THE END.